# Teaching
# French
# Culture

*Theory and Practice*

**Ross Steele**     **Andrew Suozzo**

 National Textbook Company
**NTC** a division of *NTC Publishing Group* • Lincolnwood, Illinois USA

# DEDICATION

To Howard Nostrand, whose inspirational leadership and professional commitment over many decades brought culture into the core of the modern language curriculum.

# CONTENTS

# ACKNOWLEDGMENTS

Andrew Suozzo wishes to thank DePaul University for its grant support, which enabled him to do much of the research for this book. He would also like to express his appreciation for the helpful advice of his colleague, Pascale-Anne Brault.

Ross Steele wishes to thank the Andrew Mellon Foundation for sponsoring his Fellowship at the National Foreign Language Center, Washington, D.C., to undertake research on the teaching of culture.

Ross Steele and Andrew Suozzo would particulary like to thank Howard L. Nostrand for his valuable suggestions and his generous sharing of materials.

# FOREWORD

# WHY THE CULTURE OF FRANCE AND THE FRANCOPHONE WORLD?

Learning about another culture is always a worthwhile experience because it permits an individual to learn more about the world, to look at issues in a different way, and to establish a certain intellectual distance from his or her own national values.

In today's global village, the choice of languages and cultures offered to the high school and college student is constantly on the increase. Given the considerable attention currently enjoyed by formerly "exotic" Asian cultures such as those of Japan and China, what arguments speak in favor of choosing the more traditional option of French/Francophone culture?

**Internationalism.** Precisely because the world is shrinking in this new age of powerful instant electronic communication, and because internationalism is becoming increasingly important as an aspect of education, French culture has a very particular significance. While France itself is but one nation among the many, its influence and language extend far beyond its own borders, and beyond the francophone nations of Europe (Belgium, Luxembourg, and Switzerland). In North America, French culture is the native culture of Quebec as well as some areas of the Canadian maritime provinces. France has, of course, left its mark on the state of Louisiana. In the Caribbean are two French overseas departments, Guadeloupe and Martinique, and the first black republic in the world, Haiti. Not far to the south, on the South American Continent, is French Guyana—the site of the Ariane missile launches. France's culture is widely admired by the hispanophone and lusophone countries of South America. In North Africa, in Morocco, Algeria, and Tunisia, French is widely spoken. Many of the countries of west and central Africa (e.g., Senegal, Ivory Coast, Zaire) use French as their official language and boast a number of distinguished African writers of French expression.

France has emerged as one of the prime movers of the north–south dialogue between the industrialized and the developing world, and France expresses its commitment to the Third World in the form of massive loans and subsidies as well as in the form of assistance through participation in international agencies such as the "Agence de coopération culturelle et technique."

Currently, French is spoken by an estimated 120 million people throughout the world. In Africa alone, some projections suggest that the number of francophones will exceed 200 million during the twenty-first century. Demography alone would suggest a bright future for those conversant in French and familiar with French/Francophone culture.

**Political Contributions.**    The intervention of the French navy under Admiral DeGrasse in 1783 ensured the defeat of the British commander Lord Cornwallis and the independence of the United States of America. Before, during, and immediately after the American revolution, there was intense political exchange between the French and the Americans in the persons of celebrated individuals such as Lafayette, Paine, and Franklin. In the newly independent United States, Jeffersonians initially supported the restriction of the arbitrary power of Louis XVI and the foundation of the first French Republic.

The French Revolution had an immense impact on the monarchies of eighteenth-century Europe, on the revolutionary movements throughout Europe in the nineteenth century, and in the twentieth century on the independence movements that overthrew the colonial empires and other dictatorships—ironically, even when those revolutions were directed against France itself as in the cases of Algeria and Vietnam. The discussion of the revolutionary process is unintelligible without an understanding of the political culture of freedom and democracy that grew out of the French Revolution and produced these major historical transformations.

Today France remains politically active in international affairs. The country has a permanent delegate to the U.N. Security Council and often serves as a site for the international treaty negotiations, such as the 1991 peace negotiations for Kampuchea, which were held in Paris.

**Intellectual Achievements.**    Throughout its history, but most especially since the Enlightenment of the eighteenth century, France has held a position of extraordinary intellectual eminence: first in Europe, then in western civilization, and now throughout the entire world. From the political thought of the *philosophes* (Montesquieu, Voltaire, Rousseau, Diderot) on topics as crucial as the system of checks and balances of power in a government, and the concept of the general will, through the nineteenth century social theorists (Saint-Simon, Proudhon) through twentieth century proponents of Marxism (Althusser), existentialism (Sartre, Camus), and structuralism (Barthes, Lévi-Strauss,) to the current speculations of post-modernist semioticians (Derrida), France continues to occupy a central place in the intellectual life of the world.

**France's Role in Europe.**   From the time of the Frankish Emperor Charlemagne who united a region corresponding to much of present-day France, Germany, and Italy in a single political unit in emulation of the Roman Empire to the new Europe of the EC, France has played a leading role in articulating and shaping a European destiny. Today, for example, Jacques Delors, a Frenchman and president of the European Commission since 1985, is described as having made an extraordinary contribution to a unified Europe. Within the EC, French has the status of an official language, and this situation should remain unchanged for the foreseeable future. Now, as we near the twenty-first century, France is helping to mold the new Europe and shape its relations to the rest of the world, most especially to the countries of Eastern Europe in the wake of the collapse of Marxism and, as mentioned, to promote the north–south dialogue between the rich and poor nations of the world.

**France as a High-Tech Nation.**   France, which has always been justly proud of the intellectual and artistic riches of its past, is today fast becoming one of the world's leading high-tech nations. Having renounced its previous low-tech image, France stands among the leaders in urban transportation systems, with the Paris métro and regional express trains being a showcase of new technology modernizing a long-established network. The TGV (high-speed train), the Concorde, and the Airbus mark French achievements in highly advanced rail and air systems. France's revitalized telephone network with Minitel option makes this system perhaps the world's most extended for the generalized use of information systems. Indeed, computer technology plays a major role in daily French life: the smart card ("carte à puce"), for example, was invented by a Frenchman, Roland Moreno.

**France's Economy.**   France is no stranger to riches. For many periods in European history, France was the richest nation in the west. Today France's service industry is the second-largest in the world, and the overall French economy is currently the world's fifth-largest with a rapidly expanding agribusiness sector. Its integration into the single market of the European Community is expected to render an already dynamic, diversified economy even more powerful. France exports a wide array of high-tech products including high-speed train systems destined for Texas and telephone technology intended to modernize the Mexican communication system.

**France's Artistic Heritage.**    French painting, sculpture, music, architecture, and literature are renowned throughout the world. From the soaring Gothic cathedrals to exciting postmodernist monuments rising everywhere in the Parisian area today, French soil has always been the home of unique and widely admired architectural endeavors. Several modern revolutions in painting have occurred in France (most notably impressionism, cubism, and surrealism). Its sculptors and musicians are legion. French literature, since the Middle Ages, represents one of the longest continuous written traditions in European literature. A powerful modeling force from the knightly romances to the contemporary novel and literary criticism, its interrelationship with other European literatures makes it a central part of the western literary heritage.

**Personal Reasons.**    These are as varied as there are individuals, but they often include a positive response to the beauty of the old cities, villages, and the countryside itself, the attraction of the numerous monuments and buildings dating from Roman to present times, the charm of the life-styles, a fascination with French cuisine, fashion, literature, and art, or a desire to learn the language for travel, for professional purposes, or for intellectual enjoyment.

# CHAPTER I

# APPROACHES TO
# TEACHING CULTURE

The role of culture in the modern language classroom has undergone a dramatic revolution over the past four decades. Throughout the sixties and well into the seventies, culture was still spelled with a capital "C" at most institutions and was not perceived as a significant part of the language curriculum. Despite this outlook, many educators were striving throughout this period to alter the situation, most notably in the elaboration of theory and in the development of new techniques. By the eighties, their efforts to change the place of culture had paid off: culture was temporarily included in the ACTFL Provisional Proficiency Guidelines,[1] and culture in its broadest, most anthropological meaning was deemed not only an appropriate but an essential element of language instruction. This movement has continued in the nineties with the inclusion of culture in the AATF's "A Syllabus of Competence"[2] and "The Levels of Cultural Competence."[3] What follows is a brief history of this transformation, cataloguing the explosion of theory and practice that has occurred in a very short time.[4]

## The Content of Cultural Instruction

As early as the sixties, instructors were already demanding "authenticity" in the language classroom. Given this trend, it was almost inevitable that the more perceptive educators would begin to define a different kind of cultural instruction. A key example is Wilga Rivers who, in 1968 in *Teaching Foreign-Language Skills*, maintained that culture should be understood in the broadest sense as "training in all aspects of shared community life."[5] Rivers stressed that cultural acquisition should occur simultaneously with language learning—not in an exterior manner such as through the use of "lecturettes":

> There is another approach which does not take time from the
> essential work of language learning: the insight into culture proceeds at
> the same time as the language learning—in other words, teaching for
> cultural understanding is fully integrated with the process of assimilation
> of language patterns and lexicon.[6]

Rivers was prescient in her aversion to the compartimentalization of culture lessons. She thought that culture could be conveyed by authentic dialogues that covered both the similarities and the differences between the native and target cultures. Rivers proposed a clear progression from elementary to intermediate cultural learning and advocated a selection of materials that were closely related. What was missing, however, was a clear definition of the nature of culture. Almost simultaneously, Nelson Brooks, who pioneered the audiolingual approach to language teaching, moved to fill this gap.

Brooks had been working on culture throughout the fifties and sixties. His 1968 article, "Teaching Culture in the Foreign Language Classroom," offered five meanings of culture ("biological growth," "personal refinement," "literature and the fine arts," "patterns for living," and "the sum total way of life").[7] Brooks chose to emphasize patterns of living as the most practical approach to teaching culture in the language classroom. To implement this teaching, he listed ten points that appeared "central and critical" to him in a culture's make-up—symbolism, value, authority, order, ceremony, love, honor, humor, beauty, and spirit[8]—and sought to apply these points throughout language instruction. Brooks had thus delineated an organized, rational way to present culture and had pointed to popular or small "c" culture as the most logical point of departure in the process of total cultural acquisition.

In 1975, Brooks further clarified his position in an article entitled "The Analysis of Language and Familiar Cultures."[9] Stressing the recurrent and the ingrained, Brooks defined culture as "everything in human life" as opposed to high culture, "the best of everything in human life."[10] He also reiterated the classical distinction between culture ("a way of life") and civilization ("the flowering of a way of life").[11] Brooks provided more analytical tools by dividing culture into "elements" ("a word, a tool, a food, a myth"), "nodes" ("a focal point at which two or more elements come together, especially as they relate to the individual social group"), and "parameters" ("a constant that has a given value in one context but a different one in another").[12] He also reiterated the point made by Rivers—a point that has been a constant theme in cultural instruction—that language and culture come together in meaning, that each is inadequate without the other.[13]

In the same collection of essays as Brooks's, Jacqueline Elliot, in "Analyzing French Culture and Interpreting Some of Its Manifestations," proposed four phases to facilitate the understanding and teaching of French culture: (1) "an inventory of the basic characteristics of the people of France," (2) "a study of typical situations that can be explained as consequential to the socio-cultural behaviors identified in Phase I," (3) "the discovery of new situations by the teacher and/or students through such activities as reading books, newspapers etc. . . . through direct contact with natives . . . through observation via visual and audio aids," and (4) "living or acting out selected French cultural situations to help minimize awkwardness and maximize understanding and tolerance of people who think and act differently."[14] Clearly, Elliot was also calling for a complete overview of culture and this overview was to be realized through an active learning process.

The demand for structured learning continued to be reemphasized in the seventies. Aware that capsulized learning meant a fragmented notion of culture, authors continued to advocate a cultural instruction that sought totality. Indeed, in 1977 Donald K. Jarvis in "Making Crosscultural Connections"[15] insisted that structuralism should be a key concern for professionals interested in the teaching of culture. As he put it, "Structuralism is a term variously understood, but it usually denotes the philosophical point of view that phenomena can best be understood in terms of their own environment, their place as parts in a structural whole."[16] Jarvis is obviously in the tradition of those who study culture as a closed system of significant differences that can be explained as a coherent whole.

The most significant work on the pedagogy and theory of culture in the seventies was done by Howard Nostrand and Ned Seelye. In "Empathy for a Second Culture: Motivations and Techniques" (1974), Nostrand, while recognizing the value of culture as a system of differences, was seeking the proper combination of "diversity and commonality" in cultural instruction.[17] He proposed starting from the students' objectives and then situating what caught their interest in the appropriate context of relationships. He thus became one of the earliest advocates of using student interest as a point of departure. Nostrand divided the understanding of a culture into two components: "experience of the reality and knowledge about it."[18] To achieve this understanding, he established the following repertory of experiential and cognitive techniques, both groupings starting with those techniques usable early in language instruction:

Experiential Techniques
1 Nonverbal bridges to the new culture; 2 Semi-verbal bridges (songs, games, motor and visual aids); 3 Situational dialogue and representative

monologue; 4 Literature, the cinema, and the theater; 5 Audio self-instruction, broadcasts and telecasts; 6 The mini-drama and the culture assimilator; 7 Native informants and language camps; 8 Pen pals, tape pals, and "twinned" classes; 9 Role playing; 10 The experience-based project; 11 Testing affective results.
Cognitive Techniques
    1 Observation and inference, with Socratic prompting; 2 The incidental comment; 3 Systematic exposition of a topic, including individualized self-information; 4 Participatory exposition (culture capsules and clusters); 5 The writing of simulations; 6 Analytical techniques; 7 Bibliography; 8 Techniques for synthesis; 9 Testing cognitive results.[19]

Nostrand's taxonomic procedure was continued in his "Emergent Model" (1978), a detailed definition of the corpus of cultural instruction, which became a standard and much-used reference for research in this field.[20] Nostrand delineated six approaches to teaching culture: "(1) free-wheeling, personal *aperçus*...; (2) an inventory; (3) a model of structure and function; (4) organization around main 'themes'; (5) history; and (6) cross-cultural comparison."[21] He saw a compelling need for an inventory. His own inventory merged the work of Talcott Parsons for subsystems and of Morris Opler for "themal" descriptions. Nostrand's inventory is composed of six sections (I, The Culture; II, The Society; III, Conflicts; IV, The Ecology and Technology; V, The Individual; VI, The Cross-Cultural Environment), which are accompanied by thirty-two main features or headings. The entire inventory is presented in Appendix IV. Although the classroom application of the emergent model can prove very complicated, the model has the enormous value of offering a ready reference for an abstract, coherent breakdown of French cultural life. At this point, it would, however, be necessary to update some of the features listed to take account of changes in France since the date of the model's publication. For example, a specific indication of Islam as part of French religious life is needed under II.B (Religious Institutions), and greater reference to the North African presence in France is required under II.M (Ethnic, Religious and Other Minorities). Likewise, it would helpful to add the "Ministère de la Santé et de l'Action Humanitaire" (established in 1992) to section II.F (The Intellectual-Esthetic and Humanitarian Institutions).

    In his book, *Teaching Culture*, originally published in the early seventies, H. Ned Seelye offered many definitions of culture, described classroom activities, discussed the teaching of culture, and established the goals listed below for classroom instruction:[22]

1 The Sense, or Functionality, of Culturally Conditioned Behavior

The student should demonstrate an understanding that people act the way they do because they are using options the society allows for satisfying basic physical and psychological needs.

2 Interaction of Language and Social Variables

The student should demonstrate an understanding that such social variables as age, sex, social class, and place of residence affect the way people speak and behave.

3 Conventional Behavior in Common Situations

The student should indicate an understanding of the role convention plays in shaping behavior by demonstrating how people act in common mundane and crisis situations in the target culture.

4 Cultural Connotations of Words and Phrases

The student should indicate an awareness that culturally conditioned images are associated with even the most common target words and phrases.

5 Evaluating Statements about a Society

The student should demonstrate the ability to evaluate the relative strength of a generality concerning the target culture in terms of the amount of evidence substantiating the statement.

6 Researching Another Culture

The student should show that s/he has developed the skills needed to locate and organize information about the target culture from the library, the mass media, people, and personal observation.

7 Attitudes toward Other Cultures

The student should demonstrate intellectual curiosity about the target culture and empathy toward its people.[23]

These comprehensive goals did much to point out what was missing in the foreign language classroom and constituted a model for the continuing refinement of cultural objectives by professional organizations.

While Seelye's efforts to raise consciousness about cultural differences were extensive and his efforts to bridge potential gaps were admirable, much of his approach consisted of sensitivity testing in English. This unfortunately provided arguments for those language teachers who believed that cultural instruction actually interfered with language learning. As useful as Seelye's book was in making language instructors aware that students were not equipped to be functional in their target language without a knowledge of the target culture, it did little to advance the discussion of how language and culture could be taught simultaneously. The book's very strong statement about the absence of cultural instruction in the language curriculum did however focus attention on this issue.

# Classroom Techniques

The sixties and seventies were not only a time of culture-teaching advocacy. Many instructors were developing techniques to bring culture into the language classroom. In 1961 Taylor and Sorenson developed the culture capsule to provide brief cultural selections for language classes.[24] The capsule consisted of no more than a ten-minute script focusing on one significant difference between the native and the target culture. It was reinforced by judiciously selected slides, posters, and realia and followed by questions adapted to the language level of the students. Taylor and Sorenson gave the example of the Mexican bullfight, and, in their script, they explained why what appeared to Americans as cruelty represented for Mexicans the triumph of the intelligent athlete over the brute force of nature.

Taylor and Sorenson warned against the danger of fragmentation that could accompany the culture capsule presentation format. To limit this danger Betsy Meade and Genelle Morain devised the "culture cluster."[25] Its innovation was an attempt to spread the teaching of culture throughout the week in smaller segments and to prepare a series of culture capsules that could stand in isolation or be used in relationship to one another in an unfolding series of themes. (They gave marriage as an example of how to develop a cluster.) These clusters could be presented complete with realia, visuals, and identification tasks. Clearly, the authors were striving for a coherent presentation absent in the typical culture capsule. On the other hand, they did not propose a truly cohesive cultural overview that would go beyond given topics.

In 1976 Constance Knop reviewed the culture capsule, culture cluster, and another culture teaching device that had not been invented by the language profession, the culture assimilator.[26] Knop realized that the culture capsule was limited by time and by the manner of presentation, the frequent use of English, and the perhaps excessive focus on overt behavior. She also felt that the culture cluster did not offer the students or the teacher "the opportunity to examine in depth and from different points of view a cultural act or cultural topic."[27] She favored the culture assimilator described by Fiedler, Mitchell, and Triandis.[28] The assimilator consists of a description of a critical situation, several possible interpretations, and an explanation (which confirms the "correct" interpretation and explains why the other interpretations are "wrong"). A French example would be a situation in which a student discovered that his French houseparents exhibited growing annoyance every time he had a long conversation on the phone. This would be followed by four interpretations, of which one is a "correct" interpretation of the houseparents' behavior; the justification of the "correct" interpretation would explain notions of privacy, territory, and economy that presumably provoked the houseparents' reaction. A defect of the culture assimilator is the assumption that there is only one "correct" interpretation when, in fact, there can be degrees of correctness in several interpretations. The model of only one "correct" answer does not prepare students for the different shades of opinion and the flexibility that are desirable when assessing cross-cultural situations. On the other hand, this device does bear witness to the profession's genuine desire to convey an understanding of other people's behavior that complements language instruction.

In addition to the devices already alluded to, Genelle Morain in her 1983 article in the *Modern Language Journal* catalogued the mini-drama (1968), the micrologue (1979), the "cultoon" (1979), and the audio-motor unit (1971).[29] The mini-drama is much like the culture assimilator, with the exception that it is acted out in the classroom and the action of the drama is interrupted before its resolution by the instructor, who leads the students to a full "awareness of the faulty assumptions on the part of the participants from the contrasting culture."[30] The "micrologue" is a "culturally valid text which can be read aloud in one minute."[31] The "cultoon," Morain's own development, goes through a cultural misunderstanding in a one- to four-frame cartoon and tests "visual literacy" for accurate deciphering of the cultural misunderstanding presented; the "cultoon" is presented in conjunction with a written script read aloud by the teacher to facilitate the students' efforts. The audio-motor unit, derived from Asher's "Total Physical Response," is a ten-minute listening activity "built on a single, culturally valid dramatic incident."[32] The physical response of the students is supposed to produce cultural insights.

Much imagination has gone into the creation of these devices, which function chiefly as corrective tools that constantly signal misperceptions. While there is nothing wrong with pointing out the blitheness of our students' own cultural assumptions, there is a danger that this presentation of French culture will assume an adversarial appearance. These devices repose largely on a contrastive method of cultural exposition. There is an antinomy of "us" and "them" within their very assumptions. Although the elaboration of a coherent system of difference may be intellectually stimulating to professionals, constant emphasis on how French culture differs from our own often serves to reinforce or generate hostility among students.

Another problem with these devices is the potentially ancillary notion of culture they create. They are frequently written in English, which reinforces the impression that culture is separate from language. Furthermore, if they are slated for a five- to ten-minute daily application, culture is forcibly segmented and does not grow out of language instruction; it remains an adstratum. This problem does not lend itself to an easy solution, but, as shall be discussed later, the elaboration during the eighties and nineties of multiple but complementary syllabi for varied competencies represents attempts to address this problem.

While some of the devices outlined represent more an explosion of nomenclature than a revolution in the teaching of culture, it is nevertheless apparent from their development and from the work of Nostrand and Seelye that the sixties and, most especially the seventies, were periods of great ferment in the theory and practice of the teaching of culture. This was equally true in the France of the seventies where Francis Debyser, director of the Bureau pour l'Enseignement de la Langue et la Civilisation françaises (BELC) initiated a series of workshops with researchers interested in establishing a methodological framework for the teaching of French culture. The working premise was that anthropological definitions of culture, rather than the traditional humanistic, literary definitions, provide a more unifying framework for what the language learner needs to know in order to understand the foreign country. Debyser's article "Lecture des civilisations" summarizes the outcomes of the workshops.[33]

Debyser poses the pedagogical problem by asking: "Comment mettre au point une didactique d'approche cohérente d'un ensemble aussi disparate que l'*héritage*, la *tradition*, les *institutions*, les *mœurs*, les *usages*, les *modes de la vie*, les *habitudes*, les *attitudes*, la *vie quotidienne*, les *comportements*, les *modes de pensée*, les *mentalités*, les *stéréotypes*, les *visions du monde*, les *représentations collectives*, les *mythes et mythologies*, les *idéologies*, les *productions intellectuelles et artistiques*, les *formes*, les *objets*, la *technologie* d'un peuple?"[34] He proposes that, to guide students to make their own discoveries about France and the French, representative topics from this diversity of subject matter be selected and studied from the three approaches: sociological, anthropological, and semiological. The sociological approach uses documents based on surveys to provide facts and statistics about the topic. These figures reveal the social, economic, and political context of the topic. Such factual information must be the basis on which any true comparison between societies is made. The anthropological approach is less abstract. It focuses on the daily life of the people and social groups, their behaviors and attitudes. Documents from daily life such as a restaurant menu, a real estate advertisement, a mail-order catalog, as well as opinion polls and interviews are used here. Similar documents from different societies enable contrastive analysis. The semiological approach interprets the meanings and cultural connotations expressed overtly or in the subtext of what is spoken and written in a  society. These interpretations lead to an understanding of the cultural mythology of the society, of the beliefs, the values, and the world vision that distinguish one society from another. The semiological approach when used to compare societies reveals that what at first seems different may be similar and that what appears similar may conceal significant differences.

Debyser points out that these three approaches are complementary. For example, behaviors and opinions measured by sociological surveys are part of the anthropological approach; cultural interpretation can be part of the anthropological approach as well as of the semiological approach. Debyser also points out that the danger that the anthropological and semiological approaches can be biased by the dominant cultural ideology that determines how society sees its artifacts. Nonetheless, the three approaches do offer principled and helpful pedagogical categories for selecting documents and for ensuring a coherent and integrated presentation of the topic that will give the learner insights into the functioning of the society at different levels of significance. This three-phase approach to the study and understanding of contemporary France has inspired much of the research in teaching culture by French pedagogues in "français langue étrangère." Thematic dossiers on culture topics that they prepared for foreign learners of French include documents for sociological, anthropological, and semiological analysis.

# Cultural Acquisition

This interest in culture on both sides of the Atlantic did not diminish in the eighties, when the changing format of language textbooks with communicative and proficiency goals indicated greater awareness of culture theory. The decade was particularly rich in theorization as commentators re-examined old concerns and questioned relatively recent assumptions. In classroom practice numerous techniques were devised for using authentic materials to integrate language and cultural teaching.

Among the most interesting of the cultural commentators were Salvador Benadava and Gail Robinson—each of whom was less concerned with specific techniques than with a broader notion of cultural acquisition.

Benadava consistently stressed the "communicative" aspect of culture, namely the insufficiency of the *acte de parole* as opposed to the *acte culturel*. To prove his point, in his article "La Civilisation dans la communication" Benadava cites an exercise in Archipel.[35] The goal of the exercise is to create a patient/doctor dialogue. Benadava supplies a grammatically correct example of this exercise—but an example that is culturally impossible because of its absence of phatic markers and transitional phrasing, because of the presence of an inappropriate inquiry about the cost of the consultation, and because of the omission of the requisite social security form.[36]

Benadava stresses the communicative deficiencies of a language instruction that relies too exclusively on structure. He points out that all effective comunication requires attention to three fundamental questions, which are, in fact, extralinguistic: pertinence ("la pertinence"), appropriateness ("la convenance"), and competence ("la compétence").[37] In the light of these extralinguistic considerations, he calls for the cultural education of language instructors. Paradoxically, he refuses to define himself as a teacher of "civilization" and insists that he is a language teacher. This is, however, perfectly consistent with his exposition of language teaching as instruction in communication. In effect, Benadava remains very close to Rivers's notion that culture is an integral rather than separable part of language teaching.

Benadava describes what he means by culture in "De la Civilisation à l'ethno-communication," in which he elaborates four elements of civilisation that he believes necessary in learning a foreign language: (1) "codes" (nonlinguistic signifying procedures such as gestures, silence, icons); (2) "informations" (minimum ethnographic knowledge shared by most members of the community: the Marseillaise, the franc, civil marriage, etc.); (3) "normes socio-langagières" ("the whole set of prescriptive rules relative to language use: tutoiement, criteria of familiarity, decency, vulgarity, etc.); and (4) "représentation" (a series of images, cultural in origin, attached to the referent, e.g., mayor vs. maire, turkey at Christmas, etc).[38]

To communicate this knowledge in the classroom, Benadava suggests the use of a great diversity of authentic materials and interlocutors, and creativity as in simulations, role playing, mimicry, dramas, etc. He implies that this adaptation of culture within communication is at the initiative of the instructor or the textbook author, but he does not indicate how to insert his four elements into a language course without being forced into extensive commentary. It seems unrealistic to believe that codes of gesture or silence can be readily absorbed without some exposition of their function. In fact, any such commentary would constitute a form of the "parallel" instruction that Benadava so earnestly wishes to avoid. Even some of Benadava's "informations," such as civil marriage, would require discussion to clarify the differences between the American and French attitudes. Sociolinguistic norms can in certain cases be simplified, but explanations of varying detail are required to ensure full comprehension of violations of decency, changes of register, etc. "Representation" likewise requires considerable exposition in the classroom. Despite these reservations, Benadava's four elements are obviously valuable notions to keep in mind when presenting any linguistic material, for consciousness of them can serve as a check in the potential cultural abuse of language. His call for authenticity and diversity clearly echoes the appeals of the sixties and the seventies.

Gail Robinson is primarily concerned with empathy as the point of departure for cultural instruction. In 1978, she wrote an article criticizing "hollow," i.e., acultural, language instruction.[39] She insisted that attitude was all-important in the study of language and culture. Her research showed that the study of a foreign language does not in itself create a positive attitude to the target culture. She advocated a teaching centered on personal involvement and reiterated this stance in *Issues in Second Language and Cross-Cultural Education*.[40] In this book, she stressed the critical need for "empathic capacity," which is "the ability to understand other peoples' feelings, to appreciate the details of their behavior, and to respond appropriately."[41]

In *Crosscultural Understanding*, Robinson summarizes a number of approaches to teaching culture.[42] She begins with the functionalist and behavioral approaches of Nostrand and Seelye, which she sees as purporting to facilitate cultural description and awareness of different patterns of comportment, but she holds that these approaches rest on inaccurate assumptions: namely, that

> . . . cultural behaviors and their functions can be objectively identified; that awareness and anticipation lead to greater coping; and that the important concerns of culture, i.e., what is shared, can be observed directly or inferred from observable behavior.[43]

In contrast to these approaches, Robinson presents the cognitive definition of culture that "shifts attention from the observable aspects of what is shared to what is shared 'inside' the 'cultural actor.'"[44] Culture from this approach thus becomes the "the forms of things that people have in mind."[45] Robinson finds difficulties in applying the cognitive approach to cultural instruction because it is limited to the analytic and cognitive modes to the exclusion of the sensory. She also makes the astute observation that culture viewed as a shared process would imply an approach to teaching and acquiring culture that included the internal cultural maps of the instructor and the students. Robinson completes her presentation of approaches to teaching culture with an overview of symbolic anthropology, which she characterizes as "concerned with the dynamic interrelationship between meaning, experience and reality."[46] Culture from this perspective is in a constant state of flux. Unlike the symbolic anthropologists, however, Robinson wants to fix meaning in the study of culture in order to relate individuals within the cultural system. She concludes with the suggestion that a culturally familiar point of departure is necessary to involve people in the study of another language. Like most of her predecessors, Robinson advocates the systematic presentation of material rather than a potpourri.

Central to Robinson's theoretical position is her insistence on the notion of the cultural hybrid, the cultural merge. By this, Robinson means that no one simply acquires another culture and compartmentalizes it separately, switching as need be from his or her own to the acquired. Rather Robinson sees the study of language and culture as an inevitable hybridization in which the basic culture interacts constantly with the one being acquired. It is on the basis of this conviction that she stresses the initial need for empathy to proceed in cultural acquisition.

Robinson backs up her assertions with a study on the interrelationship between stereotyping and cultural/linguistic study. Her findings illustrate that, contrary to common belief, language study does little to alleviate stereotyping. Rather, if immediate empathy is not sought, language study's normal effect is to reinforce preexisting negative stereotypes. The implications of Robinson's work are profound in that they suggest that carefully planned, systematic presentations of difference, which form the core of most cultural instruction, may well be self-defeating.

More recently Robinson has proposed a grid that can serve as a checklist for a cultural learning curriculum and for the presentation of principles and examples that illustrate a culture.[47] On the vertical axis of the grid is a checklist of categories: Knowledge/Cognitive, Affect/Attitudinal, Behavior/Skill-Getting, Pedagogy, Assessment. The horizontal axis is divided into different levels: Novice, Intermediate, etc. Each principle and example is mapped across all the categories on the vertical axis. A column is left blank for learners to insert their own examples. The curriculum is recursive with some principles and examples being recycled in a more sophisticated way as the learner advances to a higher level.

The following illustration is given to indicate how the grid would function for the principle, "Increase cultural sensitivity and develop cross-cultural understanding." At the novice level, learners demonstrate awareness of simple routines of social interaction (cognitive category), suspend judgment and show curiosity about different routines (affective category), practice skill-getting with sociocultural appropriateness and perform a few routines (behavioral category), through a pedagogical process of observation of video examples of routines in different contexts and role play.

Students have to learn to observe accurately and to refrain from immediately making ethnocentric assumptions. Observing a diversity of examples encourages suspension of hasty judgments. Focusing on similarities between two cultures can counteract learners' natural tendency to perceive differences that reinforce stereotypes. At the intermediate level, learners reflect on and show knowledge of the meanings of variations in routines (cognitive category), develop positive attitudes through respect for cultural differences by placing them within their sociocultural context (affective category), move from limited rules of sociocultural appropriateness to multiple skills with contextual and sociocultural appropriateness in specific situations (behavioral category). Assessment of the learners' competence would cover the four categories and be qualitative, as well as quantitative.

# Different Frameworks

Claire Kramsch elaborates a theoretical and practical basis for a different cultural pedagogy. Her wide-ranging commentary touches on a number of important issues. In "New Directions in the Study of Foreign Language Teaching,"[48] she calls for a broader redefinition of foreign language teaching that would require a theorization of foreign language acquisition that is more helpful in meeting the demands of learners who are more and more concerned with understanding foreign cultures. In this article she holds that to effect a more culturally appropriate pedagogy there must be a broadening of the notion of foreign language study on the vertical and horizontal levels; on the vertical level by attention to the native language counterparts of foreign language instruction and to the work of ESL departments in the United States; on the horizontal level through outreach to other fields such as anthropology, sociology, and international studies. Appropriately, in this reconceptualization of foreign language study, Kramsch states that textbooks should teach "discourse, not grammar" as a preparation for literature.[49] This concern for discourse, which embraces the fullness of a text's meaning, is central in her advocacy of the cultural dimension of language.

In a different publication with a similar title,[50] Kramsch stresses the inseparability of language and culture. Here she adopts from Attinasi and Friedrich the expression "linguaculture," which indicates the special relationship between the two, namely "constituting a single universe."[51] Kramsch makes the key point that culture is not "a fifth skill similar to reading, writing, speaking, and listening."[52] She maintains that we must "explore the cultural dimensions of the very language we teach if we want learners to be fully competent in these languages."[53] Kramsch comments on the current call in state educational guidelines for the linkage of foreign language and cultural instruction, noting with caution the American cultural biases of pragmatism and efficacy evident in these guidelines. She warns against the potential abuse of the new enthusiasm for culture, which is too often seen as the means to restore American competitiveness, as a "practical" step in recovering world primacy rather than as a means to reach a genuine understanding of others. In conclusion she reemphasizes discourse

> . . . as the integrating moment where culture is viewed, not merely as behaviors to be acquired or facts to be learned, but as a world view to be discovered in the language itself and in the interaction of interlocutors that use the language.[54]

In more recent papers, Kramsch has continued to stress the centrality of discourse with the consequence that "teaching languages as discourse and communication means precisely capturing contextual and individual variation."[55] Pointing to one danger in cultural study observed by Jonathan Culler (reproduction and transmission of the dominant culture through the foreign language), she advocates an approach through discourse to "help students critique and recreate in new ways the culture they grew up with."[56] She adopts the name Tedlock and Mannheim have given to this process: the "dialogic emergence of culture." This concept emphasizes the dynamic activity of linguacultural acquisition, an activity that is characterized by negotiation and interpretation in encounters with authentic manifestations of the target culture rather than the somewhat docile activities of absorption and replication typical of traditional methods of foreign language acquisition.

In "The Dialogic Emergence of Culture in the Language Classroom,"[57] Kramsch explores the manifestations and evasions of this dialogue in an actual classroom situation by observing several American T.A.'s discussing a German authentic document with their students. The document is an extract from *Die Zeit*, "Jugend ohne Zukunft?" (Youth without a Future?") (33, 10.8.1979), which itself was an article on an eight-hour-long television debate. She analyzes the T.A.s' choice of different conversational floors that reflect the discourse genres they wish to establish in the classroom. In her presentation, Kramsch notes that the very discussion in the classroom represents a particular form of discourse that is itself a cultural manifestation. Her discussion also illustrates the difficulty of conveying the cultural diversity of authentic materials, in part because of attempts to solicit classroom solidarity that ignore rules of the target culture but also because of the absence of exact lexical/cultural analogues to bridge the gap between the target culture document and the dominant culture, the learner's native culture. Kramsch underscores the evasiveness of culture, whose meanings are not stable but represent "a constant negotiation of genres that emerge within the discourse community of the classroom."[58] Her analysis demonstrates that the instructor's awareness of his or her own role as instructor within a discourse community becomes a key factor in the presentation of the target culture. In her new book *Context and Culture in Language Teaching* (1993), Kramsch focuses attention not just on cultural knowledge as a necessary aspect of communicative competence, but as an educational objective in its own right, as an end as well as a means of language learning.

Michael Byram is another important voice in the articulation of a model for teaching cultural studies.[59] In *Cultural Studies in Foreign Language Education*, he has argued eloquently for the inseparability of language and culture, the measurement of knowledge rather than skills, the key role of empathy in language teaching, the need to reach out to the social sciences to improve our cultural presentations,[60] and the mediating role the student must play to be a true learner of culture. Byram's work is very far-ranging. His model of foreign language education is presented and illustrated in figure 5–1 on page 73.

He is particularly eloquent on the subject of empathy, which he distinguishes very sharply from tolerance:

> Towards a foreign people, tolerance involves, in the contemporary world, willingness to work and live with people who are different, refraining from banishing them from our society as we do in the present, or even waging war upon them, as we have done in the past. Empathy, on the other hand, is more demanding. It requires understanding, an activity rather than a passive acceptance; it requires a change of viewpoint which has to be worked towards, engaged with.[61]

Citing Von Wright, he points out that "Empathic understanding is not a 'feeling'; it is an ability to participate in a 'form of life.'"[62] In this active process of empathic engagement, Byram draws attention to the fact that the students already enter the classroom as "an embodiment of the culture which they share with others,"[63] which is quite different from what he considers the deceptive term "culture baggage." He rightly reminds us that culture is not something one picks up or discards at will; people are human beings precisely because they possess a culture. The task of cultural instruction is, in part, the creation of empathy that will aid students in reassessing the schemata "which are basic to the development of the individual mind."[64] In short, they need to be helped toward negotiating the differences between their own schemata and those of the target culture, and this clearly involves an empathic engagement on the part of the learner.

Byram spurns the classroom and foreign studies goal of simple tourist-level communication and advocates a mediating function identified by Bochner for the learner.[65] Mediating individuals are those who can link different cultural groups and reconcile cultures. This for Byram is at the heart of foreign language education but unfortunately a goal that he admits is normally reached only by university students.[66] Byram sees two possible approaches to teaching a foreign culture: instruction in the native language using it as the medium of study or the integration of the target language and culture. This latter option, our principal concern, requires students not to replicate the target culture but rather to develop intercultural competence as it entails "the modification or change of existing schemata."[67] Existing classroom practices will need to be reassessed to take account of Byram's concept of the language student as mediator between the native culture and the target culture. In what ways do our practices develop the notions of self and otherness in our students? We know that emphasizing the difference between the two cultures produces an "us versus them" dichotomy and attitudes of superiority and condescension toward "them." On the other hand, we do not expect our students to approve everything in the target culture and be uncritical in their evaluation of the behaviors, attitudes, and values that characterize it. In order to appreciate otherness, one has to have a clear understanding of one's personal cultural identity. In the process of evaluating the target culture, the student will clarify understanding of his or her own cultural identity. This will lead to a definition of himself or herself in relation to others within the native culture on the basis of shared but not identical cultural values. The notions of commonality and difference in the native culture constitute the broader base necessary for the student to see more clearly what Byram calls the "existing schemata," which will be modified through contact with the target culture. This contact will develop into a series of "negotiations" or "dialogues" in which the student is the point of mediation between the two cultures. The instructor and the discourse features of the language used are key elements in the success of these "negotiations." The role of the instructor is pivotal in supplying information; in guiding the student's interpretation of target culture phenomena and relating them to the native culture; in encouraging the elaboration of an overall synthesis of the aspects of the target culture that the student encounters. This synthesis is a dynamic construct constantly changing to take account of the new experiences and expanding knowledge the student has of the target culture itself and the new interpretations the student makes of target culture phenomena. The discourse features of the language used will influence the perceptions of the target culture, whose full meanings are embedded in the deepest layers of the language with which the people of that culture communicate.

Byram's work revalorizes the function of interpretation over mere skill acquisition and places linguacultural study back in the domain of the liberal arts where imagination, subtlety, and flexibility constitute the value of the individual's effort. There is also an ethical side to his work, which, in the context of growing European unity, perceives a moral imperative in understanding and respecting other cultures. Increasing interest in cultural studies would seem to indicate that they are becoming the matrix of a new humanism that subsumes the study of both language and literature.

It is quite possible that this new humanism will propel the study of culture to the forefront of the curriculum as we move into a twenty-first century destined to be marked by ever more intensive communication and exchange between all the peoples of the world community. The mediating role of cultural study makes it precisely what is needed to create a humane, compassionate, and ethical global civilization that valorizes the richness of its diversity. The future promises that members of the language teaching profession will no longer be perceived as "just" language teachers but as cultural mediators of special value in the effort to achieve an enlightened and harmonious world culture that respects the cultural identity of its members.

# Applications

This activity is specifically for the instructor, not for the students. You need to define what culture means for you. First write your own definitions of the words *culture* and *civilization*, being as precise or vague as you see fit. Next consult at least two authoritative American English dictionaries to determine how these dictionaries define the word *culture*. Then check them for the word *civilization*. Follow the same procedure in French, consulting two French dictionaries for their definitions of *culture* and *civilisation*. Compare your own definitions and try to discover the underlying assumptions that elicit the dictionaries' definitions. Are there any significant differences between English and French definitions of culture? Most of all, do not be intimidated, because the term *culture* is still redefining itself.

You may also wish to reflect upon and define for yourself the concept of the student of French as cultural mediator between the native and the target cultures. What are some of the reactions the student might have on contact with the target culture? Can you think of some examples of schemata or patterns of thought that might be modified as a result of this contact with the target culture?

# Notes

1. See Appendix I.

2. See Appendix II.

3. See Appendix III.

4. The brevity of this exposition does not permit acknowledgment of every author.

5. Wilga M. Rivers, *Teaching Foreign-Language Skills* (Chicago: The Univ. of Chicago Press, 1968), p. 263.

6. *Ibid.*, p. 273.

7. Nelson Brooks, "Teaching Culture in the Foreign Language Classroom," *Foreign Language Annals* 1 (1968): 210.

8. *Ibid.*, p. 213.

9. Nelson Brooks, "The Analysis of Language and Familiar Cultures," in Robert C. Lafayette, ed., *The Cultural Revolution in Foreign Language Teaching* (Lincolnwood, IL: National Textbook, 1975), pp. 19–31.

10. *Ibid.*, pp. 20–21.

11. *Ibid.*, p. 21.

12. *Ibid.*, p. 26.

13. *Ibid.*, p. 25.

14. Jacqueline C. Elliot, "Analyzing French Culture and Interpreting Some of Its Manifestations," in Robert C. Lafayette, ed., *The Cultural Revolution in Foreign Language Teaching* (Lincolnwood, IL: National Textbook, 1975), p. 50.

15. Donald K. Jarvis, "Making Crosscultural Connections," in June K. Phillips, ed., *The Language Connection: From the Classroom to the World* (Lincolnwood, IL: National Textbook, 1977), p. 153.

16. *idem.*

17. Howard L. Nostrand, "Empathy for a Second Culture: Motivations and Techniques," in Gilbert A. Jarvis, ed., *Responding to New Realities* (Lincolnwood, IL: National Textbook, 1974), pp. 277–94.

18. *Ibid.*, p. 280.

19. *Ibid.*, pp. 281–82.

20. Howard L. Nostrand, "The Emergent Model (Structural Inventory of a Sociocultural System) Applied to Contemporary France," *Contemporary French Civilization* 2,2 (1978): 277–94. See Appendix IV.

21. *Ibid.*, p. 277.

22. H. Ned Seelye, *Teaching Culture* (Lincolnwood, IL: National Textbook, 1993).

23. *Ibid.*, pp. 49–57.

24. Darrel Taylor and John Sorenson, "The Culture Capsule," *Modern Language Journal* 45 (1961): 350–54.

25. Betsy Meade and Genelle Morain, "The Culture Cluster," *Foreign Language Annals* 6 (1973): 331–38.

26. Constance K. Knop, "On Using Culture Capsules and Culture Assimilators," *The French Review* 50,1 (1976): 54–64.

27. *Ibid.*, pp. 60–61.

28. Fred E. Fiedler, Terence Mitchell, and Harry Triandis, "The Culture Assimilator: An Approach to Cross-Cultural Training," *Journal of Applied Psychology* 55 (1971): 95.

29. Genelle Morain, "Commitment to the Teaching of Foreign Cultures," *The Modern Language Journal* 67,4 (1983): 403–12.

30. *Ibid.*, p. 403.

31. *Ibid.*, p. 404.

32. *idem.*

33. Francis Debyser, "Lecture des civilisations," in Jean-Claude Béacco and Simonne Lieutaud, *Mœurs et mythes* (Paris: Hachette, 1981), pp. 9–21.

34. *Ibid.*, p. 10.

35. Salvador Benadava, "La Civilisation dans la communication," *Le Français dans le monde* 184 (avril 1984): 79–86.

36. *Ibid.*, p. 80.

37. *Ibid.*, p. 83.

38. Salvador Benadava, "De la Civilisation à l'ethnocommunication," *Le Français dans le monde* 170 (juillet 1982): 33–38.

39. Gail L. Nemetz Robinson, "The Magic-Carpet-Ride-to-Another-Culture Syndrome: An International Perspective," *Foreign Language Annals* 11 (1978): 135–46.

40. Gail L. Nemetz Robinson, *Issues in Second Language and Cross-Cultural Education: The Forest through the Trees* (Boston: Heinle & Heinle, 1981).

41. *Ibid.*, p. 32.

42. Gail L. Nemetz Robinson, *Crosscultural Understanding* (London: Pergamon, 1985; Englewood Cliffs, NJ: Prentice-Hall, 1988).

43. *Ibid.*, p. 9.

44. *idem.*

45. *Ibid.*, p. 10.

46. *Ibid.*, p. 11.

47. In a group discussion. November 1992.

48. Claire J. Kramsch, "New Directions in the Study of Foreign Languages," *ADFL Bulletin* 21,1 (Fall 1989): 4–11.

49. *Ibid.*, p. 7.

50. Claire J. Kramsch, "New Directions in the Teaching of Language and Culture," *National Foreign Language Center Occasional Paper* (Washington: NFLC, 1989), pp. 1–12.

51. *Ibid.*, p. 1.

52. *Ibid.*, pp. 1–2.

53. *Ibid.*, p. 2.

54. *Ibid.*, p. 10.

55. Claire J. Kramsch, "The Role of Language in Cultural Studies," 9,2. This paper has recently been published with the same title, 135–152, in Heidrun Suhr, ed., *Post-Wall German Studies: A Challenge for the North American Colleges and Universities in the 1990's.* (Proceedings from the DAAD-New York conference held in Scottsdale, Arizona, February 6–9, 1992). New York German/Academic Exchange Service (DAAD), 1992.

56. *Ibid.*, pp. 4–5.

57. Claire J. Kramsch, "The Dialogic Emergence of Culture in the Language Classroom," *Papers from the Georgetown University Round Table on Languages and Linguistics* (Washington: Georgetown University, 1992), pp. 1–21.

58. *Ibid.*, p. 20.

59. Michael Byram, *Cultural Studies in Foreign Language Education* (Avon, Eng.: Multilingual Matters, 1989). Byram has recently coedited with Dieter Buttjes another book, *Mediating Languages and Cultures* (Avon, Eng.: Multilingual Matters, 1991) and coauthored with Veronica Esarte-Sarries a book for teachers, *Investigating Cultural Studies in Foreign Language Teaching* (Avon, Eng.: Multilingual Matters, 1991). Multilingual Matters books are distributed in the United States by Taylor & Francis, Bristol, PA.

60. Byram and Esarte-Sarries have discussed transforming the language learner into an ethnographer; namely, one who actually utilizes the procedures of other disciplines rather than one who draws on their products. See Byram and Esarte-Sarries, *Investigating Cultural Studies*, pp. 9–12.

61. *Ibid.*, p. 89.

62. *idem.*

63. *Ibid.*, p. 111.

64. *Ibid.*, p. 113.

65. *Ibid.*, p. 115.

66. *Ibid.*, p. 116.

67. *Ibid.*, p. 137.

# CHAPTER II

# EMPATHY AND THE PREDETERMINED SYLLABUS

Class A has begun its intermediate study of language and culture, and the instructor has prepared in advance a culture syllabus that will give learners an ordered and comprehensive overview of the principal features of French society. Class B has also begun the study of intermediate French. As in Class A, the syllabus announces its intention to present French culture, but it is vague about the areas of cultural instruction, and the point of departure is to be discussed by the instructor with the class. Class A begins by studying the French family but finds it rather restrictive and suffocating; the students become increasingly resistant to the unfolding pattern of French society, which their instructor presents to them as an exercise in intellectual understanding. In Class B the instructor chooses topics in which the students express an interest; they are encouraged to participate in activities such as organizing a French meal or playing the game of *pétanque* in order to allow them to experience the foreign culture. Class B is definitely more receptive to French culture, and its linguistic performance is better, but its instructor wonders what to introduce next after having discussed food, sports, and fashion. Class A, despite its lack of enthusiasm, can respond better if asked to talk about general patterns in French society, but it is clear from its answers that the French are perceived as the "others" and even, in a veiled fashion, as inferiors. Class B has a far more positive attitude toward the French, but it has a fragmented view of French society—one that corresponds closely to its very American way of understanding society; Class B has an eclectic and unbalanced view of France that will not be remedied by the erratic selection of topics presented to respond to the students' feelings and wishes.

Such are perhaps in caricatural form the models suggested by the predetermined syllabus and the empathic approach. In a way, the two pedagogies seem inalterably opposed and irreconcilable. Proponents of either pedagogy might well protest the distortions of the depiction we have given. The juxtaposition is not intended to condemn either approach, but rather to set them apart in their individual advantages and difficulties.

# Coherence versus Spontaneity

The predetermined course plan as depicted in Class A was a product of the cultural theory of the seventies, when a coherent overview of French culture became a teaching objective. In the eighties, it became clear—most notably in Gail Nemetz Robinson's book *Issues in Second Language and Cross-Cultural Education: The Forest through the Trees* (Boston, Heinle & Heinle, 1981)—that a program of cultural instruction requires an empathic response from the students if they are to be receptive to the potentially alienating situations that inevitably arise during the study of a foreign culture. While Robinson and other proponents of empathy never rejected the notion of an ordered, coherent presentation, it is undeniable that there is a spontaneity in the empathic approach that requires a greater latitude on the part of the instructor and greater flexibility in the arrangement of a course. In one sense, an empathic approach thus threatens coherence and order; predetermined structure and sympathetic spontaneity seem inevitably at odds. It is important to decide whether these approaches can be reconciled and to examine their individual merits and deficiencies in a more extended fashion than our caricature does.

# Empathy

There are pedagogical problems in the notion of empathy itself. First of all, an instructor may discover that students do not know what they wish to learn about a foreign culture; they may require extended exposure to it before they are aware of their own preferences. Another consideration is that it may not be possible to teach empathy, for this quality may be more a function of temperament than something communicated by instruction. One of the principal difficulties in creating empathy for French culture lies in the frequent conflict of values between the anglophone and francophone worlds. However well disposed students may be to the culture of France, they may still find French individualism odd and egotistical. People from American culture, which stresses conformism to achieve social goals, may find the independence of a French person irrational and perverse. There may simply be no way to bridge this gap. While sophisticated students may reach an intellectual appreciation of French individualism, they may still resent it—indeed, it is possible that no degree of enthusiasm for the general culture will ever make them comfortable with this form of self-assertion. It may be that we need to learn to suppress our reactions, our cultural aversions, rather than learn to identify with the peoples of other cultures. Self-interest and self-preservation in dealing with other groups in the human community might be offered as surer approaches than empathy. Yet these coolly rational assessments of the need to study another culture are rarely very inspiring.

Furthermore, empathy may be more our own cultural fabrication than a reality; our own culture is perhaps so deeply rooted within us that empathy may be sheer wishful thinking, a part of our own cultural mythology. Some anthropologists have gone so far as to maintain that intercultural empathy is an impossibility. How many French instructors who nourish a deep and genuine enthusiasm for France and its people continue to find the French annoying despite all the explanations and rationalizations? Unlike the Americans, the French will often judge themselves very harshly both individually and collectively. This tendency is exemplified in the particularly vicious lyrics of Renaud's popular hit, L'Hexagone, which accuses the French of cowardice, selfishness, support of dictators, and pollution of the environment—among other things. The way Renaud criticizes his fellow citizens and his country (complete with obscenity) will appear shocking and disrespectful to many Americans. In short, while there are certainly points of contact, strong affinities, and even areas of profound admiration from the peoples of the anglophone world, the overall arrangement of French life may make a general empathy an impossible task. On a more global level, French foreign policy, which often seeks to differentiate itself from that of France's allies and frequently refuses to cooperate in their international initiatives, constitutes an almost permanent source of friction and an obstacle to empathy for many Americans. Such observations might allow us to conclude more generally that hostility between different cultures may, in fact, be the norm of the human condition. Further, francophone and anglophone cultures may well be especially ill-suited for mutual comprehension and affection.

Another objection to the empathic approach is the assumption that students learn by attraction, by a search for immediate identification. For some people, however, the very attraction of things may not lie in empathy but in difference itself. Many students subscribe to a notion of French culture as exotic—"Vive la différence" implies that difference is exciting rather than an obstacle to learning. In fact, contrastive analysis, which focuses on differences, remains strongly in favor with certain pedagogues, such as Henri Besse, who proposes the following methodology in the teaching of culture:

> Les démarches proposées consistent à *confronter les étudiants*, même débutants, *à des données*, aussi contextualisées que possibles, *de la langue/ culture étrangère*, données qui, précisément, *présentent pour eux une certaine étrangeté*, afin que celle-ci alerte leur curiosité et leur vigilance autochtones.[1]

This statement clearly flies in the face of an empathic presentation and assumes that students will respond to the challenge, stimulated by a desire to resolve a mystery. Its appeal to professors, who are normally used to analyzing data and intrigued by difference, is obvious. Regrettably, one may not presume that elementary students will be intrigued; indeed, they may immediately resort to negative stereotypes when confronted by various conundrums.

The proponents of empathy might well have argued that Besse's call for contrast carries within itself the immediate danger of the "us versus them" antinomy, that his position in itself represents a manifestation of French culture in which conflictual modes of interrelating are relatively commonplace, i.e., one interlocutor defines himself *against* the other. Thus it could be observed that a pedagogy that stresses a conflictual mode of presentation may be ill-suited to the values of an American audience, which, by French standards, is intensely conformist, cooperative, and conflict-aversive. Indeed, in Besse's presentation of cultural acquisition, one finds strong traces of the French magisterial style of teaching: after the students have formulated hypotheses about cultural behavior, these hypotheses are accepted or rejected by the instructor according to their plausibility.

Despite its seduction for the instructor, the contrastive method used too early and prior to some positive identification with the target culture carries the danger of creating an adversarial relationship between the student and the target culture. Given the relatively numerous areas of potential hostility for anglophones in approaching French culture and their already negative stereotypical notions of the French, the value of initial contrast over empathy is dubious, despite its strong appeal to instructors. Later, perhaps, contrastive analysis may become desirable and, in any event, inevitable but, without the sympathy of the learner, this pedagogical approach may prove very frustrating. In any event, it would seem that we need empathy as a point of departure, even if we are not entirely persuaded that we believe it. What inspires empathy will vary from student to student. How to generate it remains the most important question.

# The Predetermined Syllabus

The predetermined syllabus, which often uses the contrastive approach, normally aims at a general overview of the culture—usually France but sometimes its former colonies and other francophone countries as well. For simplicity's sake, we shall assume that the target culture is France itself. Assuming that the general syllabus is reputable, students will inevitably encounter a very thorough exposition of French society as it is today: they will learn much about daily life and the French educational and political systems. It cannot, however, be assumed that the students will as a majority be particularly interested in all these phenomena. Indeed, if they find the beginning of the course uninteresting, they may simply tune out and regard this class as an ordeal. They may even focus on what they perceive as negative and develop a strong hostility toward the French. If this is the case, the goal of the course will have been defeated, for, while no course should seek to create an uncritical euphoria about another people, it must at least engender a positive curiosity that will lead to receptivity on the part of the learner.

The predetermined syllabus is often set up by a textbook that the instructor may not even have selected. This means that the teacher may not be engaged empathically with the presentation of France imposed by the text. Instructors are not machines; they need to be enthusiastic about their material to convey it effectively. A predetermined syllabus imposed from without in an effort to create uniform cultural learning, or even a textbook reluctantly chosen by an instructor for want of something better, may thus face the additional danger of alienating the instructor as well as the students.

Beyond doubts about student or teacher receptivity to an organized presentation of culture, there is a far more cogent objection to the systematized presentation of French culture: namely, the argument that all attempts to characterize any culture are gross distortions, that culture is too fluid and too complex to be capsulized in classroom presentations.

This objection is of a similar nature to the one that suggests that empathy is philosophically impossible, a myth of our own culture. In effect, we really have no choice in the matter: either we make an attempt to describe another culture or we give up the process altogether—just as we assume that our students can achieve a positive identification with another culture. On the other hand, this objection points to a clear danger: anthropologists have established certain categories for analyzing societies, but these categories are subject to constant challenge and revision, often on the grounds that such categories are, in fact, merely arbitrary expressions of the culture that generates them. Thus, when elaborating the facets of another culture, we must remain aware that our efforts contain a set of biases and that we cannot have absolute confidence in the full accuracy of our description. Let us also not forget that French instructors who have been to France have had personal experiences that will color the image of that country presented to the class. The value in presenting a prestructured image of France lies in the structuring process itself. Quite simply put, American culture tends toward the more immediate aspects of things and resists the whole notion of relationalism. It can be in many ways antistructural. The predetermined syllabus requires students not only to structure their view of France but almost inevitably to structure their view of their own society. It requires them to order their experiences, their perceptions of their native culture, if they are to make viable comparisons. The predetermined syllabus imposes a broader view of social phenomena, whether foreign or domestic, and encourages students, to look for relationships between those phenomena; it has the merit of resisting a fragmented perspective, but there is the danger of rapid alienation of students at early levels of study.

# Combining Empathy with the Predetermined Syllabus

The empathic approach and the predetermined syllabus need not really be viewed as mutually exclusive. How can these two distinct methodologies be combined? On both sides of the Atlantic work has been done that points to a possible fusion of the two approaches—though not without problems. Since some kind of empathy must surely be created from the onset of instruction, it is worthwhile to consider the efforts of Janine Courtillon, whose teaching in France points to a way of merging the two approaches.[2] Courtillon began her work with beginning French students by polling her class to determine what interested them in language learning. Her questions revealed that there were three strong areas of curiosity:

> les faits sociaux: comment les gens vivent ensemble—les faits idéologiques: ce qu'ils pensent, ce qu'ils croient—les faits esthétiques: les formes d'art ou de création qu'ils aiment ou produisent.[3]

Courtillon wished to establish a form of empathy within the first fifty hours of instruction—a relatively long period for an American instructor as compared to an instructor of French in a native environment and in an intensive course. To accommodate the preferences of her students, Courtillon selected documents of all sorts that were specific and contained traits that appealed to student sensitivity. At the same time, she was careful to select documents that avoided stereotyping. Essentially, she offered an example of what a talented instructor would do beyond using a specific text. Flexibly, at the determination of her students, she moved into the cultural areas that were their main concerns.

Further, Courtillon created an ordered progression in her empathic instruction through three phases: (1) perception, (2) first conceptualization, and finally (3) verification of hypotheses. She also sought to add materials that might form part of universal cultural archetypes—again based on the interest of her students. This procedure enabled her to achieve two goals in cultural instruction: the movement outward toward the other and the reflective movement toward oneself for a new understanding of one's position—both eminent goals of "linguaculture"[4] and both taught empathically yet in ordered progression.

If we take a larger view of Courtillon's efforts, we can see that initially the lack of a syllabus remains a problem, but there is also a potential solution that would permit a predetermined syllabus. If we assume that, while students and also classes have different personalities, there is surely some affinity of taste and outlook for their common culture in large groups of students. We may also assume that the media have already shaped their views of the foreign culture. The tastes and views they share would form the basis for syllabi that were at once empathic and predetermined. To create such syllabi, one might envisage a multistaged process for the larger institution. Where a predetermined syllabus already exists, surveys aimed at discovering genuine student preferences could be made over the course of a year and repeated annually to adjust to evolving student interests. These surveys could then be evaluated to find areas of commonality. Upon this basis, a more empathic syllabus could be implemented the following year. Such a syllabus would not focus simply on the manifestations of popular culture, which is often the main component of the empathic approach, but would move toward a more intellectual discussion of values and archetypes and thus reincorporate high culture into cultural instruction. Brief literary extracts could be reinserted into the cultural curriculum alongside examples of popular culture. Within any general syllabus, room can always be found for individual instructors and their students to select materials that enhance the area of cultural instruction but allow the tastes and preferences of individual instructors and students to be developed. In short, we can move toward a merger of empathic spontaneity and programmed exposition.

To achieve this merger, each teaching staff will have to reach general agreement, after reviewing student choices expressed in the survey, on what areas of culture are essential, what aspects of the culture appeal to the largest number of students, and how these features of the general culture can be connected. The staff will have to keep in mind that both popular and high culture should be part of the curriculum. It may be hoped that with an empathic, predetermined syllabus, the obstacle of cultural difference will cease to be a problem, because, once properly disposed and sympathetic, the language/culture learner will be inclined to an open-minded curiosity that is marked by a receptivity to difference rather than an animosity toward it. It is really the initial stages of instruction—elementary and intermediate study—that pose the most serious dangers of disaffection and most require a basis of empathic, structured exposition.[5]

# Applications

## Selected Topic: The French Family, an Overview

We have selected this topic because the French family is a basic element of French society and it lends itself to many levels of discussion and many different presentations. We suggest setting out each approach separately for the purpose of clarity, but, thereafter, we counsel a merger of the two.

### The Empathic Approach

This approach can originate from a series of basic questions to find out what information the students already have.

1. In general, what do students think about the family: Is it a universally identical unit, is it important to society, is it healthy, is it a repressive unit?

2.  Do the students already have preconceived ideas about the French family: Do they perceive it as identical to the American family, do they have stereotypes about it (e.g., the patriarchal model), do they see its importance to French society? Where did they get their ideas about the French family?

3.  Do the students have any factual knowledge about the French family: Average number of children, roles of the parents, models of child rearing, percentage of working mothers?

4.  Do the students personally know a French family? Would they like to question a French person about his or her family in class?

Such questions can establish key areas of student interest, knowledge, and ignorance to orient the empathic presentation and indicate what areas of the predetermined syllabus might best arouse student interest.

A next step is to provide the students with sources of information such as magazines, newspapers, books, films, and statistical sources. Upon this basis, students move away from personal impressions toward a more realistic appraisal of the French family, which in turn provides the basis for further discussion.

## The Predetermined Syllabus

The predetermined syllabus would define terms such as the nuclear and extended family. It would include the decline in the French birthrate and the transition from a paternalistic, authoritarian model to a less constrained family structure. The syllabus would cover the largely unaltered affective role of the French mother and consider the ambiguous role of the father, who no longer functions primarily as a disciplinarian. This syllabus would also point to the number of unwed couples with an increasing tendency toward fidelity and eventual marriage. It would treat the trigenerational family with the special role of grandparents. It would examine the greater attention typical among French parents to their children's academic progress—an attention fostered by the competitive nature of French education. It would also investigate the relatively low geographic mobility of the French, and the geographic proximity of most family members.

Part of the predetermined syllabus would involve a comparison with the American family. It would study the impact of geographical mobility produced by the sheer size of the United States on the American family and the resulting differences with the French family. It would reveal similar trends but marked percentage divergences in the divorce rates in the two countries and different percentages of unwed mothers and couples. It would also point out very sharp differences in the perception of the state's role in marriage, namely, that the only legal form of marriage in France is a civil marriage conducted by the mayor or his or her representative.

This approach can be complementary to the empathic approach in that it can formally articulate what one needs to know about the family, and this knowledge may be channeled into the different questions posed by the students about the French family. Thus, the predetermined syllabus can fulfill two functions: to serve as a data base or general orientation for those instructors whose students have raised certain questions, and to serve as a checklist to verify that essential areas of the family have been covered. One can evolve a general predetermined syllabus, one that would cover the family in an extensive manner and thus be adaptable to any level of instruction, or formulate specific syllabi for each level of instruction. These syllabi at a more advanced level should open discussion of more complex questions that lead to an understanding of some of the following issues: closeness of the French family (affective relations between parents and children), the geographic proximity of family members, the legal obligations between family members (*code Napoléon*), and the role of the family in different social classes.

Both the empathic approach and the predetermined syllabus can and probably should include francophone cultural presentations. Nothing impedes the instructor from juxtaposing the Senegalese family with the French family—nothing, that is, except our own ignorance. A remedy to this is to seek out francophone African students in one's institution and area and allow them to make a parallel presentation.

Below we supply level-specific applications to help you present the French family to your students.

# Elementary/Early Intermediate Level

Pose simple questions in French or more lengthy questions (as homework) in English to discover what the students wish to know about the French family and what aspects of it interest them. On the basis of these questions, select advertisements, family trees, individual photos, etc. Plan your illustrations and information so as to avoid explicit English commentary. Offer several family trees that make clear the declining birthrate—a source of intense anxiety to French demographers. If possible, select large rural families that have moved to the city over the past two generations so that the urban and rural birthrates can be compared with utter simplicity. Include family photos when possible to reinforce these differences. Emphasize these transformations in very simple French: "La famille à la campagne *était* nombreuse; la famille en ville *est* petite." In this manner complex sociological phenomena such as the rural exodus and the decline in family size can be communicated at the elementary level. Indicate the professions of the parents—again in simple French—to draw attention to shifting workplace and shifting gender roles in that workplace. Provide photographs of *crèches* to make students aware of the separation of mother and child and different social resources available in France and the United States. Provide photos of fathers ("les nouveaux pères") diapering babies and doing other "feminine" tasks to send messages about common marital behavior and the diminution of conventional roles. Illustrate with slides or photos the civil and religious marriage ceremonies that most French people go through. Provide an illustration of Muslim marriage in France to cover the customs of approximately 10 percent of the population of metropolitan France. Invite a French person and a francophone African to talk about their families in a simple manner—through illustrations and basic statements. Have students write very simple compositions describing these families or answer very brief one-word or multiple-choice questions about these presentations. Check your master syllabus or course-specific predetermined syllabus to make sure you have covered the essentials.

    In all of this, it is a given that your students should be involved in information-gathering activities. They should be encouraged to embark on various projects, such as making a collage on the French family, inviting French people they know to talk about the family, or recounting in a very simple French their own experiences with French families.

# Late Intermediate or Advanced

    Reintroduce the questions asked at the elementary level in more sophisticated oral and written forms using only French. Make the implied data of the elementary level explicit using statistical data to reinforce the low birthrate, the trigenerational family, the divorce rate, premarital cohabitation, single parenting, and families in which both spouses work. Introduce magazine *témoignages* to convey the feelings of family members about their conditions and changes in roles, and use the *témoignages* of students who have stayed with a French family or who have French boyfriends or girlfriends. Provide magazine and newspaper articles on the

French family. Find at least one film that portrays current family life. Add depth by comparing twentieth century transitions in family life in film and the written word: for example, compare Gide's cry of rage against the suffocating, authoritarian, bourgeois family "Familles . . . je vous hais" with current, rather optimistic sociological literature on the family—now viewed as a place of warmth and security in a rather hostile world. Take two Truffaut films, *Les 400 Cents Coups* and *L'Argent de poche* to illustrate the movement toward a warmer, less authoritarian family atmosphere. Investigate the family life of France's excluded North African minority, and bring in documentation or personal accounts from francophone West and Central Africa. Compare such family patterns with each other and with the American family.

Investigate family patterns according to social class, e.g., how proletarian women differ in their view of a career from middle- and upper-class women. Show the difficulties in the evolving roles of women and men as parents: fathers who don't know what to do with themselves and mother who find themselves, despite the rhetoric of liberation, playing the traditional role of the woman while being burdened with the disciplinary duties of the male. Discuss "la cohabitation juvénile," the tolerance of French parents for such arrangements, and the role of grandparents now largely reduced to affective dependence. Study a selection of recent magazine and television advertisements geared toward family consumption. Have students assess the socioeconomic status of the families normally represented, the sex roles (or refusal of those roles) depicted, the general relations between the spouses, and child-to-parent relationships. After presenting such models, have students consult the statistics of the INSEE,[6] the official French source of all national statistics on France, and sociological literature to ascertain the validity of the family images presented in these advertisements.

These applications should help you elicit performances appropriate to your students' levels of language study. Your elementary and early intermediate learners should now have had a firsthand exposure to a major feature of French society and culture. Despite their limited command of French, they will have been able to note key features of the current French family without the burden of linguistic commentary beyond their abilities. They will already possess essential data for the more interpretative work to come at a higher level of study. These students at the late intermediate and advanced levels will be able to move to an explicit discussion of the sociological phenomena that were implicit in earlier study. As they progress, they should move toward a more interpretative attitude to the data they encounter and they should assess such information as part of a general cultural matrix rather than isolated items.

# Notes

1.  Henri Besse, "Éduquer la perception interculturelle," *Le Français dans le monde* 188 (octobre 1984): 49.

2.  Janine Courtillon, "La Notion de progression appliquée à l'enseignement de la civilisation," *Le Français dans le monde* 188 (octobre 1984): 51–56.

3.  *Ibid.*, p. 52.

4.  See chapter 1, p. 28.

5.  Appendix V discusses empathy in a different framework. A reading of this chapter and Appendix V gives a comprehensive overview of the central role of empathy in cultural competence.

6.  Institut National de la Statistique et des Études Économiques.

# CHAPTER III

# STEREOTYPES: PERILS AND PRACTICALITY

**Figure 3–1. Superdupont.**

He wears a beret, a tricolor sash, and bedroom slippers; his hair is dark, he has a moustache, and though well muscled, he sports a substantial paunch and is ever ready for a "pig out." This tank-topped son of *la patrie* willingly offers his wrist as a perch for the *coq gaulois*. He knows a good wine and has a weakness for beautiful women; like Superman he can also fly. Who is he? He's "le premier superhéros à cent pour cent français"— Superdupont, the comic strip character and flying cliché.

# Autostereotypes and Heterostereotypes

Few authors have offered such a delicious conflation of French male stereotypes as Lob, Gotlib, and Alexis, the creators of Superdupont. Yet, were we to poll our students from a beginning French course, we might well discover that these students had a very developed repertoire of clichés about the French not unlike many of the notions Superdupont embodies. This is both the point and the problem. Unless students are encountering an absolutely exotic culture, they already reach the classroom fully saturated with an array of stereotypes, many deeply rooted and difficult to alter, the products of their own enculturation and media bombardment. They also demonstrate the duality characteristic of the stereotyping process: namely autostereotypes (how we characterize people from our own culture) and heterostereotypes (how we characterize people from another culture). Autostereotypes are usually positive images of our culture, whereas heterostereotypes are usually negative images of the other culture. Our image of our own culture is rarely the same as the image a person from outside our culture has of it. People from another culture do not see us in the same way as we see ourselves. Furthermore, how we see ourselves within our culture is often different from the image we want people from another culture to have of us. The national image we project is how we want other cultures to see us. In other words, the national image we convey to outsiders does not always match the insider image of ourselves within our culture.

While stereotyping is an aspect of the human gift for abstraction, it is a very dangerous kind of reductionism used to summarize perceived differences, the "national traits" of other peoples. Understanding and combatting the problem of stereotypes can lead to a better perception of other peoples by our students and resolve some of the barriers to empathy they pose. One of the key issues in cultural instruction is to find an approach that will temper these stereotypes, communicate valid cultural generalities, and allow for the individual and group diversity that makes up French culture—or any other culture, for that matter.

# Coping with Stereotypes

This is easier said than done. Fortunately, there are many approaches to the problem. Some teachers of culture, such as Laurence Wylie, assume that stereotypes are inevitable, even after cultural instruction. Wylie thus offers the very modest but appropriate goal of a refinement process that seeks "to help our students and ourselves to improve on the traditional cultural stereotypes of people from other cultures."[1]

A quick way for instructors to ascertain the principal stereotypes the class holds about France and the French is to ask students at the beginning of the course to make a list of (1) three things they know about France; (2) those things they like about the French or the French way of life; (3) three things they don't like about the French or the French way of life; (4) three adjectives to describe the French. Students can then be asked to answer the same four questions about their own culture. A brief comparison of the answers will sensitize the class to the subjectivity of such judgments and raise the question of the source of their judgments. The instructor then has the choice either of using the stereotypes elicited by the questionnaire as a reference point from time to time during the course as students get more information that will allow them to re-evaluate their judgments about the French and about the value system of their own culture or of using the stereotypes elicited as a principal theme of the course and as a basis for collective self-analysis designed to develop a contrastive study of the two cultures.

While the use of a double collection of stereotypes—auto and hetero—may be one means of drawing attention to the fundamental differences between francophone and anglophone cultures, the principal danger of such an approach lies in the destruction of empathy and the development of a real antipathy to the other culture, the "us versus them" mentality.

An example of the danger of the classroom use of heterostereotypes may be found in the presentation of some common French assumptions about Americans. If one tells students that the French believe Americans to be loud, politically naive, superficial in friendship, generally overweight, and excessively materialistic, this does not create a climate of debate or evaluation—even though this may be the intent. Normally, students react with considerable annoyance to such caricatures, and they manifest diminished enthusiasm for the study of French.

A further difficulty in the discussion of stereotypes is found in the phenomenon of "filtering." Veronica Pugibet's study of perceptions of the French by Mexican students bears witness to the radically deforming power of stereotypes:

> Le stéréotype a paru fonctionner comme un filtre car :
> —il est réducteur : *c'est un pays où* TOUT *le monde prend du vin rouge, du pain, du fromage, du pâté.*
> —il est profondément intégré: *à part le fromage et le vin, je ne vois pas ce qu'il y a de français. La veste du garçon est très française parce qu'elle est très élégante.*
> —il détache l'attribut symbolique de son lieu d'implantation vivant et le coupe de sa réalité ambiante.[2]

The reductionist nature of stereotyping eliminates the differences between the subcultures in the society, thus preventing the student from perceiving its richness and diversity. Worse, as Gail Robinson points out, once a stereotype is generated (normally from a perceived difference), one often expects or observes consistency of the stereotype in other people even "where no such consistency exists."[3]

If stereotypes are so powerful, so obstructive in any effort to achieve real contact with the French and if stereotypes are already part of the beginning students' intellectual baggage, other strategies need to be devised to allow the learners at least some possibility of refining their notions as Wylie suggests. These strategies need delineation at all levels. Any people has its own positive and negative stereotyping of itself, and these self-images are often useful in reorienting the stereotypes of them held by external cultures. Advertisements and satirical cartoons are rich sources of a culture's self-image because sales and social critique are primarily geared for internal consumption. These can be compared with advertisements geared toward foreigners such as the sale of luxury items and the promotion of tourism, which imply the marketing of certain notions of France that the French want to project to a foreign audience.

Disney World in Orlando provides an opportunity to compare French self-marketing and self-stereotyping in the French Pavilion with the image Americans present of themselves in the American Pavilion. The French describe themselves like their cathedrals—heads in the sky with feet firmly planted on the ground—to illustrate the peculiar combination of practicality and idealism that they believe characterizes them as a people. The appeal of France is that of a land in which past traditions exert a powerful attraction on the present, whereas the emphasis in the American Pavilion is on the progress made by American society since the Mayflower and American aspirations for the future. Both autostereotypes are probably unknown to most of our students and pose new reflections for them in understanding the French.

Illustrations, advertisements, and articles can also be used to discuss the image Americans have of themselves and the image they wish to project to other cultures. Students can be asked to supply their own national stereotypes and to decide how completely they agree with them. They can be asked how accurate they think the images are that the United States wishes to project internationally. The difference of views expressed by the students can be the starting point for understanding the relativity of these images and what residual truth there may be in national traits.

# Presenting the Diversity of French Culture

Clearly, in elementary French, if English commentary is to be avoided, brief presentations of different types of French people in a variety of activities are needed. At the intermediate level, however, presentation can become more sophisticated. The ordering principle in J.-N. Rey and G. Santoni's text, *Quand les Français parlent*,[4] could well be used at the intermediate level—though with some modification, as the text was intended for advanced usage. In their text, individual members of various sociological groups discuss common themes; the merit of these *témoignages* lies chiefly in allowing individuals to speak for themselves and in giving students direct contact with the French unobstructed by an authorial voice that reduces experience to generalization.

Despite the diversity this approach engenders, it is interesting to observe that in French society certain themes emerge very distinctly, e.g., reserve in relations between students and professors, gradual social ascension, a more distinct consciousness of class or milieu, a passionate attachment to regions and homes, pride of profession, etc. In other words, the vitality and uniqueness of different individuals are respected while a sense of commonality emerges—one that may be very different from representative themes in American culture.

There needs, however, to be some caution here. Many of the preoccupations elaborated are negative from an American point of view, and such awareness may create a false sense of superiority in the naive learner. In short, a sophisticated presentation may obstruct an empathic identification with the subjects. A further difficulty lies in the potential for the creation of abstract reconstructions of members of various milieus. As Michel Pierssens warns:

> Il faut finir avec le portrait stéréotypique du Français 'typique'— reconstruction abstraite sans vraisemblance—et même avec le tableau clinique purement socio-économique, qui identifie les particuliers à une série de portraits-robots (l'O.S., le cadre, l'agriculteur, l'étudiant, etc.). La sociologie, l'économie, la psychologie sociale, la linguistique, la sémiotique, l'anthropologie culturelle, etc. nous permettent des perspectives suffisamment fines pour qu'une présentation articulée de leurs résultats soit possible, sans simplification.[5]

Santoni has also warned that in the very process of assembling readings for cultural presentation, we risk propagating self-images and stereotypes.[6] Thus, considerable sensitivity is justified when presenting the social groups and attitudes that make up contemporary France.

On the other hand, such observations do not warrant our abandoning the process, but, rather, they oblige us to reflect carefully on our mode of presentation. Surveys of behaviors, attitudes, and opinions published in French and American magazines can be used to stress diversity rather than uniformity within society and to reveal similarities and differences across societies. Statistical material available from publications by INSEE (Institut national de la statistique et des études économiques) may be used at the advanced level to refine the concept of diversity. Gérard Mermet's *Francoscopie* 1993 contains a rich source of data to illustrate continuing transformations within French society which break down stereotypes, as the table on page 41 shows.[7]

Other instruments, such as advertising data, also help us to categorize cautiously the very numerous subcultures into which marketers divide the French public. Bernard Cathelat's *Les Styles de vie des Français* 1978–1998[8] illustrates how the French can be broken down into intersecting value groups that allow for considerable diversity of opinions and objectives: "La France de l'aventure, La France du recentrage, La France utilitariste." But we should also remember that this kind of categorization is a western cultural tendency perhaps at its most pronounced within France itself. Indeed, even *Le Point* has made comic efforts to describe the various "tribes" of young people within French society: la droite prolétarienne, les minets, les babas cool, les rockers, les punks, les silicon valley.[9]

## Valeurs d'hier, d'aujourd'hui et de demain

| Dans l'évolution de la société française au cours des vingt dernières années, quelles sont, selon vous, les valeurs qui ont **perdu** en importance? (%) | | Au cours des vingt dernières années, quelles sont selon vous, les valeurs qui ont **gagné** en importance dans l'évolution de la société française? (%) | | Quelles sont, aujourd'hui, les valeurs qu'il vous paraît important et même nécessaire de **sauvegarder** ou de **restaurer** pour l'avenir? (%) | |
|---|---|---|---|---|---|
| La politesse | 64 | La réussite matérielle | 60 | La justice | 71 |
| L'honnêteté | 56 | La compétitivité | 59 | L'honnêteté | 59 |
| Le respect du bien commun | 49 | L'esprit d'entreprise | 34 | La politesse | 53 |
| La justice | 44 | La liberté | 20 | La liberté | 52 |
| L'esprit de famille | 42 | La solidarité | 18 | L'esprit de famille | 50 |
| Le respect de la tradition | 40 | Le sens du beau | 17 | Le respect du bien commun | 47 |
| Le sens du devoir | 37 | La responsabilité | 14 | L'égalité | 45 |
| L'honneur | 34 | Le sens de la fête | 14 | Le sens du devoir | 45 |
| La solidarité | 29 | L'autorité | 14 | La solidarité | 41 |
| L'égalité | 25 | L'égalité | 8 | La responsabilité | 33 |
| Le sens de la fête | 24 | L'esprit de famille | 5 | L'hospitalité | 31 |
| L'autorité | 24 | L'hospitalité | 5 | L'honneur | 30 |
| La responsabilité | 23 | La justice | 4 | Le respect des traditions | 22 |
| L'hospitalité | 22 | Le sens du devoir | 3 | La compétitivité | 22 |
| Le pardon | 14 | Le pardon | 2 | L'esprit d'entreprise | 20 |
| La liberté | 12 | L'honneur | 2 | Le sens du beau | 19 |
| La compétitivité | 12 | Le respect du bien commun | 2 | L'autorité | 19 |
| Le sens du beau | 9 | Le respect de la tradition | 2 | Le sens de la fête | 18 |
| L'esprit d'entreprise | 8 | La politesse | 2 | Le pardon | 17 |
| La réussite matérielle | 3 | L'honnêteté | 1 | La réussite matérielle | 8 |

Le Pèlerin magazine/Sofrès, octobre 1991

# A Positive Image: French Idealism

Nevertheless, categorical descriptions can be only part of the solution. A sociological approach is only one way to present a society. Another alternative in avoiding stereotypes would be a presentation oriented toward themes in French life. The development of simplistic, negative stereotypes may be tempered if a basis for attraction to the target culture can be engendered among the learners. The romantic idealism that is not only a major preoccupation of French intellectuals but something of interest to the French public at large could become a source of attraction. Individual *témoignages* of real commitment are plentiful: the exploits of French doctors, the *Médecins sans frontières*, in many dangerous parts of the world offer examples of generous and inspiring actions. Such accounts also are very close to the kind of commitment found in literature and philosophy and would naturally invite readings from Sartre or de Beauvoir. Likewise, the antidiscriminatory activities of S.O.S. *Racisme* and the ecological consciousness of Jacques Cousteau all illustrate French idealism in action and simultaneously elicit identification and admiration. Indeed, at an earlier level of language learning, an overview of French society may be less important in cultural pedagogy than a deeper knowledge of some of that society's more attractive features.

# Shock Treatment: Humor and Surprise

The use of positive themes will promote identification and significantly challenge the negative stereotypes and perceptions students have developed before entering the language classroom. Nevertheless, some kind of "shock remedy" may be needed to rid students of some of their stereotypes. Indeed, that is the point of the opening allusion to Superdupont. This comic strip points to a remedy through humor, and we will present it as an illustration of an approach that could be used as early as the intermediate level. Here we propose but a brief sample technique. Taking Superdupont, one need only ask the students to catalog the ways in which he is French and begin an examination of the "verities" he reveals. His characteristics could be broken down into several significant categories:

1. apparel and accoutrements: the beret, the bedroom slippers, the *coq gaulois*, the *baguette*, the tricolor sash

2. physical appearance: dark hair, moustache, and paunch

3. moral traits: xenophobia, cunning, arrogance, respect for authority, willingness to cheat on taxes

4. his name

At the first level, an analysis of the statistical validity of these traits could be interesting. For instance, the beret, as is well known, represents a trend that peaked in the thirties and this cap is rarely worn today—except by the military[10] and, of course, by *les petits vieux*. Additionally, it can be pointed out that the beret is in itself Basque, i.e., the product of a separate language and culture that is particular to regions of France and Spain. The bedroom slippers are likewise confined to a particular class—very much a blue-collar phenomenon. The *baguette* was introduced by bakers between the two world wars[11] and, though widely popular, is a recent innovation in French life— an invention whose refined flour is disapproved of by the more health conscious section of the French population. The tricolor sash is the adornment of a French mayor during ceremonial functions and naturally ridiculous under any other circumstances—a clear illustration of superpatriotism. The *coq gaulois* can be considered a symbol of chauvinism and associated with the *cocorico* of nationalist diatribes. In short, symbolically, Superdupont is instantly a manifestation of outdated notions rather than a representative of today's French man, a comically perverse exercise of decoding.

In fact, Superdupont is also the exact opposite of the American comic strip and film character, Superman, who inspired his creation. Committed to "truth, justice, and the American way," the original Superman was precisely the embodiment of all the virtues of the American autostereotype, and, as such, the character sent completely different messages to other societies, as is evident in the French parody. Only in the films of the seventies does Superman take on any self-conscious irony and, even then, the character never ridicules fundamental American values the way Superdupont satirizes French society. Here, there is obviously an extraordinary opportunity for cross-cultural comparison.

Superdupont's physical appearance allows for an array of surprises. Most of our students probably associate being Latin with being dark. They may be quite amazed to learn that the French have nearly as many redheads as the Scots (4 percent and 5 percent respectively), more blonds (12 percent and 11 percent respectively), and fewer dark-eyed people than the English—although these distributions vary radically from region to region.[12] Any reflection on moustaches will reveal that this is quite a regular feature of the American male. The paunch leads to numerous possibilities for speculation, as the French usually impress Americans as much slimmer than they and yet more capable of eating large meals at one sitting. This allows for a spirited discussion of eating habits.

Superdupont's flaws are caricatural and not particularly restricted to any nation. Our students have a lot to learn about their own chauvinism and xenophobia. Here more subtle statistics and comparisons between the United States and France are needed: a comparison of the national emblems of the *coq gaulois* and the American eagle, a discussion about the symbols of the *tricolore* and the "Stars 'n Stripes," a consideration of the amendment to bar flag burning in the United States, a comparison of immigration levels and immigrant populations between the United States and France, etc. Superdupont's childish cunning, his excessive respect for authority (but willingness to cheat on his own taxes), his utter conviction of the correctness of France's political maneuvers (even when this includes hiring prostitutes to accommodate foreign dignitaries), all point to a kind of chauvinism that, despite its Gallic sauciness, has much in common with the arrogance of any nation.

Superdupont's name is in itself revelatory. "Dupont" has emerged as one of the cliché names for the average Frenchman. In this case, the assumption is made by the French themselves rather than foreigners; it is thus an illustration of an autostereotype. What is especially interesting is that "Dupont" is not a common French name at all—"Martin" is the most widely distributed last name in France.[13] Such an observation can be the starting point for students to create through class discussion an American stereotype similar to Superdupont. This would remind them that French autostereotypes are themselves suspect and inaccurate, that learners must come to their own judgments about what is truly French.

After a brief study about such a comic strip, a whole discussion of humor would be warranted. It would be beneficial to remind students that this character represents the French laughing at themselves, that the authors by their critical distance and the readers in appreciating the sarcasms clearly set themselves apart from the beliefs that Superdupont is supposed to embody. The laughter of a nation at its supposed national traits directly implies that the values of the French—at least those who enjoy Superdupont—are the contrary of those he represents, that the kind of Frenchman he "typifies" is considered a reactionary fool. The very pointed humor of the comic strip testifies to the fact that the French male is not a Superdupont or, at least, that a significant number of French people do not conform to the patterns he represents.

The French female is also the subject of stereotyping and romantic mythologizing by foreigners—especially male. A satirical drawing by Cabu of a stereotype of the French woman and other "typical" images of France with the caption "France is more than . . ." is used on the cover of a brochure published by the Cultural Services of the French Consulate in Chicago and the AATF. (See figure 3–2.) The purpose of this brochure is to show that there are many reasons for learning French that take the learner far beyond such reductionist, simplistic stereotypes. Once again statistical and visual data about French women from different socioeconomic backgrounds and their role in the family and in the workplace can destroy this offensive image of all French women as *midinettes*.

**Figure 3–2. The French woman as *midinette*.**

**Astérix,** the Gallic hero of the comic books written by Goscinny, illustrates many of the self-perceived national traits of the French, this time in a historical context. Those comic books have been used very successfully in language classrooms, but it is necessary for the instructor to remind students of the importance of parody in Astérix's adventures by getting them to find examples in the text and to place Astérix within the cultural framework of the French laughing at themselves.

In the Astérix books, there are also examples of humorous stereotypes of people from other European countries seen through French eyes. Another example of a foreign stereotype used for comic effect is Major Thompson, created by Pierre Daninos.[14] Major Thompson with his bowler hat and umbrella typifies the archetypal Englishman who proudly carries his values and customs with him to France, where he finds so many behaviors and events "shocking." Daninos also uses Major Thompson as a means of criticizing certain negative aspects of French life.

Humor is not the only form of shock treatment available for clichés acquired before entering the language classroom. A host of other antidotes exist. An important example may be found in body language. Many students imagine that, as Latins, the French gesticulate wildly, that they have a loose and supple body language. A few pages from Wylie and a collection of slides can correct these false images of how the French move and, by implication, who they are. An analysis of television coverage of an international summit meeting that shows the French president interacting with the U.S. president and other heads of state or of a television interview with French and Americans allows body language to be placed in a general context that is not caricatural and shows how people from different cultures have a complex system of communicating meaning, which includes gesticulation. Following Wylie's observation, communication is a "dance" between partners in which body language plays a major role. Again, the point is to provide early on in a course enough surprises and enjoyment to free the students to question their clichés about the foreigner.

Thus, by way of a conclusion, the battle against clichés is a very difficult one, largely because these clichés are deeply embedded before our students ever enter the classroom. Humor and surprise are good weapons in upsetting fixed and inaccurate notions held by students. These techniques are, however, not adequate in themselves. To create a genuine climate of empathy, French activities worthy of admiration and identification need to constitute a substantial part of any course. Studying another culture is a gesture of friendliness, a process of in-depth communication that engages the entire person. Such study flourishes in an atmosphere of curiosity, openness, and respect. Without this positive attitude, even the most sociologically refined material may produce feelings of boredom or naive convictions of superiority.

# Applications

The following activities concentrate on destroying negative stereotypes by focusing first on the physical image of the French and second on an example of French idealism, the ecological movement.

# A Visual and Statistical Image of the French

## Elementary/Early Intermediate

**Self-Awareness.** Who are the Americans? Have students compile a picture of themselves. Ask for magazine clippings illustrating Americans in all activities. Encourage diversity and make sure that the pictures include prominent minorities: African-Americans, Asians, Hispanics, and Native Americans. See to it that your students—especially those in very homogenous instructional settings—are aware of the ethnic and racial diversity of their own country.

Provide very simplified statistical tables for your students. These tables should provide racial and ethnic breakdowns of the American population, e.g., "Les noirs composent treize pour cent de la population américaine." You can even avoid the verb by using an equal sign. Make sure that the pictures illustrate different work activities, once again in an effort to avoid homogeneity and stereotypical vision. Have students describe the work or leisure activities of each individual in simple French, e.g., "Mme Olivera est p.d.g. [C.E.O.]: elle dirige une entreprise, elle travaille cinquante heures par semaine."

The ultimate goal of the self-awareness activity should be to make students realize how difficult it is to formulate simple stereotypes about their own population with the implication that the same problem will hold true for France.

**The French.** Now have the students attempt the same with the French. Help them out if necessary with your own collection of pictures and slides and make realia like magazines available for students to search for the information themselves. Whenever possible, ask students to talk about French people they have seen to gather diverse images of the French. When dealing with Caucasian subjects, be sure to include a great variety of physical types. It is important for students to realize that the French do not conform to the stereotypes of being short and dark. Be sure that some pictures represent North African Arabs (Maghrébins), Black Africans, and the citizens of Guadeloupe and Martinique as well as Southeast Asians.

You should then use simple statistical tables. First of all, as the majority of the population is European in background, the tables should illustrate facts like height, hair and eye color, and perhaps ethnic origin to make it clear that even white French people represent a very diverse population mix. Your simple statistical tables should indicate the percentage of North Africans in France, perhaps separating citizens, legal residents, and illegal aliens, but it is important for students to realize that the North African presence comprises some 10 percent of the metropolitan French population. Many of the increasing Indochinese population in France are also French citizens. It can be pointed out that in Paris the twentieth arrondissement is mainly inhabited by Maghrébins and Black Africans and that there is a concentration of Southeast Asians in the thirteenth arrondissement.

Students should also have an idea about the kind of work in which the French population engages. At this point, you can ask if there is a "français typique" and you might use an image of Superdupont, a cartoon, or Astérix to get their response. If they have gotten the joke, they have probably gotten the point.

## Late Intermediate/Advanced

**Self-Awareness.**    Students should do the same form of information gathering, but more commentary now must be infused. For instance, one can ask what kind of image of the United States the movies they see attempt to portray, how media advertising attempts to typify Americans, and who the "typical Americans" are. A discussion of the processes that generate such stereotypes can also be undertaken. One might also note the risk of stereotyping American minority groups by overlooking the differences within them. For example, within the Hispanic group, Americans have a different image of successful Mexicans and Cubans than of poorer Puerto Ricans.

Statistical tables need to be more subtle at this level, indicating socioeconomic breakdown as well as racial and ethnic backgrounds. What groups do what kinds of work? What groups show high percentages of unemployment? What groups enjoy the highest levels of education?

**The French.**    Once again a collection of illustrations of different French citizens in different work and leisure activities is appropriate. Students should be asked what kind of people the advertisements and illustrations often seek to typify, and again what forces drive these processes.

Statistical tables are once again required, but this time they need to be more expanded, taking into consideration the questions raised in the American statistical tables. Students will probably find a disarming similarity between the two societies and many common problems.

**Diversity and Assimilation.** Here students need to analyze the corresponding diversities of each nation to understand that there is no such thing as a true French or American physical type. They need to be aware of the tremendous level of immigration (initially European) into France. They need to understand that the French face very similar problems to those of the Americans in assimilating vast Third World immigrant populations from the south. They will also need to understand that the racism that has increased in France today, exacerbated by the extreme right-wing political party, *Le Front National*, is linked to this immigration, which is in part an aspect of the colonial heritage. In the final analysis, though, they should be aware that "Frenchness" is a cultural product, not a physical inheritance.

**Cross-Cultural Comparisons.** Advertisements, surveys and articles published in magazines, as well as extracts from writings by sociologists, anthropologists, and writers of fiction, and American films containing French characters and French films with American characters can be the source for an analysis of how Americans see the French and vice-versa. Students may be annoyed by the general image the French have of Americans and by the French view of America as a land of violence and excessive consumerism. But their reaction needs to be balanced by the understanding that the American view of the French can be equally annoying to French nationals. A comparison of these views will hopefully lead to a distrust of stereotypes and a greater tolerance of difference.

# Ecological Concerns

## Elementary/Early Intermediate

**Self-Awareness.** Have students compile lists of American and international organizations devoted to protecting the environment (Sierra Club, Audubon Society, Greenpeace, etc.)

**Cousteau.** Perhaps the most famous of all French ecologists is Jacques Cousteau. Most students have seen some of his films on television, and they already have a positive stereotype in his case, although they may not have really connected him with France. Have the students report on his films, identify his ship, name his crew. Since their language ability is very limited, a description of a particular film can be very simplified: "sujet—les baleines; lieu—l'Atlantique; danger—la chasse meurtrière." One can thus compile a simple table of contents for his films. A showing of one of his films can be arranged. Simple cloze reading exercises can be used to foster comprehension and reinforce language learning. In many cases, a segment of an episode would be sufficient. Students can also prepare a simplified biography of Cousteau.

**General Ecological Activities.**   The instructor might compile an illus-trated list of national parks, of some ecological conflicts in France: clashes between bird hunters and bird watchers in the Pyrenees during the large bird migration, protests at a nuclear plant in Brittany, etc. Again, very simplified headings and minimal commentary are sufficient here.

**Cross-Cultural Comparisons.**   Examine similarities between the citizens of the two nations (members of the Sierra Club and Les Verts) on these ecological concerns, again creating a sense of identification with the French rather than opposition to their concerns.

## Late Intermediate/Advanced

**Self-Awareness.**   Follow the previous steps, but this time actually look into the charters of the listed organizations or examine their recruitment literature.

**Cousteau.**   Engage in a far more sophisticated discussion of the films and activities of Cousteau, including the economics of his relationship to American distributors and the shared concerns and affections that make his documentaries so popular in the United States and in France. Note that a Cousteau museum has been opened in Paris and study the French reaction to it.

**General Ecological Activities.**   Do a more intensive study of French ecological groups and examine their recruitment literature. Have students report in detail on some of the major political clashes that have occurred within France itself on ecological issues. Develop the whole question of France's heavy dependence on nuclear power, and, reviewing the questions of acid rain and inadequate oil supply, consider why the French have been more inclined than the Americans to embrace nuclear power.

**Final Assessment.**   Show that there is a conflict in both nations over ecological issues, but illustrate that American and French ecologists have remarkably similar concerns and objectives. Again, stress that we are far more alike than different and allow for enthusiastic identification with French efforts. The ultimate objective is to give the students the opportunity to identify with shared concerns in both countries and thus be motivated to pursue their studies in French.

# Notes

1.  Laurence Wylie. "The Civilization Course" in Georges V. Santoni, ed., *Société et culture de la France contemporaine* (Albany: State Univ. of New York Press, 1981), p. 5.

2.  Véronica Pugibet, "Des Stéréotypes de la France et des Français chez les étudiants mexicains," *Le Français dans le monde* 181 (1983): 51.

3.  Gail L. Nemetz Robinson, *Issues in Second Language and Cross-Cultural Education: The Forest through the Trees* (Boston: Heinle & Heinle, 1981), p. 58.

4.  Jean-Noël Rey and Georges V. Santoni, *Quand les Français parlent* (Rowley, MA: Newbury House, 1975).

5.  Michel Pierssens, "Civilisation, culture, pratiques culturelles," *Michigan Romance Studies* III (1983): 186.

6.  Georges V. Santoni, "Stéréotypes, contextes visuels et dimensions sociales," *Le Français dans le monde* 181 (1983): 86.

7.  Gérard Mermet, *Francoscopie* 1993 (Paris: Larousse, 1993), p. 236. The information in the table is based on an opinion poll carried out by *Le Pèlerin* magazine/Sofrès, octobre 1991.

8.  Bernard Cathelat, *Les Styles de vie des Français* 1978–1998 (Paris: Stanké, 1977).

9.  "Jeunes: la France des tribus," *Le Point*, 13–19 août 1984, pp 55–60.

10.  Theodore Zeldin, *The French* (New York: Vintage Books, 1984), p. 36.

11.  *Ibid.*, p. 483.

12.  *Ibid.*, p. 44

13.  *Ibid.*, p. 35.

14.  Pierre Daninos, *Les Carnets du major* W. *Marmaduke Thompson; découverte de la France et des Français* (Paris: Hachette, 1954) and *Les Nouveaux Carnets du major* W. *Marmaduke Thompson* (Paris: Hachette, 1973).

# CHAPTER IV

# TEACHING A
# HIGH-CONTEXT CULTURE

## Problems of Generalization

It might be said that culture is something we all believe in and no one can define. People allude to different cultures with a certain blitheness, as if these were concrete, easily described mindsets, behavioral patterns, and values commonly accepted by the rest of educated humanity. Indeed there is a natural assumption that cultures are compact, monolithic entities whose readily recognizable characteristics predict the behavior of their people. Once a careful examination of these alleged characteristics begins, however, generalities break down, patterns of contradictory behavior emerge within subgroups in the culture, and many assertions are revealed to be empty stereotypes, which, in some cases, may be totally contradictory to a real portrait of the people and the culture.

Further complicating the matter is the fact that nationhood itself is a recent concept, and virtually all nations have attempted to suppress the differences evidenced by minorities within their confines. France alone provides several trenchant examples in the cases of the Provençals, the Bretons, and the Corsicans—all of whose languages and cultures have been largely suppressed to create a dominant État français. Thus, as one shifts from a macroscopic to a microscopic view of another people, as one looks at the different subcultures—i.e., the various minorities that compose a nation—generalization becomes less and less tenable. Taken to the logical extreme of this process, one is left with a collection of individual dossiers.[1]

While this position is fatal to all cultural generalizations, it illustrates the difficulty inherent in the discussion of a culture. In defining a culture, we are further constrained by the understanding that cultures are not static, and that, in today's global village of rapid communication and extensive world travel, the cultures we are studying are in constant flux, that even the millennial trends that typify "deep" culture may be in a state of rapid evolution.

# Approaches to Cultural Generalization

With these cautions in mind, we still have to find a way of approaching and analyzing French culture. An appropriate point of departure would be to consider certain levels of permissible generalization. Any discussion of culture needs to be placed under at least two headings:

1. Generalization about humanity as a whole: beliefs in justice, equity, affection, loyalty, truthfulness, respect for human life. (Of course, the specific cultural articulations of these concepts will vary widely upon investigation, but the absence of general opposition allows them to function as values or concepts that, in their vaguest formulation, might be considered as cross-cultural universals.)

2. Generalizations about given cultures. Here one must distinguish between

   a. cultures primarily confined to single nation-states (e.g., Italy, which is the sole nation to use Italian as its language of official communication)

   b. those cultures whose linguistic extensions embrace other political entities (e.g., Chinese, English, French, German, Russian, Spanish)

   c. those cultures whose language does not embrace any political entity, as in the cases of the Basques and the Kurds

   d. those cultures in which the language and culture of a colonial country have been imposed on a majority of diverse linguistic communities, as is commonplace in Africa

Obviously, francophone culture covers both *b* and *d*.

# French or Francophone Culture

At this juncture, certain choices in French culture already impose themselves. The easiest solution is to limit the choice to metropolitan France and concentrate on constructing generalizations appropriate to this single, already less than homogeneous country. The much more difficult and complex solution is to embrace the whole of *francophonie*, which includes (a) indigenous francophone groups (Quebec, Belgium, Switzerland), (b) territories where French has been successfully imposed and which have been politically annexed (Martinique, Guadeloupe, French Polynesia, New Caledonia, Reunion, etc.), (c) countries where French is the official language but is restricted largely to the urban elites and administrators (virtually all francophone Africa), and (d) those countries of North Africa (Algeria, Morocco, and Tunisia) where the use of French is widespread although the official language is Arabic.

Given the immensity and variety of *francophonie*, one recoils initially from generalization about this disparate mass of communities and countries.[2] The degree of knowledge required to make general statements of particular value is here clearly beyond the scope of any one scholar or even group of scholars. The community is so large that it defies all but the most universal and, for our purposes, most superficial generalizations. It is imperative to avoid making an unjust and culturally biased amalgam of the dynamic indigenous cultures and the remains of the colonial French culture in these countries.

One possible strategy is to start with the primary focus of attention on France and, when student interest or the course requires it, to use a knowledge of French culture as a reference point for understanding those cultures where French represents an adstratum that may be in conflict with the indigenous cultures. Indeed, the very fact that French is an adstratum means that these countries are not even truly francophone cultures. Rather than functioning as the only worthy area of study in these countries, French assumes an introductory function to their cultures; it fulfills a facilitating role as a simple step in understanding the cultural strata in francophone societies.

In our efforts to include other non-European cultures in our courses, we may well be unwittingly promoting a veiled form of French imperialism, especially in the case of Africa. Assuming that language is the basic glue that unites these diverse countries ignores the reality that French is not the indigenous tongue in most cases. The presentation of "francophonie" in French language textbooks has reduced this diversity to tokenism and oversimplified homogenization. Perhaps we should rather think in terms of area studies specifically aimed at African cultures. Here French should probably be a secondary consideration that must give way to more telling issues of societal organization, African values (if there is any such universality), questions of economics, and issues of renewed cultural self-definition that are just as common to anglophone and lusophone Africa. Professionally we are caught in a dilemma: ignoring francophone Africa encourages accusations of racism, while making the requisite acknowledgment of francophone Africa in textbooks runs the risk of "recolonializing" these nations by placing them within the French "rayonnement culturel."

Initial study focused on France may serve as an introduction to francophone countries, but we must remain very cautious about viewing France and the French language as the primary focus of attention when presenting them to our students. We should recall that French is probably spoken by no more than 20 percent of all the inhabitants of "francophone" Africa where widely used, even international indigenous languages offer French stiff competition, and local variants of French such as FPI ("le français populaire ivorien") show considerable independence from its "standard" version. It is perhaps in the interaction between French culture and the various African cultures where the most interesting studies might be undertaken, for these interchanges or negotiations could prove most instructive to us in our own attempts to create biculturalism among our students and to understand its implications.

# High-Context Culture

Cultures can be classified as high-context or low-context. A high-context culture is one in which human relations are governed by a relatively complex code of behavioral expectations, hierarchies, and obligations, one in which there are constant references to the past and to events of historical import, one in which actions and policies are seen in relationship to an elaborate context rather than in isolation. A low-context culture, on the other hand, tends to isolate specific actions, behaviors, and policies and underplays the context in which they unfold. No culture is uniquely high-context or low-context. All cultures have a contextual richness. What distinguishes a high-context from a low-context culture is the degree of emphasis and attention accorded to those practices that underscore the relational nature of behavior. High-context and low-context are also relative terms that derive their meaning from cross-cultural comparison.

Among western nations, France figures as a relatively high-context culture, whereas, when compared to one of the many Indian cultures, France may appear quite the opposite. In this framework, France may be classified as a high-context culture in comparison with the United States, which has the characteristics of a low-context culture.

A high-context culture should not be confused with a high-tech culture. The word "high-tech" refers to an intensive use of technology by the general population. Such applications can range from automatic tellers to bio-medical computer projections. In this sense, both France and the United States are high-tech cultures. Modern France prides itself in its utilization in daily life of sophisticated technology such as the Minitel (a kind of computerized national telephone directory with many other information services), electronic readers in stores, plastic public telephone cards (la télécarte), ticket-checking devices in the métro and at train stations, and, of course, the TGV (le train à grande vitesse), which has become a symbol of modern France.

How can we bring the notion of a high-context culture with its special networks of relationships to American students whose own behavior patterns have been developed within the parameters of a low-context culture? At the elementary level, it is extremely difficult to present in French a theoretical structure, a careful illustration of a phenomenon as part of a cultural whole. We can, however, present specific utterances, significant gestures, and authentic materials that elicit student interest and that illustrate general cultural patterns without commentary for the time being. We can thus lay the foundation for cultural discussion by providing the raw data for future interpretation. Some instructors at this stage may elect to give a brief presentation in English of the concept of a high-context culture in order to give students a frame of reference for the networks to which the isolated pieces of information are to be connected. Here, in this preliminary elaboration of high-context culture, the essential is authenticity of the presentation and a proper understanding of the student point of view. In regard to the latter, Nelson Brooks elaborates an extensive list of topics based on the premise that "the point of view should be that of a young person as he goes about his daily tasks."[3] The list is far ranging, e.g., "Greetings, Patterns of Politeness, Observance of Sunday, Comradeship, Flowers and Gardens, Getting from Place to Place, Odd Jobs and Earning Power," etc.,[4] and it aims at providing the instructor with a large, flexible array of topics from which to make selections according to the interests of the students. It is clear that an instructor deliberately avoiding English commentary could present a wide range of high-context cultural practices (greetings, meal rituals, educational practices, etc.) without formal com-mentary, thus giving the students an experiential exposure to the patterns of a high-context culture. Simple comparisons with corresponding American practices would sensitize students to the existence of different cultural networks.

In a similar fashion, the 1987 AATF tentative cultural guidelines pointed to simple skills for basic cultural competence, skills such as the ability to use public transportation, to cash a check, and to secure lodging as well as to a limited knowledge of the culture such as common attitudes toward public behavior and the qualities sought in French education.[5] Again it is doubtful that, without formal explanations, the behavior and concepts advocated at the early stages of language instruction can be placed within a high-context framework; knowledge acquired at this level is necessarily functional and thus preliminary to any intellectualized, abstract, systematic understanding of French culture. Its value lies in the fact that it provides an initial stock of phenomena that can be interpreted when a sufficient number of phenomena allow cultural patterns to be delineated.

To approach high-context culture seriously, the instructor must have some method of organizing the material presented to the students. George H. Hughes provides a concise summary of four cultural models in his article in *Culture Bound*.[6] Initially, he considers some of Nelson Brooks's individual questions designed to promote systematic observation—questions that are followed by individual questions. Hughes also cites Hall's ten primary message systems (Interaction, Association, Subsistence, Bisexuality, Territoriality, Temporality, Learning, Play, Defense, and Exploitation). These categories are not French-culture-specific but are intended to be universally applicable. Hughes then cites examples from the Taylor and Sorenson model designed for the construction of culture capsules. (Their model is primarily aimed at Hispanic culture and emphasizes attitudes toward time.) Hughes also reviews Howard Nostrand's emergent model.[7]

Another approach to teaching culture is presented by François Mariet, who maintains that

> . . . il faut privilégier l'étude du procès de socialisation. La famille et
> l'école, mais plus encore la culture de consommation doivent faire l'objet
> d'une attention primordiale afin que l'on substitue à des contenus
> atomisés une approche relationelle et logique.[8]

Mariet directs considerable attention to advertising and points to the segmentation and distinction that characterize a consumer society. He is sensitive to advertising's skill in homing in upon homogeneous segments of the population and sees advertising as a key tool to presenting a culture in its actuality, but he is equally concerned with stressing the group-oriented messages within the context of the whole consumer society. In other words, he insists on understanding the network of relationships that bind a particular advertisement, packaging, television broadcast, or an article to the whole. Mariet, like Bernard Cathelat,[9] proposes a perspective that emphasizes the highly relational nature of French society.

All these models provide approaches to organizing a culture. It is important to stress that, with the exception of Brooks's work, they are primarily intended to help instructors group their own information, and not as tools for the students. It is important to stress that they are all arbitrary. This is not a derisive observation; it merely signals that the description of another culture represents a choice of perspectives and that there are many choices. Clearly, an instructor should have a cultural model in mind even when teaching elementary classes in order to avoid fragmentary presentations that do not allow students to develop any notion of the "shape" of French culture. Unless American students at the elementary level have some notion that the fragments of French cultural information supplied to them form part of a greater whole with its own logic and coherence, they risk having a negative reaction to some French daily behaviors. For example, the extreme formality in addressing someone who is unknown and the concern with distance and propriety may strike an American as cold and even hostile behavior if it is not seen as a manifestation of high-context culture.

# "Relationalism"

At times, the use of these models, especially the more elaborate ones, may be daunting to the already overburdened language instructors who may understandably feel that coping with oral proficiency guidelines has already stretched their adaptive abilities to the limit. In the spirit of encouragement, there are simpler approaches to grouping the various phenomena of French culture into a coherent system. A course can be organized around the notion of relationalism as suggested by Howard Nostrand.[10] With relationalism as a unifying concept, an instructor can move through a series of salient cultural features that illustrate French preoccupation with context.

At the elementary level, one can seek simple, direct illustrations of high-context culture in common social practices. Perhaps one of the most obvious illustrations of high-context culture may be found in the elaborateness of greetings—gestural, oral, and written. The automatic handshake, the *bises*, the "exaggerated" politeness of shopkeepers with their inevitable "Bonjour, Madame," "Merci, Monsieur," "Au revoir, Mademoiselle," the baroque flourishes of letters with their various and graded closings, all convey the image of a society that insists on relationships. Other examples that can strike even the beginning language student in a direct fashion with intimations (not explanations) of a high-context culture are a general lack of casualness in the social context (especially with the polite and familiar second-person forms *vous* and *tu*), an "idealized" notion of friendship (the careful lexical distinction between *amis, connaissances,* and *relations*), and the gathering at vacation time of the extended family at the *maison familiale en province* (the French have the highest per capita number of second homes in the world), which illustrates the great value accorded to family ties and to a willingness to maintain extended family unity through extensive economic effort.

As one progresses to the late intermediate level, it becomes more possible actually to discuss as well as present examples of high-context culture. At this level, one can address such high-context notions as the primacy of history, which often verges on fatalism ("plus ça change, plus c'est la même chose") and frequently manifests itself negatively ("le poids du passé"). Obviously, asserting to a class that the French place great emphasis on history has the ring of an *ex cathedra* statement that will not be seized either experientially or intellectually without demonstration. A very practical way to illustrate the need for high-context interpretation is to take the front page of *Le Monde* and compare titles and introductions to the articles with those on the front page of the *International Herald Tribune*. The student will easily note the presence of historical and cultural (often literary) allusions in the French newspaper. A comparison of an article on a similar topic in the two newspapers will reveal *Le Monde's* attempt to situate an event in its historical setting—this is especially the case when one looks at one of *Le Monde's* dossiers. The *Trib* will be more concerned about providing the facts surrounding the actual event, the most immediate picture of the situation. By such direct contact, students will begin to experience a fundamental difference in the Anglo-American and French approaches to news—approaches that underline the distinction between high- and low-context cultures. To supply nuance, a sense of evolution to this image, the instructor ought also to supply an article on the same topic from a newer kind of newspaper, *Libération*, to illustrate French movement toward a less "relational" view of the news.

Another trenchant example of a relational culture as opposed to one that treats things in isolation may be found in tourist guides. For instance, the *Michelin Guidebooks* (*Les Guides verts*), imbued as they are with a vision of Catholic, medieval, and royalist France, are far more historical in their approach to tourism in the hexagon and far more hierarchical in their ratings of places to visit than their American counterpart, the Mobil guidebooks, whose primary concern is the easy dalliance of tourists.[11]

Indeed, as Michael Rowland points out, "The French tourist is not expected to seek the unknown but the known; not the present but the past: he is to reaffirm his patrimony but only at those points selected in advance by the Michelin editors."[12]

Likewise, the attitude of the French to their language is a perfect example of high-context culture. The "rules" of the language expounded by a French grammarian, the articles on language use that are a permanent feature in newspapers throughout France, and the *Académie Française*, which is at the top of the hierarchy of official institutions established to control the evolution of the French language and "maintain its purity," are good illustrations. Showing students an extract from an American elementary English grammar text and contrasting it with its French counterpart will provide them with a clear understanding of how much the French value interconnection and linkage, how their understanding of language is invested with a complexity that seems alien to most people from English-speaking cultures.

All the above examples lend themselves to diverse levels of utilization. As mentioned, the basic greeting patterns can be easily taught at the elementary level and other examples introduced as the students' language competence increases. It is incumbent upon the instructor to select topics suitable to the level of study; these topics will illustrate high-context culture implicitly and be the subject of explicit discussion as typical high-context phenomena.

# Hierarchy

The relationalism, the high-context nature, of French society implies another feature that is characteristically not associated with American society, although it is most certainly present: hierarchy. If one seeks a cohesive concept to group the diverse aspects of French society, hierarchical organization is another way to organize this approach. Presented here is a brief résumé of an article by Andrew Suozzo on a course centered on hierarchy and thus relationalism in French society.[13] The course was broken down into the following segments: body language, the meal, the family, education, social classes, and government. Under the first heading, which relies primarily on Laurence Wylie's research, the rigidity of French body movement is compared to the more fluid, less "disciplined" body language commonly attributed to Americans. The Russo-French comedian Jacques Tati's caricature of the head dominating the body was illustrated in the poise of various French people in examples selected from films, slides, and articles. The classical meal with its five-stage, diamond-shaped progression toward and away from the *plat principal* was used to demonstrate hierarchical orientation and interconnectedness in daily activity. In the family segment, hierarchy was tied to the *éducation du non* (severe, negative discipline practiced in some families), although allowances were made for newer, more permissive developments. Education, given the rigidity of the French national system, also served as a strong illustration of hierarchical organization. The centralization, the elaborate channeling, and the aloofness in student/professor relationships were all stressed along with the extreme competitiveness of the system. The differing social milieux or "classes" (depending on one's political perspective) were presented along that most hierarchical and truly French geometric preference, the pyramid—indeed, as an icon that is used not only to illustrate social stratification but as a diagram for age groupings, this is a most eloquent symbol, which, when compared to the bar graph and other visual images preferred by Americans, is richly suggestive about different manners of thinking.[14] Finally, in the political system, the reproduction of the elites offered an example of the power of hierarchy, and the rigid organization of the old French communist party paradoxically provided a faithful reflection of the hierarchical ordering and the structuring so endemic to traditional French society.

Suozzo's presentation was developed through realia, slides, and, most importantly, *témoignages*. What it sought was a coherent, behavioral, and cognitive approach to culture. "Behavioral" and "cognitive" here are used in conjunction, not as opposites. An analysis of behavior through illustrations, realia, and statements inevitably leads to some familiarity with the cognitive landscape of the other culture-bearer. Examples of behavior need to be related to the cognitive map that fashions the French view of the world. Indeed, hierarchy might be considered an important key to the French cognitive map.

The segments of Suozzo's course discussed above are not proposed as a definitive model but as a series of illustrations to enable instructors to begin to form their own high-context vision of France—one that may serve as a steppingstone for comparison with other francophone cultures. Obviously, much thought needs to go into the selection of examples of high-context behavior if the instructor is to avoid alienating students by confronting them with cultural differences that produce negative reactions. This can be overcome by directing students' attention to the relational networks that give these examples coherence within French culture and by stressing that every culture has to be viewed first as a system that functions within its own boundaries before value judgments in comparison with other cultures can be made.

# Applications

## Food

Food has been used as an example several times in this book. Perhaps this reflects the fact that "la cuisine" and "la gastronomie" are, like politics, a constant source of conversation in France. Food is also an excellent illustration of this high-context culture because of the French predilection for categories and order.

The distinction between "cuisine bourgeoise" and "nouvelle cuisine" is a superstructure that overarches the numerous "cuisines régionales," which have long and rich traditions.

### Elementary/Early Intermediate Level

Show the structure of simple meals and elaborate meals by collecting, copying, or photographing real menus. Stress ordering and procedure by stages. Provide essential vocabulary for the progression of the meal ("hors d'oeuvre"/"entrée," "plat," . . .) and the translations of various dishes. Have students order a meal from a selection of dishes. Make certain that they respect the proper progression. Teach the appropriate beverages and the time in the progression when they may be consumed. Have students compile French and American menus for ordinary and festive occasions. Elicit brief comparisons in French ("plus compliqué," "plus varié") about the meals. Get students to plan a French dinner for the class.

### Late Intermediate/Advanced Level

Using menus from different categories of French restaurants and extracts from French restaurant guides, discuss the value the French place on order. Compare the classical meal to a play in five acts and diagram its unfolding. Point out the need for variety to create a meal of complementary dishes unfolding over several courses. Discuss with illustrations traditions in national and regional cooking. Emphasize the importance of esthetics ("la présentation") in French cooking—an additional contextual element. Consider the French meal as an act of communication, stressing the time involved, the gathering of the family, and the place of the evening meal in the day—most normally the last social activity. Compare this to the American meal. Have students read "Le Vin et le lait" and "Le Bifteck et les frites" in Roland Barthes's *Mythologies*.[15] Select series of "totem" foods and drinks for cross-cultural comparisons, and ask students to discuss and write a composition on them in Barthes's style of analysis.

# The Role of the Past

## Elementary/Early Intermediate Level

**Housing.**   Show slides of buildings from former centuries, many of which are monuments and tourist attractions today. Show slides of old and modern housing in agricultural and urban areas. Have students investigate their own neighborhoods to see what traces of the past they see in local architecture. Compare the results.

**War Memorials.**   Show slides of French war memorials. Have students attempt to find similar memorials in their own towns. If they discover them, indicate where they are located. Compare the results.

**Advertisements.**   Collect and show slides of French advertisements that valorize the past either verbally or visually. Have students attempt the same with American advertisements. Compare the results.

## Late Intermediate/Advanced Level

**Housing.**   Housing can offer fairly provocative discussion as here it will become apparent that the two cultures are often surprisingly close in their imitation of very specific (though different) models for individual family homes. To do the subject justice, a large array of slides from both France and the United States is necessary.

**War Memorials.**   Discuss the history of France, its many conflicts, and the catastrophic consequences of the past two hundred years (Napoleonic wars, Franco-Prussian War, World Wars I and II). Review population loss and the sense of threat experienced by this European land power. Consider how the French have been locked into this historical perspective. Conclude discussion with a slide of the inscription on the "Bassin de St-Michel," which recalls the Parisian uprising against the German occupation and slides of the various commemorative plaques found throughout Paris that recall those lost in the uprising against the Nazis.

**Advertisements.**    Discuss just what aspects of the past are valorized. For instance, in the case of an idyllic representation of village life, it would be important to talk about the relatively recent urbanization of France (much later than in the United States) and the consequent attachment of most French people to specific small towns and regions. François Mitterrand's presidential election campaign poster to project his image as "la force tranquille" used the photo of a traditional village with its houses clustered around the old church steeple. Other advertisements will evoke the Middle Ages and "Le Grand Siècle." Here, as the evocations are usually positive, it is important to discuss the national pride connected to these presentations of French history, how the French see themselves as part of the ongoing flow of time. Discuss the more limited possibilities of evocation of the past in the United States—a much younger nation, the different peoples who compose the country, the potential conflicts in the evocation of the past (the story of slavery, the massacre of the Native Americans, etc.).

# Politics

Even in the low-context culture of the United States, politics is a high-context phenomenon because of the complexity of networks that are inevitable in political activity and because of past historical precedent. Both these factors are even more compelling in a high-context country like France.

In everyday discussions, the French make constant allusions to politics. Politics is a frequent topic of conversation because the French define themselves in relation to a range of political ideologies across *la droite* and *la gauche*. In France there are numerous political parties that cover a much broader range of ideologies than in the United States. Furthermore, French politics has to be seen against the background of a much longer history than that of the United States. The replacement of "la monarchie" by "la République" is one example of this.

This greater context of ideological choice is an illustration of a much more high-context view of societal options. For students at the elementary/ early intermediate level, the objective will be to imply the breadth of political choice in France. At the more advanced level, the objective will be to explore the diversity of ideologies and political commitment.

## Elementary/Early Intermediate Level

Name all the currently important political parties. Divide them between right and left and group them from the far right to the far left. Have students know the names of the main parties, their leaders, and the names of the French president and prime minister. Give students basic facts such as the bicameral nature of the French Republic (*l'Assemblée Générale* and *le Sénat*), the term of the president, and the distinction between the functions of the president and the prime minister. Show slides of campaign posters and campaign slogans.

Be sure students know basics like the French flag. Familiarize them with the refrain of *La Marseillaise* (most of the lyrics are too difficult). Introduce students to "Marianne" and remind them that our nation is personified by "Uncle Sam." Illustrate very simply that France was first a monarchy by naming some of its kings and highlight the importance of the French Revolution. Recall to students the contribution of the French to the struggle for American independence (Admiral de Grasse, La Fayette).

## Late Intermediate/Advanced Level

Discuss the more elaborate choices offered to the French elector during the first of the two rounds of voting in the national elections for the *Assemblée Générale* and the presidency. Discuss how this emerges in a society very concerned with nuances of opinion within the general context of political options. Consider whether the American two-party system or the French multiparty system is more democratic. Point out how, after the first round of voting, the French system is effectively reduced to a two-party choice between right and left. Point out the more indirect procedure for the election of senators and the seven-year presidential terms as deeply conservative trends in French politics—a concern for long-range stability. Point out, however, how quickly prime ministers can be dismissed by the president and how new governments can be formed without holding national elections. Discuss campaign posters and slogans for their direct and subliminal appeals.

Study *La Marseillaise* (written in 1792) as an expression of revolutionary fervor. Compare it with the U.S. national anthem (written in 1814). Discuss the historical settings of both and the different messages sent. Ask students for their reflections about nations that personify themselves as male ("Uncle Sam") or female ("Marianne"). Point out that the feudal heritage makes the French look at France as something nearly timeless that transcends all political regimes whether monarchies or republics and have them explore whether Americans possess this kind of view of their country.

# Other Topics

Here are some suggestions of other topics for the presentation of the high-context culture in France: the family, friendship, education, urban organization (circle versus grid), gardens (public and private), the elaborate forms of the business letter, health care.

# Notes

1. The latter case is typical of the British historian Theodore Zeldin, whose book, *The French* (New York: Vintage Books, 1984), attempts to reject any notion of "Frenchness" and urges the reader to believe in individuals, not nationalities. In an otherwise friendly review, Edmond Marc indicates the difficulty of such an approach: "Qu'ils le veuillent ou non, la sélection présentée dans l'ouvrage revêt aux yeux du lecteur une certaine 'représentivité.' Zeldin a certainement raison de dénoncer le mythe du Français moyen; mais fallait-il tomber nécessairement dans cette vision atomistique de la société? La culture et la société ne sont-elles que la somme des individus qui les composent? Cette position, difficilement tenable au niveau théorique, a cependant valeur de paradoxe stimulant et peut même être acceptable dans une optique pédagogique." E. Marc, "Civilisation: La France vue par un Anglais, Theodore Zeldin," *Le Français dans le monde* 182 (janvier 1984): 16.

2. For an overview of *francophonie*, see Louise Fiber Luce, ed., *The French Speaking World: Anthology of Cross-Cultural Perspectives* (Lincolnwood, IL: National Textbook, 1990).

3. Nelson Brooks, "Culture in the Classroom" in Joyce Merrill Valdes, ed., *Culture Bound* (Cambridge, Eng.: Cambridge Univ. Press, 1986), p. 124.

4. *Ibid.*, pp. 124–28.

5. AATF *National Bulletin* 13 (special issue, October 1987): 10.

6. George H. Hughes, "An Argument for Cultural Analysis in the Second Language Classroom," in Joyce Merrill Valdes, ed., *Culture Bound* (Cambridge, Eng.: Cambridge Univ. Press, 1986), pp. 162–69.

7. See our discussion in chapter 1 and Appendix IV.

8. François Mariet, "Un Malaise dans l'enseignement de la civilisation," *Études de linguistique appliquée* 64 (octobre–novembre 1986): 64.

9. Bernard Cathelat, *Les Styles de vie des Français* 1978–1998 (Paris: Stanké, 1977).

10. Howard L. Nostrand, "French Culture's Concern for Relationships: Relationalism," *Foreign Language Annals* 6,4 (May 1973): 469–78.

11. See Michael Rowland, "Michelin's *Guide vert touristique*: A Guide to the French Inner Landscape," *The French Review* 60,5 (April 1987): 653–64.

12. *Ibid.*, p. 663.

13. Andrew G. Suozzo, Jr., "Once More with Content: Shifting Emphasis in Intermediate French," *The French Review* 54 (1981): 405–11.

14. Since the course was given, *La Pyramide*, the new entrance to the Louvre museum, opened by the president of the French Republic as part of the official celebrations of the Bicentenary of the French Revolution, now stands as a new visual icon of the abstract, hierarchical, and geometric organization that embodies the French passion for order and reason.

15. Roland Barthes, *Mythologies* (Paris: Éditions du Seuil, 1957): pp. 74–79.

# CHAPTER V

# Anthropology and the Teaching of Culture

As the teaching of culture becomes more integrated into teaching practices in the language classroom, instructors must reach beyond their own educational backgrounds to seek new strategies for imparting cultural knowledge to their students. In this respect, social and cultural anthropology can offer particular help in defining the cultural component of a modern language course. The procedures used by ethnographers to collect data and describe a society can be adapted for classroom use. There are, however, two important caveats: (1) the selection and ordering of the content will be subject to pedagogical constraints; (2) these constraints will differ between second language courses and foreign language courses.

The teaching of the cultural component will be very different in a second language course in which the learner is living in the target culture environment—France or a francophone country—and has many opportunities for direct cultural experiences that can serve as data for classroom discussion and activities. In a foreign language classroom, the learner's experience of the second culture is mediated by the instructor, who will probably be a native speaker of English, and by the instructor's personal rapport with the target culture. The learner's experience of the target culture is also mediated by the information contained in the textbook and other ancillary materials from the print and electronic media chosen by the instructor and, in a learner-centered curriculum, by the learners. In this chapter, we address the foreign language classroom situation, which is the context in which most language educators work in the United States when teaching French.

# Language and Culture

Despite general acknowledgment of the relevance of anthropology and ethnographic descriptions, language educators and writers of textbooks and materials have not made great use of them. In part, this is because the relationship between the language and the culture components of a foreign language course has remained at the level of motherhood statements like the following by Lehmann and Jones: "One cannot properly learn another language without learning something about the cultural and social contexts in which it is used and the values of those who speak it, nor can one communicate accurately with a speaker of another language if one filters the information received through one's own monocultural experience."[1] No contemporary language educator would disagree with this overall statement as a basic principle. If we read it closely, however, certain points lack precision and could give rise to disagreement. How is "properly" to be defined in "one cannot properly learn another language"? Note the vagueness of "without learning something about the cultural and social contexts." How much is "something"? Does this word link language and culture tightly together or does it allow them to be separated in an arbitrary association? The expression "communicate accurately" allows for many interpretations. How does one define accurate communication? Should the focus be on accuracy, which evokes a grammatical emphasis, or on fluency and the ability to communicate effectively, underscoring successful transmission of the meaning of the message? At the surface level, the statement by Lehmann and Jones appears to support the importance of culture in language teaching. At a deeper level, however, a close reading of the statement does not bind culture to language, the relationship between culture and language is unspecified, and instructors can continue to allocate as large or as small a proportion of the language course to culture as they wish.

We are after all called *language* teachers and we have traditionally seen our "raison d'être" as primarily teaching the language, even when we accept that culture is at the basis of language. For this situation to change, the relationship between language and culture has to be analyzed in specific pedagogical terms with reference to precise educational objectives and learner needs in a cross-cultural perspective. To remind instructors of the indissociability of language and culture, Claire Kramsch has adopted the term "linguaculture."[2]

Despite the shift from grammatical to communicative competence as the goal set for learners by today's language teachers, the period during which communicative competence has been the goal is quite short in comparison to the decades during which grammatical competence was the goal and native-like accuracy was expected. Perhaps that is why, even though communicative competence is now the objective, much of language use in the classroom is of the rehearsal type to develop accuracy. Those decades during which form was all important still cast their shadow over interactive approaches to language learning that focus on the communication of meaning. It might be suggested that until we give full acceptance to meaning as central both to communication and to language use in society, then we are not prepared to see culture as central to our language teaching practices.

# Definitions of Culture

The anthropologist Clifford Geertz defines culture as "an historically transmitted pattern of meanings embodied in symbols, a system of inherited conceptions expressed in symbolic form by means of which men communicate, perpetuate and develop their knowledge about and attitudes towards life."[3] Language is the principal means by which these meanings are expressed. In our approach to language teaching, do we make the learners aware of these systems of meaning and symbols? If not, then we are artificially separating language from its source of reference and teaching it in a vacuum.

This concept of culture as a "pattern of meanings embodied in symbols" has overtaken the behaviorist concept whereby culture is construed as patterns of behavior acquired under the influence of the social environment. Behaviorist theory inspired the stimulus–response repetition approach to language teaching enshrined in the audio-lingual method, which became discredited because learners did not pass beyond repetition to develop the capacity to communicate. The audio-lingual method focused on form and gave little importance to the content of that form, i.e., to meaning. Similarly, behaviorist descriptions of society were principally concerned with observation of behavior and not with the meanings of the behavior.

In the teaching of both language and culture, analysis did not go beyond the surface level to explore the system of meanings that constitute the everyday life and knowledge of individuals in their social context. Culture notes in foreign language textbooks were isolated pieces of information that were neither coordinated into a systematic body of knowledge nor linked to the language. They were facts presented from the viewpoint of an outside observer and not illustrated from within the culture. Culture notes did not encourage the transition from description to the discovery and interpretation of beliefs and values held by the members of the target culture.

The method of analysis proposed by Geertz can show us a way to pass beyond description to interpretation and the integration of culture into language teaching: "Believing, with Max Weber, that man is an animal suspended in webs of significance he himself has spun, I take culture to be those webs, and the analysis of it to be therefore not an experimental science in search of law but an interpretive one in search of meaning."[4] In this perspective, culture is the key to successful language learning. The culture component has no longer a secondary role in a foreign language course. Meaning is the link between culture and language.

# Shortcomings of Survival Goals

Although attention is given in a communicative competence approach to some pragmatic aspects of language use, the acquisition by the learner of language skills continues to dominate. Language is generally presented in the context of a tourist in the foreign culture—usually an American who is in Paris or another French city for the purpose of learning French. Linguistic survival and the ability to satisfy needs and overcome communication problems are the main concerns. This instrumental view of language does not require an understanding of the "pattern of meanings embodied in symbols" in the target culture. Tourist language exchanges are, for the most part, value free. The student learns how to ask questions and to respond, learns the second language vocabulary items appropriate to the situation, and achieves most of his/her survival communication goals.

In this approach, what information have the learners gained about culture apart from the fact that objects have different names and that the people have some different customs from theirs? Has there been any understanding of the reasons for and the nature of the difference? This would seem doubtful. And it is quite possible that the absence of this understanding actually reinforces a negative dichotomy between "us" and "them": "our" language and customs are natural and normal, "theirs" are strange and irrational. We are a long way from a widely proclaimed benefit of foreign language learning: namely, that it promotes tolerance of other peoples!

Tourist language avoids ideological issues. Knowing how to say things in the second language does not require a change in the learners' beliefs; they are in no way challenged to understand why the French organize their society differently or even to recognize the existence of different values. Supplying bits of tourist survival information in an arbitrary fashion does not present a meaningful, holistic view of the foreign culture's value system, which could challenge the learners' ethnocentric beliefs. Learners bring to the foreign language class a set of cultural attitudes and values that have been formed during the socialization process of growing up in their society and during the educational process in their native language. Many of these attitudes and values have never been questioned and are assumed (wrongly) to be universal. They are expressed often unconsciously through everyday life and language and constitute the learners' ethnic identity. Learners instinctively reject anything that troubles or challenges this monocultural, monolingual identity because it threatens the essence of their being. If a foreign language can be acquired without upsetting these attitudes and beliefs, the learners retain their cultural security within a closed universe. They are quite prepared to express interest in folkloric aspects of the foreign culture, which can be enjoyable and nonthreatening. But when they have to question their ethnocentric views of the world, they feel threatened and their reaction is usually negative. By concentrating on the communicative language component and using the culture component as incidental illustration, we are contributing to maintaining the learners in the false security of their ethnocentricity. France and other francophone countries will provide them with entertainment and a fund of anecdotes but with no serious challenge to reexamine their own assumptions, to grow as intellectual and moral beings.

# The Goals of Cultural Learning

How then can we lead students through the experience of learning a foreign language to an understanding of and, hopefully, an empathy with the foreign culture? We have seen that a course based primarily on the acquisition of communicative language skills will not achieve this goal. Michael Byram proposes a model of foreign language education consisting of four mutually supporting parts[5] (see figure 5.1).

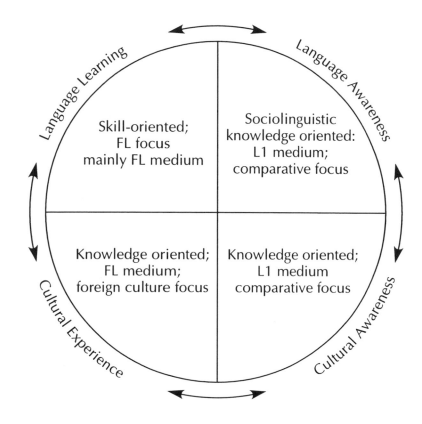

**Figure 5–1. A model of foreign language education.**

Without entering into a discussion here on the use of the native or the target language, although a limited use of the first language can be legitimated when the aims of the foreign language course are broader than the acquisition of communicative language skills, it is worthwhile to reflect on certain aspects of Byram's model. Its virtue is to place what Byram calls "cultural studies" at the core of a foreign language course that has general educational goals. Byram contends that by emphasizing vocational goals and concentrating on teaching language skills, language teachers have lost sight of the broader educational goals of their courses. By moving cultural studies to the center of the curriculum, the educational goals come back into focus, and we can expect that our foreign language learners will develop an understanding of the foreign culture and so become linguistically and interculturally competent

To achieve this outcome, the necessity of presenting viewpoints of the foreign culture from both outside and inside it should be obvious. In most textbooks, the viewpoint is from the outside. The learner observes the foreign culture with an outsider's viewpoint, reinforced with cognitive learning procedures. This does not necessarily cause any shift from the learner's own culture or any transformation of the learner's cultural schemata. Schemata of knowledge are the generic concepts that an individual, while growing up, has internalized in memory and through which the meaning of new experiences is filtered. On the other hand, the insider's viewpoint will present the foreign culture in its own terms and the learner will experience the emotions of participation in another world of customs and traditions. This affective aspect of culture learning is important in modifying the learner's schemata from a monocultural to a bicultural perspective.

The learner as an outsider has a stereotypical view of the foreign culture. Contact with insiders from that culture reveals to the learner, probably for the first time, that his or her own culture can also be seen in stereotypical terms. The learner thus becomes aware that how we are seen by other peoples is not necessarily the same as how we see ourselves. This sensitization to the concept of "otherness" first necessitates a change in values, which will be oriented by discussing and analyzing in class the notion of stereotypes and autostereotypes. How do we see our culture? How do we present our culture to people from another culture? How do these people see themselves? How do they want us to see them? As a result of this discussion illustrated by a range of authentic materials, the learners will begin to understand themselves more clearly as individuals living in a society that functions on the basis of mutual agreement on a set of shared cultural meanings. They will also begin to perceive the culturally shared meanings according to which the members of the other culture live. Consequently, two of the educational aims of foreign language instruction are achieved: an increased understanding of one's own culture and competence in the target culture.

This process also shows the importance of moving from a general level of comparison between two cultures to an individual level. Stereotypes exist at the level of unrefined generalities. Variations at the individual level exemplified by a range of persons from different generations and subgroups within the culture relativize the stereotypes. Insiders reveal a complex network of attitudes and relationships that are meaningful in the overarching context of the society's traditions and value systems. Furthermore, complexity and individual differences give increased opportunities for each learner's empathy to be stimulated as (s)he relates personally to a particular lifestyle or individual. In any group of learners, there is a diversity of personalities, tastes, and interests. The whole group cannot be expected to empathize with an image of the target culture presented through a general, homogenized example of a contented, "typical" French family unit. Empathy is not a passive feeling. It is aroused by participation in an activity or by involvement with one or several individuals whom one finds attractive. Empathy requires understanding and a change of viewpoint. Cognition alone does not enable the learner to experience the target culture from within. A combination of cognition and affect is necessary to transform the learner's monocultural schemata of foreign peoples and cultures.

A parallel can be drawn with two ways in which we as individuals can react to a group of other people. One way is to observe them as an ethnographer from an outsider's viewpoint. We remain detached and note various patterns of behavior. On the basis of these observations, we make hypotheses about the reasons for their behavior. The second way is to interact with individuals in this group. In interaction, we no longer remain detached. Our emotions become involved and our empathy or antipathy is stimulated. Through this direct experience, we discover that some or perhaps all the hypotheses we had made on the basis of analytic observations are false. We discover that the individuals in the group may share some values but they also have personal experiences and aspirations that explain part of their behavior. Through interaction, our interpretation of their behavior becomes more refined. There are many nuances. The generalizations we had first formed have lost their absolute truth value. We become more cautious about making such generalizations and more tolerant of individual differences.

# Implementing Cultural Content at Various Levels

How then can we design the curriculum of a foreign language course to guide our learners to an understanding of the range of people in the target culture and of the meaning systems and their associated symbols in that culture?[6] Anthropology can help us define the content. The content has to be adapted to the linguistic level of the language learner. It would be utopian to hope to make an exhaustive presentation of the target culture. The presentation does, however, have to give a balanced overview. Aspects of the target culture have to be selected in such a way that they present a structured series of functional contexts showing how meaning networks are organized. There has to be a mixture of general aspects that provide factual knowledge and individual case studies that provide the subjectivity of experience, i.e., analysis at the macro and the micro level. Ethnographic descriptions present the people, the society, and the country. These three categories could provide a framework for topic selection, combining them in different proportions at the beginner, the intermediate, and the advanced levels.

# People

At the beginner level, the "people" category would constitute the largest proportion, as the early learner's interest and empathy are usually stimulated by a curiosity about the lives of other people. Conversations give appropriate language opportunities for communication at the beginner level. People reveal their values through conversational interaction. The participants in the conversations would be chosen from different sociocultural groups. Individual and family relationships would be explored. Learners would be trained to observe what is explicit and what is implicit in the conversations. Recognition of the implicit content of conversations would be the entry point to the process of interpreting facts and acts. At the intermediate level, different varieties of language used by different social groups would be a significant part of the people component. Gender and generation roles within social categories would also receive attention. At the advanced level, a study of value patterns in social relationships and in interaction between insiders and outsiders would deepen the interpretation of people's behavior in the target culture.

Gail Robinson has done particularly valuable work that can be used for the "people" category. Highly aware that anthropology can propose a helpful methodology of analysis but that it does not necessarily create cross-cultural understanding, Robinson sought a more positive application of this discipline in language learning. She elaborated the ethnographic interview for language students in *Crosscultural Understanding*[7] and, in 1991, supervised a third-semester study of students in Spanish who were trained to conduct ethnographic interviews as part of the course. These students learned the technique of eliciting open-ended questions designed to obtain the interviewee's point of view. Student response to attitude surveys taken before and after the course suggested that the ethnographic interviewing techniques taught and the interviews conducted contributed significantly to greater cross-cultural understanding and to a more positive attitude toward language learning.[8] Equally gratifying was the fact that these students had carried out the task at a relatively early level of language study.

# Society

In the society component, social institutions and cultural artifacts would be studied. At the beginner level, those institutions and artifacts that most directly affect everyday life and customs such as school, transport, housing, eating, dress, and the media would be selected. These would be exemplified, and the beliefs and value systems they symbolize would be suggested. At the institutional and cultural level, ideological orientations are easier to see. The interpretation at the beginner level would establish broad clusters of beliefs and values, which would be refined when these societal phenomena are reexamined and new ones such as political institutions, literature, and art are introduced at the intermediate and advanced levels. We would recommend that societal phenomena be recycled at different levels to allow a deeper understanding of their function in the overall network of shared meanings that shape the cultural identity of members of the target culture. Raymonde Carroll's suggestions in *Évidences invisibles*[9] are very pertinent to advanced study of French society. She recommends choosing points of cultural conflict for analysis, distinguishing cultural and societal subsystems, distinguishing between myths of collective self-concept and actual behavior in an effort to determine relative constants that are culturally specific.

# Country

The country component of the course would include geography and history. A historical dimension is necessary to make learners aware that present social practices are the result of an evolutionary process over centuries that has fashioned the customs, institutions, and traditions of the target culture. It is important to apprise learners of the concept of change so that they do not freeze the target culture in its current manifestation, thus isolating it from chronological developments. An immobile, timeless object can quickly be reduced to a stereotype. A balanced presentation at the beginner and intermediate levels will have led learners to realize that the target culture is an organic whole, meaningful in its own terms, and that a justifiable evaluation of it has to be made on that basis. At the advanced level learners can be encouraged to develop more refined strategies to make critical evaluations of beliefs and values. Certain subgroups within the target culture criticize its dominant beliefs and values. Learners can analyze the criticisms made by these insiders, compare them with critical judgments of the target culture made by outsiders, explore the ways in which criticisms by outsiders are influenced by native culture value assumptions, and thus arrive at an enlightened personal opinion of the target culture.

# Connotations

Throughout the whole course, every opportunity must be taken to contextualize learning through the use of authentic materials and to highlight the connotations of the language used in them. As well as enhancing the general language awareness of the learner through a distinction between denotation and connotation, connotations form a pedagogical bridge from language to culture. When learners incorrectly attribute to a second language word a native language meaning, they have stayed within their own culture and failed to make the transition into the target culture's universe of meanings. Much work has been done on linguistic interference from native to target language, but this has generally been on the level of form. More work needs to be done on meaning interference because this reveals incorrect cultural transfers and takes us to the core of the language/culture nexus. This is where the learner can have direct experience of the relationships between language and culture and can gain insight into the cultural component of meaning. The same object does not have the same meaning in the cultural context of the native culture and in the cultural context of the target culture. Behaviors that may seem the same in the native culture and the target culture have a different significance within the frame of reference of each culture.

# Descriptions, Explanation, and Interpretation

Current practice is to present unconnected pieces of information in a descriptive mode. This does not of itself produce the change of viewpoint necessary to an understanding of the target culture. In order to progress to a deeper level of understanding and knowledge, the learner has to pass from description to explanation and interpretation. At the explanation and interpretation stages the meanings and values symbolized by behaviors, artifacts, and institutions are made explicit. The following pedagogical stages of the target culture have been suggested for the process of explanation and interpretation. (1) an observation and description phase: information presented in functionally interrelated authentic sociocultural contexts; (2) experience through the medium of the foreign language used in participatory activities and in authentic communicative situations filmed on video or in documentaries and feature films; (3) explanation of the explicit data; (4) collaborative interpretation of the implicit values and meanings leading to deeper understanding; (5) elaboration of a body of "informed" knowledge about the target culture. Parallel to each stage is comparison with the native culture so that the learner acquires new competencies in both cultures.

# Educational Outcomes

Anthropology proposes methods for defining course content and for analyzing societies that are helpful for language instructors, but these methods do not of themselves create cross-cultural understanding. Anthropology also informs language teachers of the significance of nonlinguistic symbols that carry cultural meanings. In the classroom, video is a powerful medium for highlighting the message-transmission role of the nonverbal elements in human interactions, as well as nonlinguistic cultural forms of expression such as art, architecture, music, and dance, which play a functional role in the meaning networks of a society. Here, language instructors can engage in collaborative cross-disciplinary projects with members of other faculties. The learning space of foreign language study may thus expand from the isolated, hothouse, language-concentrated world of the foreign language classroom to the open, free-growth world of humanistic learning and personal enrichment.

Current practices in language classrooms focus on behavioral outcomes, the ability of the learner to perform in the target society. More attention needs to be directed to the process by which learners make value judgments about the target culture and how these can be transformed into enlightened cultural perceptions. Only when we have designed a curriculum that integrates linguistic skills and the growth of cross-cultural understanding within the framework of the cognitive, affective, and cultural development of the learner can we hope to achieve the general educational outcomes that are ascribed to foreign language instruction.

# Background Information for Instructors

Writings by the anthropologist E. T. Hall, especially his early book *The Silent Language*[10] provide helpful insights into ways in which instructors can introduce learners to the target culture and heighten their cross-cultural awareness. The studies made of village life in France by Laurence Wylie—*Village in the Vaucluse*[11] and *Chanzeaux, A Village in Anjou*[12]—show how beliefs and values structure the organization of daily life. The video made by Bernard Petit of interviews with residents of the "Village in the Vaucluse"[13] gives the insiders' viewpoint twenty years later and also raises for discussion the notion of change. Raymonde Carroll's book *Cultural Misunderstandings*,[14] written from an anthropological perspective, gives an insider's account of the French–American experience, which could serve as a model for exploring cross-cultural misunderstandings between Americans and people from francophone cultures.

# Applications

## Sensitivity to Language/Culture

### Elementary

It is important to show your students that words that would appear to be interchangeable from one language to the next evoke different images. We thus propose a simple exercise that allows the learners to modify their own cultural images. The instructor supplies the students with a list of words and asks them to supply the correct English translation or analogue whenever possible. Beyond translating, students must then collect illustrations of the words from their respective cultures in order to compare the French image with its American counterpart.

Here are some possible themes. Food and food vending: le petit déjeuner, le déjeuner, la charcuterie, la boucherie chevaline; public space: le jardin public; finances: l'argent; transportation: la voiture, le train, l'avion.

Beginning with food, it should be apparent that "le petit déjeuner" and "le déjeuner" are very divergent from American patterns, that the "charcuterie" really has no precise equivalent and that a "boucherie chevaline" is largely unthinkable. You need to ask your students for their reactions and to help them interpret why these differences exist.

The French "jardin public" (park) allows you to comment on aesthetic notions that are less significant in the United States. The symmetry and elaborate display of French parks represent different values.

French paper money will illustrate the priority the French place on high culture and allude to the potentially inflammatory prospects of choosing political heroes, as is the case in American currency. High culture here plays a unifying role that it does not enjoy in the United States.

Transportation, though very similar, still evokes different word associations. The higher proportion of smaller cars in France indicates different energy priorities and, in the heart of the cities, parking problems, because the old apartment buildings do not have garages. Different makes of cars have different connotations. The old "deux chevaux" has special peasant connotations. The French travel by train much more than Americans do. French trains are rapid and efficient. Both the train and the airplane as illustrated by the TGV and the Concorde bear witness to a fascination with high technology—something that many Americans view as particular to their own culture. Such achievements allow students to think about the fact that America is just one of many high-tech cultures and that it has no monopoly on scientific know-how and futuristic planning.

# Symbols

## Elementary/Intermediate

Have your students find illustrations for the following symbols: the French flag ("le tricolore"), the *coq gaulois* (a symbol of France that derives from the early Celts), Marianne (the symbol of the Republic), the "fleur de lys" (originally the symbol of the monarchy); students may have seen the "fleur de lys" on the license plates of cars from Quebec with the words "Je me souviens"), and the Eiffel Tower ("la tour Eiffel," symbol of Paris and France). Ask students to give a meaning to each one and, when possible, to supply its American analogue. Allow for very subjective interpretations and considerable inaccuracy, which will be corrected in class discussion.

## Intermediate/Advanced

Once again have students find illustrations of these and other symbols such as the *bonnet phrygien* and the *croix de Lorraine*, discuss their meaning, and indicate American analogues. This time, however, they will need to discuss the historical origins of the symbols and their research should reflect the level of study. In the case of American analogues, they will need to talk about the significance of Uncle Sam as opposed to Marianne and the *coq gaulois* as opposed to the American eagle. Their work should be evaluated collectively and increasing precision and accuracy about the usage of the symbols will be required.

# Time

## Elementary/Intermediate

Have your students find out French meal hours and their duration, the arrangement of the school week and the length of the school day, the normal hours of the workday, the times and extent of annual vacation leave, and the number of national holidays. This should enable them to begin to realize that time is ordered differently in France and allow you to touch briefly on some of the reasons for this difference by highlighting the emphasis on a qualitative notion of time.

## Intermediate/Advanced

Take these same categories but go into greater detail, e.g., the value of the midday and evening meals in the socialization process, the diminishing importance of lunch, the concluding nature of dinner (not a prelude to other activities), the different convictions about the regularity of study with the weekend often viewed as too long a break for elementary school students, the value of leisure with its concomitant notions of renewal and "recueillement" and stronger emphasis on personal development as opposed to work. These topics allow for considerable debate and call into questions some of the most typical values of American society: speed and efficacity. Have your students put their reflections into essay form for general class discussion.

# Notebook

## Elementary/Intermediate/Advanced

On the basis of a series of interrelated films and/or readings, have students keep a notebook of observed behaviors and their interpretations of them. After each viewing or reading, they should note on separate pages the behaviors and their attempt to interpret them. Students can review their interpretations and modify them as their knowledge increases. After the students have collected initial data on behaviors, the instructor can supply headings for classification such as individualism, sociability, hierarchy, aesthetics, etc. The interpretations may well be highly subjective, but the point is to provoke reflection rather than to arrive at a definitive interpretation. A report should conclude this activity, the timing of which is best determined by the instructor. There should be a general class discussion about the interpretations the students have reached.

# Discovering the Subtext

## Elementary/Intermediate

Students learn to recognize an implied message in a short dialogue, e.g., a polite refusal of an invitation, pleasure at a compliment disguised as self-denigration, growing impatience, hidden reproach, genuine interest. Students can respond by multiple choice or very brief written answers.

## Intermediate

Using authentic materials, students identify a limited number of expressions from different sociolinguistic registers: vulgar, uneducated, standard expression, high register. Ask them to identify the register via multiple choice or in their own words. Also have them paraphrase or summarize a dialogue in standard French if it is in another register.

## Advanced

Using authentic materials, students analyze the social context of an extended conversation or statement. Ask them to identify the sociolinguistic register explaining their choice and let them indicate the concerns of the speaker(s). They should try to bring out the full context of the discourse. Political speeches can be very useful for this activity.

# Diversity of Discourse

## Intermediate/Advanced

Select topics that elicit a variety of viewpoints in French society. Assemble written transcripts of discussions or use a video or film of a discussion. Television talk shows can be very useful. Illustrate that there is controversy and disagreement on many subjects. Remind students that foreigners often have the impression that French people are in profound disagreement during discussions when they are only indulging in "l'art de la parole," which is a core value in their culture. Have students analyze the different linguistic formulations that reflect different perspectives based on class, economic situation, and ideological positions.

# Social Critiques

## Intermediate/Advanced

Collect protest literature from marginal or aggrieved groups in French society: women (though they constitute the majority of the population), workers, the unemployed, the young, the elderly, immigrants (especially North African and Black Africans), gays/lesbians, resident ethnic minorities (Basques, Bretons, Corsicans), farmers, etc., in order to make it clear that France is not a monolithic society. Have students paraphrase the nature of the grievances of specific groups and compare their complaints with protest within American society.

# Interaction

## Intermediate/Advanced

It can be very difficult in the foreign language classroom to create direct interaction with representatives of the target culture. Several forms of interaction are possible:

1. A French visitor is invited to talk about his or her life in France. The students are encouraged to ask questions to elicit further information on likes and dislikes and differences the visitor has noticed between life-styles and opinions in France and the United States. After the visitor's departure, the class discusses the attitudes and opinions revealed

through the visitor's talk and answers and the reasons for these (age, gender, status, class, etc.). It is essential to remind the class that they are the attitudes and opinions of *one* French person and not of *all* French people.

2. A discussion on a theme of general interest ranging from friendship, love, and family to ecology and energy policy can be planned in advance and native speakers can be invited to participate—preferably native speakers who do not share the same viewpoint on all matters.

3. French clubs can supply an atmosphere for either planned or informal discussion between natives and nonnatives.

4. A "réunion francophone" could be organized with actual culture bearers to convey specific points of view on different topics.

# Notes

1. Winifred P. Lehmann and Randall L. Jones, "The Humanistic Basis of Second Language Learning," *The Annals of the American Academy of Political and Social Science. Foreign Language Instruction: A National Agenda*, Richard D. Lambert, special editor (March 1987): 187.

2. Claire J. Kramsch, "New Directions in the Teaching of Language and Culture," *National Foreign Language Center Occasional Paper* (Washington: NFLC, 1989): 1.

3. Clifford Geertz, *The Interpretation of Cultures* (London: Hutchinson, 1975), p. 89.

4. *Ibid.*, p. 5.

5. Michael Byram, *Cultural Studies in Foreign Language Education* (Avon, Eng.: Multilingual Matters, 1989), p. 138. Available through Taylor & Francis, Bristol, PA.

6. See our discussion in chapter 1, pages 8–9, of Francis Debyser's tripartite model combining a sociolinguistic, an anthropological, and a semiological approach.

7. Gail L. Nemetz Robinson, *Crosscultural Understanding* (New York: Prentice-Hall, 1988), pp. 73–74, 102–124.

8. Gail L. Nemetz Robinson, "The Role of Ethnography in the Foreign Language Classroom," *The LARC Update* (The National Foreign Language Research Center at SDSU) 2 (November 1992), p. 3.

9.  Raymonde Carroll, *Evidences invisibles: Américains et Français au quotidien* (Paris: Éditions du Seuil, 1987) and referred to later in this chapter in its English translation. *Cultural Misunderstandings: The French–American Experience* (Chicago: Univ. of Chicago Press, 1988).

10. Edward T. Hall, *The Silent Language* (Garden City, NY: Doubleday, 1959).

11. Laurence Wylie, *Village in the Vaucluse*, 3rd ed. (Cambridge, MA: Harvard Univ. Press, 1981).

12. Laurence Wylie, *Chanzeaux, a Village in Anjou*, 3rd ed. (Cambridge, MA: Harvard Univ. Press, 1966).

13. Bernard Petit, *Laurence Wylie in Peyrane* (Brockport, NY: Educational Communications SUNY College at Brockport, 1983).

14. Carroll, op. cit.

# CHAPTER VI

# Using Authentic Materials

The use of a wide range of authentic materials has become common-place in modern language classrooms. Authentic materials are a means of "direct" access to the target culture because they were initially conceived for target language speakers. This "direct" access, however, is mediated in varying degrees by their pedagogical use for teaching the target language, which was not part of their original conception. The global media and information explosion has made authentic materials readily available to the instructor. The challenges for the instructor are how to select among the materials available and how to use them most effectively to teach French culture and language.

Authentic materials integrate culture and language and thus facilitate the integration of culture and language teaching. They can be classified in three general categories: print documents, which are read; audio documents, which are listened to; and visual documents, which are looked at. They are found principally in the print and electronic media of the target culture. Some documents use only one medium to be decoded for meaning. Examples are a newspaper article with no visual illustrations, which requires only the reading skill; an audio recording of an interview, which requires only the listening skill; a slide, which requires only the viewing skill. Other documents require combinations of the reading, listening, and viewing skills to understand their message(s). For example, a newspaper article can consist of print and visual elements (a written text and a photo or a graphic illustration); a videoclip combines spoken and visual elements (a song and filmed action); a videofilm combines spoken and visual elements (dialogue and filmed action).

Documents that contain more than one information-carrying element are easier to understand, especially for students at the beginning levels. Having set the goals for the course and identified the learning needs of the students, the instructor chooses the most relevant authentic materials available. The instructor may choose to use in the course authentic documents from only one medium or may choose a combination of documents from different media. In the latter case, the course is described as a multimedia course. These documents can be used singly at appropriate times for illustrative purposes, or they can be grouped together in one or several thematic "dossiers (socio)culturels" that form the basis of the course.[1]

Authentic materials stimulate motivation for learning because students appreciate that they are learning "real" language used in the target country as opposed to pedagogical language for the classroom. Through these materials they can experience the target culture. Melvin and Stout have shown how authentic materials can be used to "discover a city" as a substitute for a trip to the city in the target country if the students cannot travel there.[2] Authentic materials allow students to expand their existing knowledge and to take greater control of their own learning by pursuing their own interests. Authentic materials not only provide information on the target culture but also contain expressions of attitudes, feelings, opinions, and ideas. They can be compared with similar authentic material from the students' native culture for information content and the behaviors, attitudes, and values that this material reveals. Information on the two cultures is thus compared *in the context of each culture*. This sensitizes students to the internal coherence of each cultural system and promotes better-informed cross-cultural judgments. Authentic documents show the diversity of phenomena, behaviors, and attitudes in the target culture. This diversity diminishes the possibilities for the student to reduce the target culture to an oversimplified, homogeneous, stereotypical model.

Textbooks often fix their object of study in an immobile time frame. The target culture is, however, not a static object but is constantly evolving. Authentic documents enable the instructor to update the contents of the textbook and bring into the classroom the most recent changes in the target culture. As France becomes increasingly integrated in the European Community, new sources of national preoccupation and new social tensions emerge. Relevant authentic materials reflect these movements of opinion, which in turn will effect changes to the country's value system.

In a pedagogical perspective, it must be remembered that the same authentic document does not spark the same interest from every student all the time. This is why it is recommended that, from time to time where possible, a choice of documents be given to the class to work with. On these occasions, students—individually, in pairs, or in small groups—are asked to discover something about the target society from the documents they have chosen. Because the students approach their chosen document(s) from different standpoints, they look for and find different things. This action phase should be followed by a reflection phase in which (under guidance from the instructor who supplies additional information and comment when necessary to correct false assumptions arising from incorrect interpretations of a document) students give justifications for their opinions, make predictions about the target culture, and draw conclusions about what Nostrand calls its "ground of meaning."[3] This reflection phase is important in order to make explicit the cultural implications of the document in the broader context of the target culture's value system. In this way, students working with a range of different types of authentic documents develop their critical thinking skills as well as a deeper knowledge of the target culture expressed through the target language.

# Authentic Materials from the Print Media

Newspapers, magazines, cartoons, comic books, brochures, posters, notices, and tracts offer rich sources of authentic materials. Textbooks, especially for beginner courses, contain a wide range of realia from print media that are intended to create an "authentic atmosphere" of the target culture and to stimulate language-learning activities. Textbooks have not, however, sufficiently exploited the possibilities the realia offer for sociocultural-learning activities, that lead to a discovery of cultural patterns and the value system of the target culture. Every authentic document has a cultural as well as a linguistic script. The linguistic script draws its meaning from the cultural script. The cultural script is the door to understanding the target culture. As Nostrand points out, authentic documents that are used in isolation from the context of the target culture become trivia and do not increase the students' understanding of the target culture's patterns of thought.[4] To sensitize students to the important sociocultural context of the authentic document, they can be asked to suggest what the document reveals about the target culture. Their observations can be used by the instructor to underscore the centrality of the sociocultural context as the basis of the shared meaning(s) of the document for the speakers in the target culture. The shared meanings are what makes communication possible between those speakers. They are what the student has to recognize and interpret in order to understand the target culture.

Authentic documents from the print media are frequently used to develop the reading skill in the early stages of language learning. Students are taught strategies for global or for detailed reading comprehension. Once again, however, the students' concentration is more often on bottom-up processing of the information, on decoding the language to understand the message of the text, than on looking for the sociocultural information in the text. To make students aware of this type of information, a helpful activity is to give them a newspaper in French or a page from a newspaper and ask them to scan it for different types of texts that give information about the target culture. The births, deaths, engagements, and marriages section, for example, gives information about family organization, class structures, attitudes to these major events in family life, religious beliefs, etc. This information is given through the formal language register of the "faire-part," which is itself an illustration of a value system. The different types of advertisements in the newspaper not only give vocabulary for objects that are part of daily life but also reveal attitudes toward those objects and what the French expect of them. The classified advertisements for accommodations and housing reveal a different organization of living space and different expectations from those in the students' culture. The classified advertisements for employment can be the entry point into discovering the hierarchical organization of a range of trades and profes-sions, the status of these based on the educational qualifications required (and the educational system that delivers these qualifications), and the different life-styles and values of different professional groups. The layout and the content of the newspaper itself give information about its principal category of readers, their sociocultural status, their expectations, and their values.

Comparing two newspapers, one from the native culture and one from the target culture, reveals a range of similarities and differences in the two cultures. As with the comparison of all types of authentic documents from two cultures, however, care must be taken to compare similar documents in order to make equivalent observations. In the case of newspapers, those compared must have a similar sociocultural readership. For example, Le Monde would be compared with The New York Times or The Washington Post. Le Figaro would be compared with the main daily newspaper of a large American city. A comparison of the amount of space each newspaper accords to its principal sections gives information about the importance of these topics in the value system of its readership. How much space is given to news of other countries, to sport, to cultural activities? In the sports section, what sports are featured? Are they the same in the two papers? If not, can you explain the differences? News stories on the same event can be compared in the two papers. Are there different emphases in the reporting of the event? Why? To show that different emphases reflect not only different national values, the news stories on the same events in different French newspapers can be compared. In this case the differences can be explained by different ideological and political positions, which reflect the diversity of opinions and political views in France and which do not necessarily have direct equivalents in American society. This activity, as well as illustrating different value systems in the two cultures, heightens students' awareness of the relative truth value of "factual" reporting and the ideological subtext in authentic documents. The instructor's role as mediator between the document and the student is vital while the student is acquiring a body of information and strategies necessary to analyze the document within its cultural frame of reference.

To build up a balanced repertoire of information on the target society, students should work with a range of documents containing sociological and anthropological information. Sociological documents give facts and figures. Anthropological documents describe how life is lived, how society is organized. Much information is supplied by opinion polls, which are a constant feature of the French press. The French have a deep fascination with the images that opinion polls give of them and new trends in those images. Students need training in how to read these opinion polls, how to interpret the results, and how to use the information these polls supply.[5] If this information remains as isolated facts and is not integrated into a developing, overall view of the groups that constitute French society, then the purpose of using opinion polls as authentic documents has not been achieved.

Advertisements are another type of authentic document that gives insights into French attitudes and values. Advertisements illustrate many aspects of daily living and cultural practices. They can be classified thematically and by degree of complexity. Simple advertisements can be used with beginners to introduce them to the everyday life of the French and to strategies for decoding their explicit and implicit messages. In the print media, advertisements usually combine a written text with a visual element that illustrates and reinforces the message(s) in the written text. Television advertisements usually have a basic narrative structure. Comparing advertisements on similar objects or themes in the target and the native cultures reveals not only different attitudes to consumerism but also different sociocultural values. The primary goal of advertising, whether in the print or the electronic media, is to convince the reader, the listener, or the viewer of the truth of the claims made in the advertisement and of the necessity of possessing the advertised object, or of adopting the opinion expressed in political and similar advertisements. During the analysis of advertisements, students need to be alerted to the techniques of persuasion used by the authors of them so that they do not become gullible consumers and can evaluate the ideological subtext.

There are many types of authentic print documents not found in newspapers and magazines that can motivate student interest in the target culture and provide windows onto the ways it functions and why it functions in those ways. The instructor's choice of them will depend on the nature of the course and the level and interests of the students. Posters and tourist brochures (which can also be obtained through sister-city linkings), restaurant menus, transport schedules, stamps on mail, bank notes, labels and instructions on pharmaceutical products, tracts distributed by political and advocacy groups, and documents produced by government agencies are some examples. In this last case, the identity papers and cards carried by a French person and an American can be used to illustrate the different relationship between the individual and the State in the two cultures.

A major event that takes place in France and attracts international attention such as the Bicentenary of the French Revolution in 1989 or the Winter Olympic Games in Albertville in 1992 can also be the focus of a sociocultural analysis using authentic materials in French and accompanying them with related authentic materials in the native culture. In the first example, this could lead to a research project on the concept of freedom and democracy in the two cultures. Since the students' attention is being directed to the sociocultural context of the authentic materials and not to the language structures that can be used for formal language learning, comparisons with similar documents in the students' mother tongue are necessary in order to increase awareness of cross-cultural value systems. Awareness of the values in our own culture that condition our opinions and judgments as outsiders of the target culture is a necessary prerequisite to a balanced evaluation of the key values of the target culture.

"Bandes dessinées" are particularly popular in France.[6] They also convey information about French attitudes and values. Although their use of slang and colloquial expressions may hinder the students' linguistic comprehension, the visuals and the simple narrative facilitate understanding of the situation and the events. The series of adventures by Astérix, written by Goscinny and illustrated by Uderzo, are a transposition of contemporary French attitudes and values into the confrontation between the Gauls (the French) and the Romans (the foreigners, the invaders). Astérix, the hero of the Gauls, symbolizes the values of individualism, "débrouillardise," and national pride that the French ascribe to themselves. The comic nature of his adventures enables Goscinny to mock the French obsession with those values.

Minitel gives direct access to the huge range of databases and Minitel services in France, which provide an electronic source of authentic materials.

Using a Minitel terminal or a modem-equipped personal computer, an instructor with a subscription to one of the American providers of Minitel services can consult France's electronic white and yellow pages, get information on French train schedules or on Parisian shows, obtain tourist information for a visit to Martinique, read summaries of current French newspapers and magazines, or telecommunicate with a variety of consumer and professional services in France. Online sessions can be recorded for offline uses in the classroom as an information resource and as a means of extending cultural awareness.[7]

# Authentic Audio Materials

Audio recordings were the principal means of giving students practice in listening comprehension of authentic spoken discourse until video became easily available. Students listened to recorded conversations, interviews, and radio broadcasts and learned to decode intonation, pauses, and other paralinguistic features that convey meaning in addition to the words used. Video, whose visual element facilitates listening comprehension, is a more effective means of developing students' listening skill, especially in the early stages.

Radio broadcasts can be used not only as listening practice but also as sociocultural documents. Radio programs contain a variety of segments that range from news broadcasts and current affairs to talk shows and entertainment. These different spoken texts elicit different techniques of observation and interpretation of sociocultural data. Extracts from them can be used as documents to illustrate a course on aspects of contemporary French society.

At the intermediate and advanced levels, various types of interview documents (oral, oral transcriptions, written) can be used to develop students' inferencing skills. After identifying the opinions and the justification for them expressed in the interview, students can be asked to assess these opinions from a sociocultural perspective and to evaluate whether the person(s) being interviewed would be likely to hold a given list of other opinions. Rey and Santoni have elaborated models of opinion evaluation grids that can be used by students for this type of document.[8]

Recordings of songs and French popular and classical music can be used as documents for social and cultural analysis. The special status of the French poetic song represented by such singers as Georges Brassens, Jacques Brel, Léo Ferré, Barbara, and Édith Piaf, and by new generation singers such as Patricia Kaas and Jean-Jacques Goldman[9] shows the importance of the lyrics as well as the accompanying music for a French audience. These lyrics express French attitudes to life and values. Videoclips combine song with a visual presentation of the singer and the themes of the lyrics. An analysis of the visuals in the videoclip is a way of delineating French aesthetic and moral attitudes.

When French music is part of a course on big "C" culture, recordings of French music illustrate French musical traditions. Comparisons can be made with the preoccupations expressed in the other art forms of the corresponding period. Likewise, comparisons of the classical music heritage in France and in other countries reveal a distinctly French style that reflects a French preoccupation with form and the distilling effect of the intellect over the emotions. The polemic that raged at the end of the nineteenth century between the supporters of Debussy's music and those of Wagner's music of uncontrolled passions illustrates the fundamental French preference for "la mesure," refinement and balance, over "les extrêmes," excess and prodigality.

# Authentic Visual Materials

Slides serve two main purposes in the modern language classroom. They inject the sense of sight in the learning process, and they bring the target culture into the classroom. Slides of drawings, illustrations, and photos can depict daily life from past centuries and slides taken in France today can portray the diversity of contemporary daily life and customs. Slides provide necessary examples in big "C" culture courses on French painting, sculpture, and architecture.

Students need to be trained to develop their viewing skill so that they can draw appropriate sociocultural information from slides. They need to develop their ability to observe and to integrate what they observe into a descriptive and interpretative model of different aspects of the target culture. Santoni has shown how a selection of slides can lead students to recognize representative characteristics of the life-styles of members of different social classes in France.[10]

Cottenet-Hage, using two slides of French posters, describes a process whereby students can be encouraged to "penser la culture," to realize that language and culture are to be decoded through each other and that meaning depends on the cultural context.[11] The process, which can be inductive or deductive, is activated by a set of questions that the students answer, with the instructor's help where necessary, to discover the socio-cultural context of the language. The ensuing collective discussion tests hypotheses, makes comparisons with the students' native culture, and illustrates that the functioning of a cultural system is logical but logical in an arbitrary way. The use of authentic documents thus combines language and culture and develops the students' capacity to "comprendre l'autre, non seulement sa langue mais son identité telle qu'elle a été façonnee par une Histoire et une Culture."[12]

Some instructors find the traditional format of slides easier to use than a laserdisc if they only intend to show several slides in a class. The laserdisc, on which a large number of visual documents can be stored and rapidly located, is a powerful adjunct to a computer in the development of interactive video programs for big "C" and small "c" cultural courses.[13]

It has been said the video revolution has finally brought Francophone countries and spoken French into the classroom authentically. Native French speakers can be seen and heard communicating and going about their lives in an authentic sociocultural context. The context of situation and the paralinguistic features that play an important role in communication are readily observable and help the students understand the different layers of meaning in the exchanges between the speakers. The scene on videotape is really authentic only when the participants are not aware that they are being filmed and the film is not edited. But even then the shooting decisions made by the camera operator and the angles and distance of the camera shots modify the authentic reality of the scene. Scenes that are staged with native-speaker participants in France and videotaped for pedagogical purposes may give an impression of authenticity but are, in fact, images of French life mediated by the pedagogical author in collaboration with the camera crew and the tape editor. In this case, the subjective deformation of an authentic scene can be considerable. Such videotapes may be useful for formal language learning but are flawed as sociocultural documents. Despite the drawbacks, video is a huge leap forward from the time when the learner had only a sparsely illustrated textbook filled with grammar exercises and an instructor with a limited command of spoken French as the link to French language and culture.

Altman in *The Video Connection: Integrating Video into Language Teaching*[14] gives a wealth of practical suggestions and activities for using video in the language classroom. Other research has shown that students watching video to develop their listening skill spontaneously use top-down processing of information but that their attention span for processing is very short. It could be expected that top-down processing would make students more aware of the sociocultural dimension of what they are watching. Our students, however, have grown up watching hours of television each day and, as a result, only see the big picture and do not see much detail. The instructor therefore needs to teach them strategies that extend the top-down processing they habitually use to the observation of telling examples of sociocultural behavior.

The parameters for selection of video extracts for their sociocultural content will differ from those used for language practice.[15] Once again, the instructor's selection will be made according to the course goals and the students' level and needs. Videos can be integrated into the course for their small "c" or big "C" content or to show students examples of the cultural dimension of language. They stimulate activities for individual, small-group, or class viewing.

Videos, like satellite TV programs such as the international francophone channel TV-5, are available in ever-increasing numbers. Many instructors find the choice overwhelming because of the time it takes to preview the video for content and difficulty, select an appropriate extract, analyze it, and devise student activities for it. In American colleges equipped for screening satellite TV programs in French, instructors have observed that few students watch the programs voluntarily unless there is a class activity or assignment based on them. Preparation of a viewing guide that directs students' attention during video and TV screenings outside the classroom would seem to be advisable. "France Panorama" (Eagle Communications), using news and current affairs programs from the French TV channel Antenne 2, and "France-TV Magazine" (University of Maryland/Baltimore), also using French TV news and culture programs, are two series of videocassettes produced with pedagogical guides.

Films produced for the cinema and TV have been successfully used for the information they contain about French society, its attitudes, and values. Film is clearly its own aesthetic universe but this does not obviate the fact that, like literature, it can also be a rich source of cultural documentation. Whether the film belongs to the realistic or to the fictional genres, cultural presuppositions underlie all its modalities of representation. A comparative study of a French and an American film, one of which is a "remake" of the other such as A Bout de souffle and Breathless or Trois hommes et un couffin and Three Men and a Baby or Le retour de Martin Guerre and Sommersby clearly reveals different social, cultural and aesthetic values in French and American society. Likewise, a comparison of an American and a French review of the same film can be the basis for a discussion of what different cultural attitudes may have provoked a favorable or negative reaction to the film by the reviewer.

In conclusion, the quantity and diversity of authentic materials now available for teachers of French and their students, while making the target culture much more accessible in the classroom, has brought new challenges: how to make the best selection of them and how to use them most effectively. The temptation is to immerse the learners in a sea of authentic materials and let them make their own choices. As we have indicated, however, authentic documents are not self-interpreting. The instructor needs to supply the learners with strategies and guide their observations until they have developed a sufficiently coherent concept of the target culture to be able to take increasing control of their own learning. Authentic materials provide a varied and stimulating contextualized content for the process of discovering key aspects of French culture, but without synthesis and valid interpretation this context will not provide a coherent framework of cultural understanding.

# Application

## Intermediate/Advanced

It is preferable for an authentic document, whenever possible, to be given to the students in its original form because the context of its original existence as a document destined for native French speakers is part of its sociocultural authenticity. The document presented on page 98 has had to be reset for technical reasons. In its original form it was in the book review pages of the "Culture" section of the weekly magazine L'Express.

One reason for choosing this document to illustrate applications of authentic material is to demonstrate that an authentic print document can come from any section of a newspaper or magazine. The choice of the document depends on the use to which it will be put. This document could be used as the starting point to stimulate interest in a section of a course in French history, political science, or sociology, in a course about frequent cultural references in a French person's "bagage culturel," or about the transformation of events into myths that reflect key values in French society. The Bastille has become an icon of French Revolutionary history for the French themselves and for the entire world. American students know of the Bastille though the expression "Bastille Day" to name the French

HISTOIRE
# Le génie de la Bastille
Comment la Révolution fit d'une prison
dépeuplée le symbole honni de l'Ancien Régime.

De la Bastille, on croyait bien tout savoir. Elle fut le symbole de l'absolutisme, le lieu terrible et sombre où s'entassaient les victimes des lettres de cachet, héroïquement conquis un certain 14 juillet 1789 au prix d'un peu de sang. Cherchant à rétablir les faits, le livre de Claude Quétel s'attache à démonter les mythes. Certes on a torturé en cette Bastille, mais une seule exécution y eut lieu en quatre siècles. Ironie de l'Histoire, ce fut sous le règne d'un des seuls rois que la mémoire collective s'accorde à reconnaître comme « bons », Henri IV. Pour le reste, c'est une prison comme les autres, qui voit passer au fil des temps des criminels de toutes sortes : du crime contre l'Etat au crime contre la religion, en passant par toutes les délinquances.

Combien de légendes autour de cette prison lorsqu'elle tombe sous les assauts du peuple de Paris? On s'attend à y trouver tout un monde de victimes du régime despotique. La réalité est plus triviale. On n'y découvre que sept prisonniers : quatre faussaires, qui, prudemment, fuient, deux fous oubliés là et un obscur comte de Solages, rapidement promu héros de la liberté.

Et pourtant on connaît la suite : la Bastille érigée en symbole et la date de sa prise, indirectement, en fête nationale. Bref, au moment où elle tombe, la Bastille n'est plus « un objet de pierre mais un concept, un rêve, une religion ».

C'est tout l'imaginaire de la Révolution qui s'y cristallise. Il fallait trouver derrière ces murs et leurs prisonniers un symbole et une justification.

**PIERRE BOURETZ** ■

• **La Bastille. Histoire vraie d'une prison légendaire,** *par Claude Quétel. Robert Laffont, 504 p., 185 F.*

national holiday, which the French call "la fête nationale du quatorze juillet." Often students know something about the history of the Bastille, although their knowledge is colored by a biased Anglo-American interpretation of the events.

Students need to bring to the text a reading skill that allows a rapid, top-down assessment of the content, which will assume its full meaning as their awareness of the historic/cultural dimension of the text expands. Students can be asked specific questions about the meaning of events, institutions, and historical characters cited in the text in order to develop their awareness of the historical context. For example, at the intermediate level a simple grid consisting of three headings—"L'Ancien Régime," "La Révolution," and "La Bastille"—could be given to the students, who fill in the names of the events, institutions, and persons mentioned in the text. Likewise another grid could be constructed to distinguish between fact and myth as presented in the document.

At the advanced level, students could be given the task of researching historical interpretations of the storming of the Bastille such as its value as symbol of the Ancien Régime precisely because it had, though not at the time of the Revolution, served as the most notorious place for the incarceration of intellectuals and other socially prominent individuals who were often victims of the infamous "lettres de cachet." Students should be made aware that the version of the taking of the Bastille they have just read in this document downplays the symbolic value of the Bastille *prior* to the Revolution by implying that the Bastille acquired its nefarious symbolism after the Revolution as an expedient to justify otherwise pointless violence. This version also ignores the fact that the practical defensive purpose for the Parisians' assault on the Bastille was to acquire needed gunpowder for their muskets in order to resist the foreign mercenaries in the employ of the king, who were surrounding Paris. The significance of the Bastille as a French icon should be discussed in relation to other icons associated with the French Revolution and the values it espoused.

For a comparison with the students' native culture, the following topics are suggested: Revolutionary violence and the quest for liberty (Boston Tea Party); the symbolism of historical monuments and places (Independence Hall in Philadelphia); the image of both France and the United States as countries representing to the world the key value of *liberté*/freedom (*Les droits de l'homme*/Declaration of Independence, Bill of Rights).

The process engaged in studying this authentic document has been to move from the information in the text to a broader contextualization of its specific details, to an interpretation of its cultural meanings, and finally to a cross-cultural comparison that entails a discussion of native and target culture values.

# Notes

1.  Marie-Claude Fargeot-Manche, "Utilisation de documents culturels en classe de langue," *Le Français dans le monde* 178 (1983): 64–68.

2.  Bernard S. Melvin and David Stout, "Motivating Language Learners through Authentic Materials," in Wilga M. Rivers, ed., *Interactive Language Teaching* (Cambridge, Eng.: Cambridge Univ. Press, 1987): pp. 45–56.

3.  Howard L. Nostrand, "Authentic Texts and Cultural Authenticity," *The Modern Language Journal* 73,1 (1989): 51.

4.  *Ibid.*, pp. 49–52.

5.  See Ross Steele and José Pavis, *L'Express: Aujourd'hui la France* (Lincolnwood, IL: National Textbook, 1992), for information on how to read opinion polls for classroom use, especially pages 36–48.

6.  "Spécial: Bande Dessinée," *Le Français dans le monde* 200 (1986).

7.  The Telematics Commission of the American Association of Teachers of French has established a database of innovative pedagogical uses of Minitel sources.

8.  Jean-Noël Rey and Georges V. Santoni, *Quand les Français parlent* (Rowley, MA: Newbury House, 1975).

9.  Sherry Dean, "French Popular Music," *AATF National Bulletin* 17,2 (November 1991): 2.

10. Georges V. Santoni, "Stéréotypes, contextes visuels et dimensions sociales," *Le Français dans le monde* 181 (1983): 84–94.

11. Madeleine Cottenet-Hage, "Enseigner la langue, enseigner la culture," *Le Français dans le monde* 250 (1992): 66–69.

12. *Ibid.*, p. 69.

13. The interactive video program created by the M.I.T. Athena Language Learning Project, *A la rencontre de Philippe*, authored by Gilberte Furstenberg (Yale University Press, 1993), uses an extremely flexible and imaginative methodology that involves students in a story with several possible endings. The story, filmed in Paris, and the hypercard extensions, are rich documents for sociocultural analysis.

14. Rick Altman, *The Video Connection: Integrating Video into Language Teaching* (Boston: Houghton Mifflin, 1989).

15. Elizabeth Joyner, "Choosing and Using Videotexts," *Foreign Language Annals* 23,1 (1990): 53–64.

# CHAPTER VII

# THE RETURN
# OF HIGH CULTURE

The affirmation of popular culture throughout the seventies and eighties was clearly a compelling necessity. Cultural instruction could not be restricted to *belles lettres* and the fine arts, for this was far too myopic a view of France as a whole and constituted an arrogant dismissal of French daily life. Further, the inherent snobbishness and elitism of this approach were clearly obstacles to reaching a large student population whose interests were less esoteric and less intellectual. This narrow mold had to be shattered to make room for the realities of the larger world.

## Oral Proficiency and Culture

Other forces were also at work. The emphasis on oral proficiency that became dominant during the eighties inevitably found itself focusing on culture with a small "c." The immediate communicative needs of elementary and intermediate students—students who could rarely hope to exceed the "novice" learning levels—tended to focus on the speech acts that would facilitate the transactions of everyday existence. Indeed, high culture courses and the language skills required for abstract discussions on the cultural achievements of the French seemed in many ways more suited only to very advanced students.

Despite its undeniable value, one of the pitfalls of an oral proficiency orientation is the potential for the reduction of cultural data to tourist information. Survival and thus the banal exchanges that must take place to permit an individual to be functional in France take priority over other pedagogical considerations. At this level, the student may easily ignore the cultural achievements of the French. The instructor, focused by necessity on the linguistic skills of the learners, loses sight of the big "C" culture. Just as the profession finds itself on the threshold of a truly oral-proficiency-based curriculum, it finds itself in danger of falling into total banality, of reducing culture to a kind of simplistic folklore.

At the elementary level, the new—and highly desirable—oral-proficiency-based textbooks generally seek to present information that is "typical," i.e., the most representative cases they can find for French people. While this is a laudable effort at authenticity and accuracy, it also runs the risk of stereotyping. Not everyone fits into the bourgeois family, however reassuring this may be to most language learners and instructors. A society is never uniquely composed of "typical" people, and, in a curious way, the "typical" may describe no one at all.

A further problem of the popular culture approach lies in the potential betrayal of humanist values inherent in any presentation that ignores high culture. Foreign language instruction should not merely be viewed as a "practical" skill. If the primary goal of teaching students a foreign tongue is to facilitate activities such as ordering lunch, the rich intellectual exchange that can be a source of strong motivation for language learning has been entirely jettisoned. Banality reigns supreme.

Furthermore, the French themselves have always accorded a special place to high culture—which they normally call *civilisation*—in their own self-assessment and self-valorization. To ignore high culture would require us to refuse to define the French fully, for it would be disregarding a key element of their overall culture. Given the importance of *civilisation* for them, we should look at the way it is marketed for domestic and foreign consumption, for by such activities the French define themselves.

# Culture in French Media

The media are a key aspect of the valorization of high culture in French life. Major national newspapers of all political affiliations participate in creating a privileged role for culture and in maintaining the very notion of the prime spokesperson of that culture, the French intellectual. *Le Monde*, the newspaper of the intellectual, administrative, and managerial elite, always includes a "cultural" headline on its front page. *Le Figaro*, the newspaper of the bourgeois right, contains pages under the heading *vie des spectacles*, which deal with the theater, café-theater, music, film, radio, and daily television events. *Libération*, which was initially identified with the attitudes and values of the student leaders of the events of May 1968, always features extended articles of cultural analysis, whether they be about a rock group or a museum exhibition. One need only consult *Le Monde*, *Le Figaro*, and *Libération*, on the death of Michel Foucault in 1984 to discover that the passing of a French intellectual is headline material. It would be inconceivable to imagine the analogues in any English-language press. (Would the deaths of Norman Mailer or Saul Bellow produce any comparable effect?) Ironically, high culture is such a part of French life that one might go so far as to say that, in one way, it actually constitutes an aspect of popular culture.

Regional newspapers also participate in this same valorization of cultural life. Weekly magazines such as *L'Express*, *Le Nouvel Observateur*, *Le Point*, and *L'Evénément du Jeudi* devote large sections to "la vie culturelle." Further, Parisians and tourists alike purchase either *Pariscope* or the *Officiel des spectacles* to learn what is happening in Paris each week. Although films are usually the largest sections, there are headings devoted to theater, variety shows, restaurants, clubs and discothèques, music and dance of every sort, and children's entertainment. Again, try to find an analogue of these exclusively cultural publications in any American city. Normally speaking, Americans find such information in certain sections of their newspapers, mainstream or alternative, not in a separate weekly. T.V. *Guide* is the closest to the French model, but it is uniquely devoted to television viewing and has its French equivalents in *Télé 7 Jours* and *Télérama*.

This valorization of cultural life is not limited to the print media. The television show "Apostrophes" hosted by Bernard Pivot, which ran from 1975 to 1990 and was watched by a huge audience, had as its format the discussion of the latest books. Its replacements, "Caractères," hosted by Bernard Rappiand and "Bouillon de Culture," hosted by Pivot, are similarly successful. There is a consistent effort to intellectualize public life even on the "boob tube." In fact, the philosophical discussion becomes a model of socialization, and, to some degree, projects the old notion of the "salon" (both philosophical and literary) to the nation as a whole.

Even the French private tourist industry works in this direction. The series of *Guides Michelin* in particular seeks to provide directions for tourists to undertake a cultural exploration of the *patrie*, and it is no secret to any reader of these guide books that high culture is the dominant theme. Invited to explore the Roman, medieval, and classical past, the diligent (and obedient) tourists are drawn into a process of cultural initiation or allowed to reinforce and broaden their own cultural awareness.

# Development of the Role of the Intellectual

Indeed, the whole elevation of high culture is very old in France—as a form of enculturation both for French people and for foreigners. The reign of Louis XIV (1643–1715) marks perhaps the beginning of France's self-conscious "mission civilisatrice," as Versailles with its rich court life characterized by a profusion of the arts and architectural grandeur became the model for all European monarchies. This whole process is reinforced throughout the eighteenth century by the *philosophes*, most notably Voltaire, who in his *Siècle de Louis* XIV invents the notion of cultural history, and, of course, assigns modern primacy to France. Exported most notably to Russia and Prussia, French civilization and language become at this point the dominant culture of Europe. The French Revolution was next to export a new political culture to the world, with France once again enjoying the role of model in the unfolding of human civilization.

Despite the existence of the role before the term, the nineteenth century will invent the successor to the *philosophe*: namely the *intellectuel*, an epithet coined during the Dreyfus affair. And so the intellectual torch will be passed from writers like Zola who defended Dreyfus to Sartre and Camus and then to the "nouveaux philosophes" and to thinkers of international stature like Barthes, Foucault, and Derrida. In short, the whole notion of the intellectual is primarily and logically identified with the French, as they invented the term. This notion also underlines the important social role of such individuals in that society—a role that is often derisive and insignificant in anglophone society. If we choose to ignore this elevation of high culture in France, we actually choose to misunderstand the culture.

# Government Support of Culture

In very recent times—since the Fifth Republic—the French government has paid very particular attention to culture. Institutionalizing the phenomenon, de Gaulle created the "Ministère des Affaires culturelles" and named André Malraux as "Ministre d'État" to this post. The latter, inspired by his beliefs in the eternal aspect of culture, created "Maisons de la Culture" in all of France's major cities, and thus contributed to the decentralization of the theater—a development that far outlasted the influence of the "Maisons" themselves.

De Gaulle's successors, Georges Pompidou and Valéry Giscard d'Estaing, also maintained a Ministry of Culture, though not at the level of a state ministry. Both presidents, however, forged ahead with cultural projects, Pompidou in realizing the controversial museum of contemporary art and culture that now bears his name and Giscard in laying the plans for the Musée d'Orsay. With the election of the socialist candidate François Mitterrand in 1981, culture was restored to a more central place in the government. Jack Lang, former director of the Festival du Théâtre in Nancy, became minister of culture and the international messenger of French culture as the symbol of intellectual independence in a world dominated by Anglo-American culture.

It should also be noted that the French seem to expect certain cultural traits in their presidents. De Gaulle unabashedly considered himself an intellectual and his *Mémoires de guerre* are a vast political reflection on the two world wars rather than a series of "factual" anecdotes. Pompidou, former student at the École Normale Supérieure, published an anthology of French poetry and was well versed in modern art. Valéry Giscard d'Estaing, beyond his political writings, did a popular television show on Guy de Maupassant. François Mitterrand has written numerous books of political and personal reflections, and his love of bookstores is well known in Paris. The cultural expectations the French have of their political leaders should be conveyed in a French course for foreigners, for this illustrates a very significant feature of the national mentality.

We must also be aware that the French government has never ceased to be concerned with the exportation of its culture to other nations. It is almost impossible to imagine a U.S. government sitting down and worrying about an issue like the "rayonnement culturel"; indeed there is no equivalent concept in English. This need to maintain culture at home and to spread it abroad is a very dominant French preoccupation. It is also backed by French institutions throughout the world, most notably the Alliance Française, which, enjoying quasi-governmental status, is charged with the domestic and international dissemination of French language and culture.

# Current Trends

At the level of the ordinary citizen, high-cultural practices even seem to be increasing.[1] Curiously, the new practices embrace a variety of forms both "legitimate" and "illegitimate"—a tendency that exhibits more independence among the French themselves. The sixties generation, for instance, may still cling to its enjoyment of rock and roll while appreciating other forms of music. The mixture of high and popular culture has now become more pronounced and is governed by a certain eclecticism. In short, high culture is still very significant but the hierarchy of cultural practices is now much less evident. New cultural technologies like audiovisual entertainment have inevitably altered that structure. This does not mean, however, that the French have abandoned high culture.

Given the role culture—and particularly high culture—plays in French life, whether at the individual or institutional level, we cannot simply relegate it to some more remote advanced level of French studies, although it is obviously easier to discuss it properly at such a level. If we aim for cultural proficiency even at the beginner level, we must find ways of communicating high culture to the very beginning student as well as the advanced. With this in mind, the mission of the nineties will lie in preserving the importance of popular culture in language instruction while simultaneously incorporating high culture into every level of the language-learning curriculum. Below are some suggestions to this effect.

# Applications

## High Culture and Politics: Elementary/ Intermediate Level

### The French Presidents as Intellectuals

1. Create a chart with all the presidents of the Fifth Republic. Have students learn their names and the dates they held office.

2. List the publications of each author; in Giscard d'Estaing's case, his television series on Maupassant should be added. Have students undertake the same project from presidents Eisenhower through Kennedy. Have students compare impressions in a very simple French: "plus/moins littéraire, plus/moins intellectuel, plus/moins sympathique, etc." Allow them to make simple statements about what a French president does in intellectual domains.

3. Identify the monumental endeavors of several of the presidents to enshrine culture and/or leave significant architectural works behind them, most notably Pompidou (Le Centre Pompidou) and Mitterrand (L'Institut du monde arabe, L'Arche de la Défense, La Pyramide du

Louvre, L'Opéra de la Bastille, La Grande Bibliothèque de France). You could list Le Palais du Centre National des Industries et des Techniques (CNIT) at la Défense for de Gaulle, the initiation of the Musée d'Orsay for Giscard d'Estaing. Students will discover that U.S. presidents, in fact, lack the authority to undertake such projects, that their initiative is limited to presidential libraries, which often do not bear witness to a desire to leave any enduring architectural monuments to posterity. The students may wish to ponder the significance of this omission in presidential powers and its implications about the relationship between political power and culture in the United States.

**French Valorizations of High Culture in Earlier Times.**   After looking at contemporary efforts at cultural monuments by French presidents, go back to the seventeenth century to Versailles. Show the palace and Louis XIV's portrait by Rigaud. Again, this can be handled very simply: "Voilà Louis XIV; voilà Versailles; c'est son palais, c'est le symbole du prestige culturel du roi et de la France au dix-septième siècle." Bring in Voltaire's *Le Siècle de Louis* XIV to reinforce the king's role and perhaps familiarize your students with the name Voltaire. Similar exercises can be done with Louis XV and the Place de la Concorde, Napoléon and the Arc de Triomphe, Napoléon III and Georges Haussmann and the Louvre and the Tuileries to bring home the architectural monumentalism expected of a French ruler be he president, king, or emperor.

# High Culture and French Daily Lives: Intermediate/Advanced Level

Ask the students to be a group of French university students in Paris discussing what to do in their leisure time. Choose three probable activities: (1) the cinema, (2) the theater, (3) art exhibitions. Use realia to illustrate the options. For example, the film selections are discussed using *Pariscope* rating systems, i.e., brief, simplistic critical evaluations in the form of stars. Have them discuss the films, the location of the theater, and the price of tickets. Be sure to have your selections illustrate the large number of foreign (especially American) films available to the Parisian audience. Teach the students the difference between "version originale" and "version doublée." Show the program of the Cannes Festival to illustrate further the role of cinema. Point out your city's own film festival if it has one. Do the same for the theater. Again use *Pariscope* to show the diversity of offerings ranging from the *Comédie Française* and other state-subsidized theaters in

Paris and its suburbs (including Ariane Mnouchkine's *Théâtre du Soleil*) to commercial theaters. To remove the students from Paris, you could use the program of the Avignon festival. Work in explanations about theater choices. Likewise, for art exhibitions indicate Paris's principal museums, their contents, and their locations. Show pictures of them. Have a discussion about the current options by illustrating briefly and simply the kind of art that is currently receiving special status in an exhibition. Use simple vocabulary and essential terms to classify it.

# Literature: All Levels

## Familiarization with Literature

It is difficult enough to familiarize advanced students with literature, and so the instructor's natural reaction with students at earlier levels may well be "Why bother?" It is, however, not at all impossible to allude very briefly and yet frequently to great works of French literature without intense discussion. Starting with the pithy maxims of the seventeenth-century moralists, one has a vast selection of brief, pointed statements that can be used to build a body of references that will prepare students for the frequent literary allusions in the media and in discussions. The instructor, midway into an elementary course, may thus wish to introduce a "quote of the day" or "quote of the week." Why not supply a statement like Pascal's "Le cœur a ses raisons que la raison ne connaît point" (perhaps with the lesson on *avoir* or on negations). "Il faut cultiver notre jardin," "L'enfer, c'est les autres," etc., all supply terse but provocative remarks that draw student attention to the existence of literature, initiate them to its allusive role in French culture, and yet require little commentary. It doesn't hurt occasionally to allow them to see a film version of a play—even with subtitles—to offer them the vibrancy of a performance. Segments of the latter may be done as cloze exercises to reinforce vocabulary.

## Presenting Literature as an Introduction to Other Forms of High Culture: All Levels

Any allusion to authors is an opportunity to introduce other forms of high culture such as architecture, sculpture, painting, and music. The briefest mention, for instance, of Chrétien de Troyes or Marie de France allows the instructor to present photos of castles and cathedrals, photos of richly sculpted bas-reliefs and free-standing statuary, illustrations of medieval life from copies of paintings and illuminated manuscripts, models of armored knights, and brief selections of medieval music. Again, at the early level, these are very simplified presentations with minimal commentary. Their function is to expose French high culture to the students and to awaken their curiosity. Literary allusions serve as an entry point for a wider exposition of cultural life.

## Literature as Cultural Study at the Advanced Level

Here we provide examples of authors from several periods and use a common methodology for the cultural explanation of their works. It should not be assumed that we are implying that a cultural approach is the only one to literature. There is no need to do these works in their entirety if time is short. Segments can be used to illustrate cultural settings and attitudes.

### Jean Racine: *Phèdre*

1. *Cultural matrix.* For Racine, this means his upbringing, his class, his studies at the Petites Ecoles at Port Royal and at the Collège de Beauvais, and the audience for which he produced: primarily the aristocracy and the king. Any discussion of audience requires commentary on the French court and the role of the monarch as patron of the arts. It would also involve a discussion of royal absolutism and the overwhelming dependence of the author upon his ruler. (One would need to cite Louis XIV's relationship to Molière as well as to Racine.)

2. *Lexicon and conventions.* The students would have to learn briefly about the emergence of *préciosité* and how the lexicon of this "salon" movement would come to dominate cultivated expression. They would then need to understand how *préciosité* restricted the lexicon and how *bienséance* correspondingly narrowed the range of permissible representation. They would have to understand these restrictions in the context of an authoritarian, absolutist culture and see the relationship between political constraint and artistic expression.

3. *Values.* This entails the whole network of assumptions, of moral judgments behind the play. Racinian morality is largely pessimistic, and it implies predestination and the overwhelming, irresistible force of concupiscence manifested in degrading passion. If students are to understand the behavior of the main character without being excessively judgmental and to have some understanding of the rather bleak worldview of the *grand siècle*, they must achieve some understanding of these values that are alien to them. It is often helpful to point out the rival value system of Corneille and to explain that, with its affirmation of the individual, even in tragedy, it exemplifies the historical moment of the

Fronde, the period that directly precedes Louis XIV's personal rule. Similarly, one may point out that Racine's values are more appropriate in a world of royal absolutism.

4. *Ancillary materials*. These include illustrations of period architecture, painting and sculpture, and musical selections to convey the mood of the times. The rigidity and regularity of Versailles and its garden need to be illustrated. Louis XIV's choice of his equestrian statue at the palace needs to be compared to the very baroque model by Bernini that he rejected, and, of course, the Rigaud portrait of the king is *de rigueur*. Lulli's music would supply an example of royal taste in music, just as *Phèdre* exemplified his taste in drama.

## Voltaire: *Candide*

1. *Cultural matrix*. This includes Voltaire's background as a child of the Parisian bourgeoisie and his aspirations to the nobility and intellectual life. On a broader level, it includes the continuing authoritarianism of the French monarchs, the increasing mercantilism and ever-growing wealth of French society, the powerful influence of English culture and Voltaire's own stay in that society, the emergence of the Enlightenment, and Voltaire's position as culture hero of the new movement.

2. *Lexicon*. This means an explanation of Leibnitizian philosophical tenets—especially the expression "the best of all possible worlds"—and a general familiarization with terminology, most importantly the word *philosophe*.

3. *Values*. Again, this requires an explanation of Enlightenment objectives. Definitions from the *Encyclopédie* (*philosophe, christianisme,* etc.) should be compared with the treatment of such ideas and institutions in the text. Student reading should reveal that the work is a general program for the values of the Enlightenment.

4. *Ancillary materials*. These would include further examples of classical architecture, love of geometry, painting ("The Dinner at Sans Souci" and a salon painting featuring Mme de Pompadour).

## Honoré de Balzac: *Le Père Goriot*

1. *Cultural matrix*. Balzac's own background and career would begin the exploration. A brief portrait of Restoration society is also helpful, with its doomed efforts to return to the old order and the illegitimacy and falseness of that society, which had at that point become far more a

capitalist than a feudal society. The emergence of the Romantic movement is a third aspect: superstition, religious devotion, and the reaction against the Enlightenment.

2. *Lexicon*. This entails an investigation of the rich specificity of Romantic writing. It requires stressing the explosion of vocabulary that occurs from the novels of the Enlightenment to those of the Romantic period and the new terminology, such as *l'homme à passion*.

3. *Values*. Again, this focuses on showing the transition from Enlightenment to Romantic values, i.e., from the *philosophe* to the *homme à passion*, to the uneasiness with both capitalism and feudalism, since the society espoused one while practicing the other.

4. *Ancillary materials*. These include examples of Romantic art and architecture: the death of classicism in architecture, the paintings of Delacroix.

### Albert Camus: *L'Etranger*

1. *Cultural matrix*. This begins with Camus's youth as a child of poor French colonists in Algiers. Study should include Europe between the world wars: the general collapse of confidence in all the old orders, the rise of fascism and communism as solutions to the human condition. One aspect is the reception of Camus's work in post–World War II Europe.

2. *Lexicon*. Introduce new existentialist terms such as *l'absurde* and its new style of writing of particular dryness that corresponds to the perceived aridity of life.

3. *Values*. The students can explore the elaboration of a new value system based on personal experience and judgment as well as the repudiation of transcendental justifications for behavioral choices, the rejection of Marxism as a form of determinism, and the conflict with Arab nationalism as it decolonized North Africa.

4. *Ancillary materials*. Mid-twentieth-century to postwar architecture, its severity, restraint, and lack of ornament and postwar painting and music are topics to cover.

### Marguerite Duras: *L'Amant*

1. *Cultural matrix*. Some relevant background would include Duras's childhood in Indochina; French colonialism at the beginning of the twentieth century, most especially in Indochina, French anticolonialism since the late sixties, and French feminism; and also the romantic communism of many French intellectuals of Duras's period.

2. *Lexicon*. This requires a familiarization with colonial locations and a general geographical knowledge of French Indochina.

3. *Values*. Students may explore the postcolonial, anticolonial atmosphere of leftist militancy in post–World War II France; they may examine the articulation of a particular feminism, self-affirmation.

4. *Ancillary materials*. These would include photos of French Indochina and films by Duras.

# Film

Perhaps the most current way to introduce high culture, films can be used at almost any level. We supply two well-known films as examples of cultural explication.

## Jean Renoir: *La Grande Illusion*

**Elementary/Early Intermediate.**    You will have to allow your students to view a subtitled version for them to understand the plot of the film. This should not deter the instructor from doing some exclusively French activities. First, one needs to supply a historical background. Here, this means a simple schema in French illustrating World War I—the dates, maps of the fronts, statistics on casualties, and, perhaps, prisoner of war camps. Second, an equally schematic portrait of social classes is required; provide your students with a checklist and ask them to match characters with classes. Who is an aristocrat, who is of the people, etc.? Also ask them to identify the class of the German in charge of the prison. Prepare a checklist of physical and moral descriptions of the French prisoners of war. Without commentary, you will have given your students an overview of class structure; this perspective will be largely implied rather than stated.

**Late Intermediate/Advanced.**    At this level, the instructor should strive to make what was previously implicit explicit. Besides the pertinent historical background about the war itself, a discussion in French of European class structure before World War I is a necessity. Then an elaboration of class structure in France is required. At this point, you can ask your students to discuss the milieus or classes of the various characters. You should pose questions about the linguistic cues. Why does the French officer, who is about to risk and lose his life in order to create a distraction that will allow his comrades in arms to escape, refuse to use the familiar form in addressing them? Why does that same officer actually get along better with his German captor? Why does the German commander, who is obliged to shoot the French officer, nevertheless deeply mourn his demise? What is said about the class structure of European society, and what is the *Grande Illusion*? After discussing these questions, the instructor can then better explain how World War I represented the death of the old Europe.

# François Truffaut: *Les 400 Coups* and *L'Argent de poche*[2]

**Elementary/Early Intermediate.** These films should be viewed in tandem to illustrate major changes in contemporary French culture. Again, beginning students must have access to subtitled versions and the presentation will be primarily implicit. The two themes to be stressed are the decline of an authoritarian culture, here largely illustrated in public school life, and the decentralization of France. To develop these themes, ask simple questions about the school life of the characters in both films. In the first, students can characterize the instructor very simply in French: "brutal, sévère, sadique, méchant, etc." They can also compare him to the teachers in the second film, who again can be described easily in simple French: "gentils, sympathiques, sensibles, tendres, etc." They can also describe the schools: all male/both sexes, grim/colorful . . . and the lives of the children: sad/happy, doomed/promising. Also point out that one film takes place in Paris and the other in the provinces—in the very geographic center of France. Give the dates of the films to make it clear that things have changed and ask simple questions about which is better, clearly distinguishing between the present and the past.

**Late Intermediate/Advanced.** The instructor can now go into depth on the French educational system: how it was a product of the Third Republic, how it originally separated the sexes, how it is much more severe than the American system, and how thoroughly centralized it was and still is. Thereafter, *Les 400 Coups* can be placed in its appropriate time frame with observations about educational authoritarianism in pre-1968 France. Next discuss *L'Argent de poche* as a manifestation of reform, of a new, more humane pedagogical and general culture. This film will allow you to explain what it meant to be a *soixante-huitard*. The two films taken together can make the whole revolt of the late sixties into something very comprehensible.

Coupled with the declining authoritarianism is the movement toward decentralization. Here the instructor can discuss de Gaulle's attempts to give new impetus to the regions of France as well as the policy of administrative decentralization promoted by the Socialist government elected in 1981. The symbolic message of L'*Argent de poche* can thus be evaluated in the light of today's France and students can be asked about the relationship between authoritarianism and centralization. They can be encouraged to look at American society to see the differences in education produced by different levels of government (state and local), to ask themselves what issues are paramount in their system, and whether centralization is a meaningful solution or an aggravation of a severe problem of standards. In short, these films can be used to engage students in a dialogue on French and American education and can lead them to reflect on how state organization and cultural values affect educational systems.

## Marguerite Duras: *Hiroshima Mon Amour*

Because of the somewhat graphic physical and sexual detail of this film and the complexity of its themes, it is more suited to late intermediate/advanced university students.

This film is ideal in the creation of empathy in a class that has strong pacifist inclinations. To present it properly requires an introduction to post–World War II intellectual concerns: namely, an aversion to the forces of mass destruction, themes of loneliness and isolation, and interrogation about guilt and innocence. It also requires a discussion on collaboration with the Nazi occupiers during the war to examine the anxieties of the female protagonist. The film's presentation of a racially mixed couple also introduces the themes of cultural intermixtures (allies and enemies) and the breaking of sexual taboos. This is a film of enormous reactive value, which is why it probably should be interpreted subjectively, allowing students to free-associate their impressions. The instructor can have them do this in class, and then try to reorganize their reactions into a coherent series of categories that will point to a number of central themes in modern France, and, indeed, the modern world. A class project, working from the original script, would be to write a segment of their own film script in a similar genre. A word of caution: If your students are highly conservative, this is obviously a film to avoid.

# Conclusion

These are but a few of the possibilities for reintroducing high culture to the French classroom. They are intended to illustrate that high culture is a vital part of French cultural instruction and that any high-culture "artifact" must necessarily elicit commentary that illuminates the broader culture.

# Notes

1. The authors of an inquiry of the Département des Études et de la Prospective du Ministère de la Culture et de la Communication state that "Du moins en moins de Français demeurent totalement à l'écart de la culture : le pourcentage d'individus qui possèdent des livres ou des disques, qui lisent des livres ou écoutent de la musique, a globalement tendance à croître." *Les Pratiques culturelles des Français* 1973–1989, p. 7.

2. Andrew Suozzo wishes to acknowledge the 1979 N.E.H. Summer Institute at SUNY–Albany under the direction of Georges V. Santoni as the source of this comparison.

# CHAPTER VIII

# ASSESSMENT OF CULTURAL COMPETENCE

A great amount of research has been done on ways of assessing the levels of linguistic competence of foreign language learners but very little has been done on the assessment of their cultural and intercultural competence. This is because either the cultural component of language was ignored or, when it was accepted as part of language, it was not considered necessary to test it.

The assessment of linguistic competence was traditionally focused on knowledge about language and language form. The audio-lingual movement began to shift the focus toward language use, but grammatical knowledge remained the primary concern of language testing. The communicative movement has seen increasing emphasis placed on appropriate language use in various sociocultural contexts. The ACTFL language proficiency guidelines were the landmark in shifting the emphasis from linguistic competence to communicative competence by assessing what the learner can *do* with language. Knowledge about the language is not eliminated, because what one can do with language depends on one's control of the three key elements of language (lexis, grammar, and phonology). Assessment of the learner's communicative proficiency subsumes knowledge about the language.

Despite the now general acceptance that language is embedded in culture, that meaning is constructed and negotiated by speakers in culturally defined contexts, French language textbooks written with communicative or proficiency goals have continued to present exercises and activities with linguistic competence as the dominant component of communicative competence. Cultural competence is not made explicit. Textbooks constantly assess linguistic competence but rarely assess cultural competence beyond behavioral surface manifestations of the culture. They do not test the learner's knowledge of the deeper system that links surface manifestations into meaningful networks of values or the learner's empathy toward the other culture and ability to interpret intercultural differences appropriately.

# The Elusiveness of Cultural Competence

The ACTFL Provisional Proficiency Guidelines (1982) included a fifth section on culture (reprinted in Appendix I) after the sections on speaking, listening, reading, and writing. The final version of the Guidelines (1984), however, did not include the culture section. The explanation for this omission was that sociolinguistic competence was part of oral proficiency. This is true, but the sociolinguistic competence required for speaking proficiency levels is only a small part of sociocultural competence.

The authors of the Provisional Proficiency Guidelines on culture used the same proficiency levels as for the other four skills: Novice, Intermediate, Advanced, Superior, Near-Native Competence, Native Competence. The global definition of each level established a clear progression: Novice = limited interaction; Intermediate = survival competence; Advanced = limited social competence; Superior = working social and professional competence; Near-Native Competence = full social and professional competence; Native Competence. Nevertheless, the detailed descriptions of each level lacked the same clarity. They contain a number of French phrases used in daily life, which reveals a language rather than a cultural emphasis. Furthermore, there is no obvious reason why certain cultural features precede others in the progression from Novice to Near-Native Competence.

It is by no means certain that the development of cultural competence can be organized into a hierarchical progression that matches the components in the progression from one level to the next of oral proficiency. There is general consensus on the components of language, on what constitutes progression in control of them by the learner, and how this control can be measured. There is no similar consensus about culture and considerable doubt whether gaining cultural competence is a step-by-step process. The temptation is to start with simple cultural manifestations at the Novice level and to introduce analysis of these manifestations at higher levels. The weakness of this approach is that it concentrates on cultural trivia, what Kramsch calls "the culture of the four F's: food, fairs, folklore and statistical facts."[1] Because the four F's are different from the native culture, they are perceived as strange or bizarre. This approach does not encourage the learner *from the outset* to see the differences within a meaningful system of behaviors, attitudes, and values that has internal coherence. The perceived differences reinforce negative stereotypes that are not changed by analysis if and when the learner reaches the higher level. What is the point of knowing that the Minitel exists in France unless you know what it is used for, how it has affected the daily lives of the French, what their attitude is toward it, and how it fits into the new technological revolution that is a source of French national pride? Many Americans are shocked that the French eat rabbit, but do they know that the French are equally shocked by the huge quantity of milk Americans drink? Such "eccentricities" can be explained within each culture's system of values but not when presented as isolated behaviors.

Knowledge of simple sociocultural information such as "street designation before name (*Rue de la Paix*) and telephone number groupings in pairs in French provinces, i.e., 32-49-63" or the ability to "express wants in culturally acceptable fashion in simple situations: *Je voudrais une chambre avec salle de bains. Un coca, s'il vous plaît. Je voudrais envoyer cette lettre aux* Etats-Unis. *C'est combien?*" or to "identify very common products, prices in local currency, and ask questions on conditions of promotion or sale, such as *Combien coûte cette écharpe?*" (ACTFL Provisional Proficiency Guidelines for culture, Intermediate level[2]) may not be a necessary prerequisite for an understanding of salient features of French society (for example, the hierarchy and the sharper sense of separation between social milieux or the more abstract concept of relationalism) that distinguish it from U.S. society. An outsider of both U.S. and French societies has observed that the French expressions cited above reveal more about central values of American society than of French society: bathrooms/cleanliness; the U.S. drink icon; the importance of the United States; money and the favorite U.S. pastime of shopping.

Surely a primary goal of cultural instruction should be a reflection on, and an interpretation of, the forms and values of another society as compared to one's own. It would therefore seem more helpful for students to be given information enabling them to develop a holistic and sensitive view of some of these forms and values early in their course so that they can situate the simple cultural manifestations they meet in their textbooks within the general matrix that gives the other society its artifacts and its meanings. In the ACTFL Provisional Proficiency Guidelines for culture, a characteristic of Near-Native Competence is that the learner "has internalized the concept that culture is relative and is always on the lookout to do the appropriate thing; no longer assumes that own culture is 'the way it is.'" There seems no compelling reason that this cannot be a characteristic of cultural competence at the Novice level and there is definitely no reason whatsoever that this should not be a characteristic of the Intermediate level.

The Commission of Professional Standards of the American Association of Teachers of French published in 1989 "A Syllabus of Competence" for teachers of French. The full text of the culture chapter of this syllabus is reproduced in Appendix II. In it, cultural competence is defined as "a combination of three interrelated parts: the sociolinguistic ability to communicate, certain areas of knowledge, and certain informed attitudes."[3] The committee, chaired by Howard L. Nostrand, that produced this chapter drafted a Working Paper in 1992 for the AATF Commission of Professional Standards in which the levels of sociocultural competence to be evaluated are defined according to the ACTFL scale. The Working Paper, reproduced in Appendix III, is the most concerted effort of the profession to produce viable guidelines for the levels of sociocultural competence to be evaluated. It will be noted that in addition to the categories "Sociolinguistic Ability" and "Knowledge of the Culture Area," which were components of cultural competence as defined in "A Syllabus of Competence," a new category designated "Knowledge of Cultural Analysis" has been added, starting at the Intermediate–Mid level. This document is proposed as the basis for certification of teachers' sociocultural competence. The Advanced level, subsuming all preceding levels, would correspond to Basic teacher certification and the Superior level to the Superior certificate. In 1993, the AATF Culture Commission drafted a provisional document called "The Cultural Component of Foreign Language Learning: A Common Core of Cultural Understanding and Knowledge of the French-Speaking World." For further discussion, see Appendix VI.

# Small "c" and Big "C" Culture

In a chronological perspective, the concentration of the profession's efforts on the production of an adequate description of sociocultural competence was the result of the difficulties of the authors of the ACTFL Proficiency Guidelines to find a solution to the assessment of cultural proficiency. Before appropriate techniques for assessing cultural proficiency could be devised, it was necessary to define what was being assessed. The focus of the ACTFL Proficiency Guidelines on language also resulted in culture being defined in relation to language and an emphasis on sociolinguistics and small "c" culture. This was also a reaction to the traditional domination of big "C" culture, especially in its literary manifestations, in modern language departments. The new emphasis on language use rather than knowledge about language stimulated the development of small "c" culture as the location for communicative language learning activities.

Big "C" culture, however, is also part of cultural competence. A valid assessment of cultural competence must include both small "c" and big "C" culture. The problem is what proportion each part should have at each level of cultural competence. Some would claim that at the early levels it should be solely small "c" culture. Others would hold that big "C" culture has a role from the beginning because it provides the overarching framework that gives small "c" cultural practices their meaning. Others would retort that big "C" culture learned as discrete cultural facts is quickly forgotten, encourages overgeneralizations, and does not change students' monocultural attitudes. The separation in most modern language departments of big "C" culture courses and small "c" culture courses does not facilitate links between them. Until formal links are made between them through innovative syllabus and course design, it seems unlikely that the dichotomy between big "C" and small "c" culture can be overcome and the holistic assessment of a student's level of cultural competence can be achieved. Newer teaching approaches such as a semiotic approach, which teaches students to recognize and interpret linguistic and nonlinguistic signs in a cultural context, and an approach to teaching literature from a cultural studies perspective are other ways of integrating big "C" and small "C" culture.

# Testing Instruments

Research into the most valid ways of assessing a student's progress in learning a language has produced a range of test types and test items that can be used or adapted to assess cultural competence. Formative assessment gives information that will help decide how the learning of the individual student or of a group of students will progress most effectively from that point. Summative assessment gives a comprehensive and systematic picture of the achievements of the student.

The main test types are diagnostic tests, achievement, prochievement,[4] proficiency, performance, norm-referenced, and criterion-referenced tests. They can be administered orally, in writing, or on a computer at various stages of the course. The instructor chooses the test type that corresponds to the goals of the course and may use more than one test type during the course. The duration of the test may range from a short-answer quiz to a role-play to a written essay.

Within these test types there is a diversity of test items of which some examples are multiple choice, true/false, cloze, open-ended, discussion, interpretation, summary, essay, and task- or performance-based items. Some items produce objective answers that are easy to score, while others, which ask for expression of opinion or a truth evaluation, produce subjective answers which cannot be scored as easily or as reliably. The latter, however, have greater value in assessing cultural competence. Discrete-point answers can show part of what the student knows but do not reveal whether or how the student has integrated this knowledge into a cross-cultural framework of attitudes, beliefs, and values. Discrete point testing has to be complemented by other forms of testing in order to evaluate cultural competence.

How will the instructor choose the appropriate forms of student assessment from among this wide variety of test types and test items? The choice will be based on the course objectives, the course content, and the way it is taught. Having specified the objectives, the instructor will define what has to be assessed to evaluate the degree to which students reach those objectives and what forms of testing make this evaluation most valid. The forms of testing should be flexible (that is, they should depend on the learners' needs), motivating for the learners, and mindful of the short-term and the long-term learning objectives. Most important, assessment should be integrated into the teaching and learning process.

Rebecca Valette, in her pioneering chapter "Culture and Literature" in *Modern Language Testing*[5], gives very useful examples of test items classified according to the four cultural goals she recommends that the classroom teacher adopt: cultural awareness; command of etiquette (the polite codes of behavior in the target culture); understanding of outward cultural differences; understanding of cultural values. She provides examples of multiple-choice items aimed at assessing the acquisition of high culture or "civilization" and others designed to assess a more anthropological awareness of culture.

Rather than expand Valette's list of test items and give additional examples of them, we will discuss the bases on which the instructor can choose test items to assess sensitization to the target culture, knowledge about the culture, and culture through communication.

Assessing knowledge of facts and comprehension of content is a cognitive activity in which memory has an important function. The student observes the target culture as an outsider and can learn about it through his or her own language or through the target language. Assessing culture through communication is an assessment of cognitive, behavioral, and affective factors. The student experiences the target culture through the target language as an insider. The student goes beyond learning about the culture to learning the culture, goes beyond knowledge about certain features of the target culture to the essence of the culture that is experienced through communication, performing activities, and learning in the target language. The student penetrates beyond the word to the world view expressed by the target language.

In moving from factual knowledge to culture through communication, assessment moves from measuring knowledge to evaluating competence. Measuring knowledge is most frequently individual assessment. Evaluating competence will also include assessment through pair and group activities while at the same time encouraging cooperative learning.

# Assessment of Sensitization to the Target Culture

At the beginning of a course with cultural goals—and this includes language courses—the instructor needs information on what the students know about France and the French (or francophone countries and their inhabitants) and what the students' attitudes are. This information allows the instructor to adapt the course content to the students' level and needs and to devise strategies to promote informed cross-cultural attitudes. To get this information, a diagnostic test is appropriate.

Psychologists have devised numerous tests of attitudes and beliefs. These can be used profitably in the foreign language classroom, particularly with students at the more advanced level. The instructor is often limited by time, however, and, in many courses, does not require the degree and quantity of information these tests supply. A general qualitative impression can be obtained in the following ways, but the students must be clearly told that they are not being graded on their answers, that the activity only has a diagnostic purpose that will enhance the relevance and the outcomes of the course for them.

Students are first asked to write the five most important things they know about France. (In courses on francophone countries, the instructor will adapt this and the following activities accordingly.) This can be a general knowledge question or it can be restricted by the instructor to a particular topic related to the course. The question's lack of precision usually produces a wide range of answers, which enables the instructor to get a general idea of the areas of awareness existing in the class. Next, students are asked to write the five adjectives that best describe France for them and the five adjectives that best describe the French. By quickly classifying these adjectives into two categories expressing a positive or a negative attitude, the instructor will realize what attitudes need modification to achieve a positive cross-cultural outcome. This process can be engaged explicitly, by drawing attention to pertinent examples that are discussed, or implicitly by the choice of examples used during the course.

A variation of this activity is to give students a sheet with the letters of the alphabet listed vertically and to ask them to write against each letter one or several words beginning with the letter that evokes for them something about France or the French. A simple example would be P = Paris. The students' answers will be scattered over many topics and this diversity will enable the instructor to gauge the general knowledge and some attitudes of the class. The scattered answers will also reveal any major areas that are lacking in the students' general knowledge.

These activities will call forth a number of stereotypes prevalent among the students, but the instructor who learns at the beginning which stereotypes are most prevalent among that particular group of students is better equipped to act on them in a positive fashion during the course.

Another activity is to tell students they have to make a presentation on their country and its people to a French person who has never visited the United States. They have to list the five topics they will talk about. The instructor will review the lists, noting the topics chosen and how much account has been taken of the foreigner's cultural identity. This information, which shows how the students see themselves and their country, is important for the instructor to have when planning activities to promote cross-cultural perceptions. It reveals how this group of Americans perceive themselves and their country. Their perception is basically ethnocentric. But how do the French perceive them? A variation of this activity is to tell the students they have to make a presentation on a specific topic, for example, the cultural achievements of their country and its people.

These activities, which can be done in English at the beginner level, are a rapid way for the instructor to get vital information for planning the course to promote more alertness to cross-cultural issues. The students' answers reveal both a cognitive and an affective reaction to France and the French. The course will give the students more knowledge, but this is not sufficient to effect significant change to monocultural attitudes. Discussion that helps students understand the reasons for their affective responses is necessary to promote more enlightened attitudes.

Some students in the class may come from bicultural/bilingual backgrounds. They should be encouraged to talk about their cross-cultural experiences in these discussions. Some students may have been to France and should also be encouraged to share that experience with the class. The different perceptions revealed by these experiences increase students' awareness of a pluralist perspective on another culture, which is necessary if egocentric stereotyping is to be modified.

The difficult choice for the instructor is to decide the amount of time to give to content and to promoting cross-cultural attitudes. The decision depends on the goals of the course, but these must be seen in the broader context of a humanistic education. Do we want our students to be knowledgeable but ethnocentric and intolerant of foreign attitudes and beliefs? The initial activities to assess the students' sensitization to the target culture can stimulate students to think about France and the French and about their perceptions of their own country. This stimulus is, however, only the starting point for the process that will produce more enlightened attitudes. Time should be allocated to this process during the course. The instructor might simply refer, from time to time during the course, to the information obtained in the initial activities when course materials reflect attitudes and alert students to the cognitive and affective connections they had not been aware of. The instructor might repeat the initial activities in a modified form at some point during the course and discuss the results to heighten students' awareness of cross-cultural comparisons and corresponding attitudes. The instructor might lead a discussion or assign an activity at the end of the course in which students review if and how their attitudes toward France and the French have changed as a result of what they have learned during the course. Each course is part of an overall process during which the student develops an informed personal perspective on France and the French and sees the world from a new perspective, during which the student moves from a monocultural identity to some degree of a bicultural identity and becomes aware of the commonalities and the differences between cultures.

# Assessment of Factual Knowledge

The traditional form of the culture course is a series of lectures that survey aspects of French and francophone culture. The culture course is a content course that aims to impart information or facts. The content can consist of big "C" culture topics (history, literature, the arts, etc.) or focus on one topic, for example, French painting. These courses usually adopt a historical perspective (France from its origins through the centuries to the present). Sometimes they treat only one century or period, for example, the nineteenth century or French Impressionist painting. Similarly, these courses can consist of a survey of small "c" culture topics (geography, daily life, education, technology, social/political/economic institutions, etc.) or focus on one topic, for example, political life in the Fifth Republic. Unlike big "C" surveys, these surveys are usually presented with a synchronic perspective, i.e., France today. Both strategies concentrate on the "big picture," which, however, tends to encourage generalization and reinforce stereotypes.

The content of these courses and the forms of student assessment are usually decided in advance. There is rarely any negotiation with students at the beginning of the course to determine which topics would interest them personally. Such negotiation would enhance the students' involvement and motivation and help counter the criticism of tedium they often make of the lectures in survey courses. Because it is unlikely that all the topics will interest them equally and because the topics are about a foreign country to which they are attached to a greater or lesser extent, they do not become personally involved and quickly forget the facts they have memorized for the end-of-the-course examination. In this case, the course does little to increase their cultural competence or their cross-cultural sensitivity. The expectation is that students will have acquired a range of cultural and sociocultural references that will help them understand and appreciate the "bagage culturel" that French speakers have in common. Note that this "bagage culturel" varies according to the social class the French person belongs to. Nonetheless, there is a shared "bagage culturel" resulting from social enculturation and a centralized primary and high school education system that binds the French together as a cultural group. In conversation and in writing there are frequent unconscious, spontaneous allusions to the shared contents of this "bagage culturel," which the foreigner must learn to recognize and interpret.

In survey courses, the end-of-course examination is the usual means of assessing what the student has learned, but it does not necessarily predict what the student will remember or use in the longer term. This examination usually contains discrete-point items or short-answer or essay items or analysis of a written or visual document. Discrete-point tests establish a model of right/wrong, true/false that may be appropriate for testing some factual knowledge but is not a good preparation for tolerance of cross-cultural differences, where degrees of opinion are more appropriate. Short answers and essays based not on general questions but on structured questions require critical thinking on various levels of interpretation rather than a "correct" answer. This kind of testing provokes greater alertness to cross-cultural issues. Analysis of a document also requires interpretation and expression of opinions.

A variety of forms of assessment can be given during the course. Students can be asked to gather information for a project, write a paper, and, if the lecture is accompanied by a tutorial, to make a presentation in class. Encouraging students to do these assessment activities on topics that interest them personally not only extends their knowledge but can also increase the satisfaction they derive from the course.

Lectures can be enhanced with audio and visual ancillary materials. As well as illustrating the content of the lecture, multimedia materials can be used to stimulate interaction between the instructor and the students. If the lectures are given in an electronic classroom, students can be asked to give their opinions and reactions to be recorded and tabulated so that the evaluation of their own reactions may become part of the learning process. In a small "c" culture lecture on young people in France, the instructor can use French opinion polls. Students can be asked to answer the same questions. Their answers can be immediately tabulated electronically, projected on a screen, and compared with the answers given by the young people in France. The similarities and differences revealed by this comparison can be the source of discussion and cross-cultural analysis. When multimedia materials have been used in lectures, they can also be used for assessment purposes. For example, on a big "C" culture test students can be asked to classify pictures of buildings according to their architectural style or century and to comment on the distinguishing characteristics of each style; in a small "c" culture test, students can be asked to classify and compare pictures illustrating the life-styles of representative French families from different social classes or explain the commonalities and the differences.

# Assessment of Culture through Communication

Assessment of linguistic competence concentrates on the formal aspects of the word, denotation, collocation, and the combination of words into correct sentences. Linguistic competence is "knowing that." Students are viewed as learners and the primary goal of assessment procedures is to measure the accuracy of their language output.

Assessment of communicative competence focuses on language as an instrument for a variety of outcomes. It evaluates the students' linguistic savoir-faire, what the students can do by means of verbal and nonverbal language. Communicative competence is "knowing how." Students are viewed as communicators, and fluency as well as accuracy are evaluated by the assessment procedures.

Communicative competence subsumes linguistic competence. Cultural competence subsumes communicative competence. Cultural competence extends beyond the denotation of words to their sociocultural connotations[6] and includes sociolinguistic and discourse competence. Another feature of cultural competence is sensitivity to the attitudes, beliefs, and values embedded in the target culture. Sensitivity does not mean adoption of those attitudes, beliefs, and values. It means recognition of them, the ability to interpret them within the context of the evolving system of deep meanings that give the target culture its coherence, and the ability to respond to them with understanding and a varying degree of empathy. Cultural competence also includes knowledge and interpretation of big "C" and small "c" cultural features of the target culture as outlined in previous sections of this chapter. How to assess such a hybrid competence as cultural competence remains a challenge for our profession despite the meritorious solutions proposed by the AATF Commissions. In particular, the relative importance of each feature of cultural competence in assessing the levels of cultural competence has yet to be determined. The means of assessing these features have to be refined so that they can be tested across the nation for validity and replicability. Assessment of cultural competence is extremely complex, because the student is no longer only a learner, no longer only a communicator, but an individual with a personal and cultural identity defined by his or her life up to the time of assessment.

Evaluation of sociolinguistic competence is the part of assessment that is most advanced. This is because it is the principal component of communicative competence that has been the goal set by the profession and highlighted by the ACTFL Proficiency Guidelines since the early 1980s. Students' ability to use with fluency and accuracy the language register appropriate to the type of situation, to the location and the topic of exchange, and to the sociocultural characteristics of the interlocutors or writers can now be assessed with considerable reliability. Students are assessed on their knowledge, their skills, and the strategies they use to communicate successfully in a variety of contexts and for a variety of purposes. Distinguishing features of this assessment are contextualization and the two-way process of social interaction (initiation and response) by verbal and nonverbal means or by writing.

The next areas of assessment that we suggest require research are techniques for evaluating the ability to interpret connotations and for evaluating awareness of the value system of the target culture. The significance of connotation has been shown by semiotic analysis of texts. Roland Barthes's book of short essays, *Mythologies*, introduced French readers to the concept of semiotic analysis as a means of discovering and interpreting the connotative meanings of objects and symbols in their daily lives. Connotations are the sociocultural layers of meanings that have been added to the precise meaning (denotation) of words over time. Analysis of those layers of meaning is a way of understanding the target culture and penetrating its value system. At the novice level, a comparison of the simple meanings and uses of such an everyday item in the students' own culture as "cheese" with what is evoked for a French speaker by "le fromage" alerts them to the sociocultural dimensions of meaning and the different connotations of words in different cultures. As students advance in their learning of French, they should be presented with a variety of oral and written texts for which comprehension depends on understanding the connotations certain words and artefacts have for native French speakers. Connotations depend on context. So it should be possible to determine students' different levels of competence by assessing their ability to interpret appropriately the connotations of certain words in different texts in the target culture.

Interpreting connotations leads to the discovery of the value system that gives the connotations their full sociocultural meaning. This can be demonstrated by a meaning analysis of the text on page 129 from the cover of the French weekly magazine *l'Evénement du jeudi* of 6 February 1992. This text is also an example of the type of text that could be used to assess student competence at the Superior level.

The first degree of analysis could test sociolingisitc competence. Students need to understand lower language registers: the key word *piston*, which is slang for U.S. "pull"/"clout"; *fac*, which is student slang for U.S. "college" or "university"; *télé*, which is a frequent popular abbreviation of "télévision" (which Novice students would know); *copinage*, a derivative of *copain*, which is slang for "the old-boy network" or "getting (unfair) help from friends." *Coup de pouce* ("favoritism"), while not slang, is part of a more colloquial register of expression.

The next degree of analysis could test sociocultural competence. Students need to understand the educational system ("du lycée à la fac"); the difference between civil service and private enterprise ("de l'administration à l'entreprise"); the political opposition between Paris dominated by a right-wing mayor (Jacques Chirac) and the French State under the leadership of the socialist President François Mitterrand here comically identified by his nickname, the colloquial word *Tonton* ("Uncle"), which suggests benign rule by an avuncular figure; and the allusions to contemporary scandals in easily identifiable institutions or sports. *Radioscopie* ("X-ray") announces a detailed exposé of favoritism in the workings of the Republic, which here has a derogatory connotation because of the qualifiers "du copinage et du coup de pouce." The final sentence ("But, after all,

# LA FRANCE DU PISTON

Du lycée à la fac, de l'administration à l'entreprise, de Paris-Chirac à l'Etat-Tonton, de la médecine au rugby, de l'armée à la télé . . . Radioscopie de la République de copinage et du coup de pouce. Mais, après tout, sans piston, la société serait-elle encore vivable?

without pull, would life in society still be bearable?") seeks a wink of complicity by suggesting acceptance or approval for what has previously been condemned.

The value system expressed here is one of profound ambivalence and it points to a pattern discussed by Laurence Wylie in which French children are taught to be obedient and respectful of rules but then in adolescence are encouraged to break them. This is, of course, an expression of "le système D" ("la débrouillardise"). French people are expected to respect and admire the State and to follow the innumerable rules and regulations it promulgates. Simultaneously, they are expected, according to the rules of an unwritten social code ("le système D"), to do whatever they need to do to get around the obstacles posed by excessive bureaucracy. The adult French person is expected to have the morals of a scout and the pragmatism of a Machiavelli. "Le système D" is a form of social grease necessary to make French society function. Only a fool or a foreigner (!) would be naïve enough to believe that society could function efficiently without the occasional and necessary help of the people you know who have power. This cover text suggests to the readers their own complicity in behavior they might be too quick to condemn without self-reflection. This text is a conservative text by its paradoxical implication that corruption is essential for the smooth

functioning of society. Students who know about the polemical style of
L'*Evénement du jeudi*, which perceives itself as adopting a center-left aggres-
sive attitude to those who hold power and influence in French society, will
not expect a conservative thesis in the cover story. They will assume that the
implied reader complicity is an expression of an ebulliently provocative
style designed to seize reader interest and, obviously, increase sales of the
magazine. This text could also be the impetus for a cross-cultural analysis,
because it invites dialogue and interpretation of the value systems of
French and American society. From a French perspective, it pits American
puritanism and naïveté against French worldliness and savoir-faire. From
an American point of view, it demonstrates French willingness to tolerate
corruption and the inability of an old-world society to clean its own house.
At the Superior level, the student, instead of adopting an attitude of
condescension to French practices, should engage in a process of cultural
negotiation carefully weighing the distortions that each society's perspectives represent on this issue. A cultural dialogue entails an awareness of the
more elaborate and imposing weight of the State and its social obligations
for a French person and the compelling need to get around them. Although
influence peddling is not uncommon in America, the whole notion of a
"système D" has not been articulated because the State has not been
perceived as having the same overwhelming influence.

In summary, the test for the student has been to identify the
sociolinguistic and sociocultural information in order to interpret the
message(s) of the text and to understand the text as an emanation of
another culture. In other words, the student has been asked to show not
only "what" the text means but how it means. As a result, the parameters of
a cultural dialogue have been established between the values expressed in
the text and American values—a set of negotiations between two value
systems. By engaging in this process, students place themselves in the
position of what Byram calls "cultural mediators," individuals who are
prepared to diminish cultural conflicts through understanding and thus to
contribute to the new syncretic world society now emerging as the twentieth century draws to a close.

To reach this level of cultural analysis requires a preparation through a
broad exposure to a variety of activities to develop sociolinguistic and
sociocultural competencies that may be assessed and thus reinforced. To
this purpose, Howard Nostrand has edited a paper for the AATF Professional Standards and Proficiency Commissions entitled "Testing the Sociocultural Outcome of Language-and-Culture Learning" (October 1991) that
proposes a tentative list of fifteen test types, which are reproduced below:[7]

# Types of Questions on the Sociocultural Component of Proficiency or of Teacher Competence

## A. To test sociolinguistic ability

### Type 1. Oral interaction in a situation of controlled difficulty.

At the Intermediate–High level (ILR 1+), the examinee can be asked to play the role of a traveler, making the distinction between formal and intimate second-person terms, and to:

a. obtain the information to reach a given destination via public transportation.

b. secure lodging for the night.

c. order and pay for food and drink.

d. make a purchase.

e. conduct a simple phone conversation.

f. take notes on information such as price, location, departure time.

At the Advanced level (ILR 2), the examinee can:

a. request politely a given object or favor.

b. offer or receive a gift or an invitation.

c. apologize.

d. introduce self or a fictitious person.

e. discuss a current event or policy, a field of personal interest, a leisure-time activity of one Francophone country or area.

At the Advanced Plus level (ILR 2+), the examinee, after listening to a brief newscast, can be asked to summarize it.

Note: The above examples and further indices of cultural competence at all levels will be found in H. L. Nostrand, "Basic Intercultural Education Needs Breadth and Depth," pages 153–159 of Ellen Silber, ed., *Critical Issues in Foreign Language Instruction* (N.Y.: Garland, 1991).

**Type 2. Written questions on proper behavior.**

Questions on social conventions that govern conversing, dating, invitations to meals, common formulas for social letters. Examples:

a. Comparez la distance habituelle entre interlocuteurs francophones et anglophones.

b. A quelle(s) occasion(s) les hommes français s'embrassent-ils?

c. —Mr. et Mrs. Jones ont fait la connaissance des Durand, qui les invitent à dîner chez eux un soir à 20h30. A quelle heure doivent-ils y arriver? Doivent-ils apporter quelque chose? Si oui, quoi?

d. —Quelqu'un vous fait un compliment sur votre costume. Vaut-il mieux le remercier, ou répondre sans accepter le compliment? Pourquoi? (Parce que c'est la coutume; ou, parce qu'il semble vaniteux d'accepter une louange.)

# B. To test knowledge of the culture and society

Several abilities are more important than the retention of facts, notably:

• To recognize a culture pattern when it is illustrated.

• To describe a culture pattern, and to ascribe it to the proper part of the population.

• To predict what pattern is probable in a given social or business situation.

• To "explain" a culture-related act by relating it to a consistent feature such as a major value, a habit of mind, or a prevalent assumption.

• To identify a foreigner's faux pas, or misconception of a situation.

**Type 3. A photo or drawing showing a culture pattern.**

—What does it exemplify?

—Commentez ce tableau. Indique-t-il une attitude qu'on rencontre en France?—Exemples:

a. Une maison, volets fermés, barrière devant, grille fermée.

b. Un Français qui discute, en gesticulant, avec un agent de police à côté d'une voiture mal garée. Ou bien:

c. Une voiture garée devant un panneau "Stationnement interdit."

### Type 4. A verbal description of an unlikely situation.

—Is this situation common in the culture?

—Trouvez-vous cette situation probable ou invraisemblable? Expliquez.—Exemple:

"La famille Dupont va passer l'été à la maison comme d'habitude, puisque le père n'est qu'un modeste fonctionnaire."

### Type 5. A question of fact, either in true/false form (or a correct answer listed among distractors) or one requiring a brief answer.

In either case, facts can be chosen which involve a broader understanding. The latter format can ask for a sentence on significance: geographical, historical, political, economic, inter-ethnic, etc.

a. Nommez (ou trouvez sur une carte muette) un nombre donné des pays ou aires où le français est la langue natale ou la langue officielle. Depuis quand, dans chaque cas, a-t-elle ce statut? Questions sur les capitales, les ports ou autres villes importantes.

b. Questions sur la géographie physique: fleuves, montagnes.

c. Questions d'histoire: dater un événement, identifier un personnage.

d. Questions sur des coutumes répandues. Par exemple, —Nommez une fête nationale française célébrée en l'honneur d'une date historique; d'une classe sociale; des morts.

e. Questions sur les idées-forces ou présuppositions qui se manifestent dans les comportements et les institutions. Exemples:

—Nommez (ou définissez sommairement) un nombre donné des valeurs majeures des Français, ou d'un autre pays de la Francophonie.

—Dans le paragraphe suivant, expliquez brièvement les expressions imprimées en caractères gras.

### Type 6. A "culture assimilator": An instance of improper behavior to be explained, e.g., through a multiple-choice question.

—Mr. Smith, vendeur, a pris rendez-vous avec un P.D.-G., et la secrétaire lui a rappelé que son patron était un homme très occupé. Il arrive à l'heure convenue, dit au P.D.-G. qui il est, et ne perd pas de temps à sortir de sa serviette une proposition de contrat. Sa visite est vouée à l'échec. Quelle a été son erreur?

a. Dire "Je suis M. Untel" était superflu et semblait pompeux.

b. Porter une serviette chez le P.D.-G., c'était rivaliser avec lui en importance.

c. Demander un contrat semblait mettre en question l'honnêteté du P.D.-
G.

d. Il fallait prendre le temps de causer avant de parler d'affaires.

**Type 7. Cloze procedure, with the deletion of words that customarily express a value, an attitude, an emotional reaction; or, deletion of conventional ellipses or abbreviations such as in a want ad.**

—Remplacez le tiret par l'expression consacrée (à résonnance culturelle; ou, usuelle dans le reportage sur une élection ou un événement sportif).
—Remplacez les abréviations (e.g., dans une petite annonce).

**Type 8. Knowledge of sources of information.**

—What reference works, bibliographies, or databases would you consult to answer a given question about the mentality of the people or the culture area?

**Type 9. A report on reading (either oral or to be proctored if written).**

—Mentionnez les idées que vous retenez de la lecture d'un nombre donné de livres ou d'articles sur la France ou un autre pays francophone, ou sur l'analyse culturelle.

**Type 10. A literary passage with features to be identified.**

—Dans ce passage, mentionnez un détail que vous trouvez intéressant du point de vue (a) linguistique, (b) littéraire ou stylistique, et (c) culturel. Expliquez chacun de vos choix.

# C. To test knowledge of how to observe a culture analytically

**Type 11. A photo or drawing of a situation showing social behavior in an unknown culture.**

—What custom can be inferred?
—Quelle coutume peut-on déduire de ce tableau? Exemples:

a. Person(s) at table, using knife and fork to peel a fruit.

b. A woman at a grocery, carrying a small shopping bag (un filet).

### Type 12. A statistical report lacking source and date.

—Ce reportage suffit-il comme documentation d'un essai? Expliquez.—
Exemples:

a. Selon un journal réputé, la statistique montre que la population des villes a dépassé celle de la campagne en France au milieu des années 1930.

b. Un conférencier a dit récemment que la Communauté européenne consacre 67% de son budget à l'agriculture.

c. La région la plus riche de la Communauté européenne, si l'on applique les critères usuels, est six fois plus riche que les régions les plus pauvres.

### Type 13. A brief description of a field procedure to comment on.

Example: Is it useful to keep field notes in chronological context besides organizing them? Why, or why not?

### Type 14. An audio text for observation of linguistic behavior.

a. —Dans ce texte oral, quel mot a été employé pour exprimer, par exemple, la joie?

b. —Dans ce texte oral, quelle(s) forme(s) d'intonation diffère(nt) de celles de votre langue?— Exemple: le type d'énumération, dans une phrase telle que "Cet ennuyeux parle constamment de son arthrite, de sa toux, de son foie…" où chaque avant-dernière syllabe est prononcée au niveau aigu 4 des 5 niveaux, et la finale au niveau 2, relativement grave.

## D. To test the reflective aspect of intercultural attitudes

### Type 15. A conflict situation briefly described.

a. A proposed point of view to defend or criticize.

b. What should be done, if anything, about this situation?

# Assessing Cultural Competence by a Student Profile

Because assessment of cultural and intercultural competence subsumes many other competencies, it is obvious that one test will not suffice to test a student's level of competence. Rather, we suggest that tests, given over time, of the competencies discussed in previous sections of this chapter should be used to constitute a profile of the student's cultural and intercultural competence. Attempts made so far to assess cultural competence by one overall test have probably been unduly influenced by success in assessing each language skill in that manner.

Research has been able to identify a relatively stable content for language skills, which makes it possible to assess reliably the student's competence in them. The context of cultural competence is not so readily identifiable and is fluid because it is the result of "negotiations" between the native culture and the target culture. Cultural competence is not a skill. Assessment of the four language skills can be based on performance. Cultural competence involves many choices and is a projection of the learner's personality. Assessment of it is a continuous process that requires a subtlety that parallels the learner's cognitive and affective relationship with the target culture and his or her sensitivity to intercultural perspectives. The learner's reactions to different elements and experiences in the target culture will represent greater or lesser awareness, more refined or more limited sensitivity. This is in keeping with the human personality, which does not react uniformly to all social and intellectual phenomena but rather responds with alacrity to some and indifference to others. Consequently assessment of cultural competence will be valid only when the continuous development of the components of this competence is viewed in its totality. Establishing an evolving profile of the learner's cultural competence is a means of assessing quantitatively the components of this competence and qualitatively the level that has been reached.

An analogy of the difference between assessing competence in the four language skills and assessing cultural competence could be drawn between assessing driving ability and assessing the performance of a concert pianist. To be able to drive a car successfully, it is not sufficient to know how to start the car and use the steering wheel and the brakes and to know the rules of the road. This knowledge has to be coordinated and applied in the physical performance of the driving act. The driver's skill can be assessed objectively by this performance. A student of music who wishes to become a concert pianist, in addition to learning to play the piano, must have a knowledge of musical theory and of the different styles of the piano repertoire consisting of the works of the great composers of piano music through the centuries. The student will have a varying degree of empathy with those styles. The path to making a successful career as a concert pianist takes the student through a series of competitions in which his or her performance is judged against the performance of other pianists. This performance is assessed not only on the technical accuracy with which the pianist plays but also the pianist's interpretation of the score. While the assessment of the technical accuracy can be objective, the assessment of the interpretation is subjective and will vary from one judge to the next with their appreciation of the pianist's style of interpretation. Just as the pianist's interpretation of the works of some composers will be judged more successful than that of the works of other composers, so the student's demonstration of cultural competence will vary with his or her personality, intellectual affinities, and affective responses to that component of cultural competence being assessed.

The subtlety required in the assessment of the overall quality of the student's cultural competence cannot be provided by computer testing of it. An increasing number of computer programs are available that claim to teach aspects of sociolinguistic skill and cultural knowledge.[8] For example, the screen shows a list of possible responses to an utterance in French and the student selects the response that is sociolinguistically appropriate in the situation. A hypercard program contains many items of big "C" and small "c" culture that are cross-referenced and allow students to develop their knowledge in these areas. The advantage of such computer programs is that they allow for individualized learning. Not all students answer the same items incorrectly. When the student gives an incorrect response, the feedback program makes available an immediate explanation of the mistake and additional items to reinforce the correct answer. This is why computers can be very helpful in establishing a profile of the students' competence based on the incorrect responses and the final performance on specified activities and tests.

However alluring the prospect may appear, a computer with banks of objective test items designed to assess the components of cultural competence remains inadequate to the task precisely because these items lack the necessary subtlety to assess the qualitative dimension of cultural competence. As we have pointed out, the subjective nature of the interpretation of attitudes, beliefs, and values in the target culture, which is linked to the personality of the learner, is a significant factor in the assessment of overall cultural competence. A continuing qualitative profile of the learner's cultural competence is necessary to complement the quantitative computer profile in order to obtain an equitable assessment. The distortions possible in assessing the student's overall cultural competence based on a *single* quantitative test and a *single* qualitative evaluation are evident.

The new diachronic and multifarious cultural testing proposed here seeks to avoid such distortions and inequitable "misassessments." Its objective is to promote forms of assessment of cultural competence that reflect more accurately and with greater sensitivity the complexities of the individual personality in its negotiations with new value systems and conceptual orderings. It will be difficult, if not impossible, to ever reach an absolutely "objective" level of cultural testing. However, a quantitative and qualitative profile based on multiple assessments offers the encouraging possibility of reaching a fairly reliable evaluation of a student's cultural competence.

# Notes

1. Claire J. Kramsch, "New Directions in the Teaching of Language and Culture," National Foreign Language Center Occasional Paper (Washington: NFLC, 1989), p. 1.

2. See Appendix I.

3. See Appendix II.

4. Prochievement testing is a combination of proficiency and achievement testing that aims at a more holistic way of assessing specific tasks.

5. Rebecca Valette, *Modern Language Testing* (New York: Harcourt, Brace, 1967).

6. Robert Gallison demonstrates how a culture expresses itself through "mots à charge culturelle partagée." See Robert Gallison, *De la langue à la culture par les mots* (Paris: Clé International, 1991).

7. Howard L. Nostrand, ed., "Testing the Sociocultural Outcome of Language-and-Culture Learning," third draft, unpublished report to the AATF Professional Standards Commission and Proficiency Commission, October 1991.

8. For a stimulating exposition of the cultural uses of the computer in foreign language pedagogy, including the interactive videodisc, see Judith G. Frommer, "Language Learning, Cultural Understanding, and the Computer," *Papers from the Georgetown University Round Table on Languages and Linguistics* (Washington: Georgetown University, 1989), pp. 332–43.

# CHAPTER IX

# THE
# STUDY ABROAD PROGRAM

Studying abroad in France is potentially the most effective way to achieve a deep understanding of French culture, but such an understanding is by no means automatic. Study abroad completely changes the situation of French as a foreign language and culture taught in the classroom. When students are in a francophone country, the majority of cultural learning will occur outside the classroom and the challenge for the instructor is to integrate this informal and unsystematic learning into a formal context so that they do not end their stay with a series of fragmentary impressions but, rather, have begun to organize their impressions into a more coherent understanding of France. All this requires conscious forethought and planning and a keen awareness of the objectives of the study program.

## Predeparture Concerns

### Who Should Study Abroad?

Presuming that the objective is cultural and linguistic "fluency," the degree of student preparation becomes very important. If the program is relatively brief—a ten-week quarter, for example—it is essential to select students with a reasonable background of study in French. One year of college study or its high school equivalent (normally two years) really should be a minimum in this instance. An absolute or near total beginner will simply not have the time to acquire the linguistic skills needed in such a period; without a strong linguistic foundation, the learner's cultural skills cannot be sufficiently developed.

Longer programs, especially those of at least a year in length, are sufficient to provide the average student with adequate time to acquire cultural and linguistic fluency.[1] But it must be pointed out that length is no absolute guarantee: a strict, intensive program of French language learning must be constantly enforced, student exchanges with native speakers must be encouraged, and national "ghettoization" discouraged. Behaviors and national assumptions will often need to be explained and discussed during the stay.

# Who Studies Abroad?

Before taking any group to France or a francophone country, the instructor should be aware of the students' interests, academic and social, and, most especially, their majors and career plans. While to some degree every program is created before students join it, it is still essential to look at the participants and to attempt to slant the program to their needs. A group composed largely of business students has very different goals than one composed of those preparing to teach French. While both are interested in acquiring the language and culture of France, the specific uses of the language and culture that they foresee in their own lives will be radically different and will color their concerns. Programs need to exhibit flexibility in this regard.

# How Long to Stay?

Unfortunately, this question cannot be answered in the ideal world but in the very practical one of financial concerns that bear down on both students and institutions. A full year is ideal for linguistic and cultural apprenticeship. As it may take up to two months for students going to France for the first time to adapt to the rhythm and ways of French life, short stays, while they can be very productive for those whose mastery of the language is well advanced, are not the ideal format. If this is the only alternative, well-prepared students can make enormous progress: most will reach a true functional competence and the very gifted will reach a much higher level. Generally speaking, however, six months is needed for those who arrive in France at the intermediate level to reach cultural and linguistic "fluency."

# How to Prepare the Students for French Life?

It is very naive to believe that one can fully prepare students for changing cultures, especially if they have never left the United States before, but much can be done to alert them to situations that may be frustrating. Very particular attention must be directed to informing them about their lodgings and French behavioral expectations, especially if they are staying with a family. They need to be informed of the kind of food they will be offered, and to know the requirements and rhythm of their host educational institution. It is very important to try to avoid—if possible—taking students who have strong negative attitudes toward the French, for they will probably only reinforce their prejudices during their stay. The most important service an instructor can do is to cultivate legitimate areas of enthusiasm toward France. This is best accomplished by knowing the students' study goals and by pointing out what one suspects may advance those goals as well as discussing the students' general interests and how they can best be satisfied abroad.

Information on travel arrangements and visa limitations on their stay is essential. Experience confirms that one cannot overlook the simplest matters such as telling the students that they will need French currency immediately upon arrival, that they will need to buy a plastic "télécarte" to use the public phone system (even how to put it in the machine is a source of puzzlement to some). If the group is going to Paris, basic advice about the métro is essential: how to acquire free maps, how to read them, the need to keep one's tickets at all times, the various ticket options, and the complexities of using the bus as opposed to the métro. Wherever the group is going in France, a general overview of the local transportation system needs to be supplied in advance as well as a map of the country so that the students can locate themselves in relation to its geography. They emphatically require precise financial information; in many cases, however, you will not be able to prevent naively optimistic expense projections. Some of the students will inevitably have serious money problems during their stay. A largely prepaid tour is a way of diminishing but not entirely eliminating this problem.

# What Is "Culture Shock"?

Prior to departure, the instructor should talk to the students about "culture shock," explaining that this is a general term to indicate a sense of uneasiness and occasionally even panic that many people experience during the initial phase of their stay in a foreign country. The students should be made aware that this is a perfectly natural reaction when one is faced with different social customs and when one is unaware of how to accomplish daily activities in a new environment. They should be told that culture shock will diminish and finally disappear as they learn more about how the surrounding society functions and what that society expects of them as social beings.

To avoid or limit culture shock, they will also need to adapt to the absence of some of their home creature comforts such as air conditioning, private bathrooms, elevators, etc., for these privations are often particularly disconcerting to Americans. One should encourage the students to focus on the things they are encountering that are unavailable in the United States rather than losing themselves in complaints about amenities.

One may also reassure students by explaining that the term *culture shock* is in itself an expression of the hyperbole so typical of American culture, that a French person might simply see it as a form of *malaise*, thereby avoiding the psychological blockage inherent in the more hysterical American description of this common human experience. It should also be pointed out to them that, unlike "very foreign, exotic" Asian cultures, France is a modern society rather similar to the United States, that they will not be helpless there, and that there are few things that they were already doing at home that they cannot do immediately in France. Ironically, some of their frustrations will come from the fact that the American and French societies are on the surface quite similar. At the beginning, they will not perceive the subtle differences that will get them into difficulty and perhaps lead them to misjudge the French.

# Initial Adaptation to Life in France

Once in France, both in class and in counseling, much reinforcement and many explanations will be necessary.

# Accommodations

Students participating in homestays will need different degrees of advice, because the families or individuals who lodge them will be very diverse. Early on, students will have to understand different notions of personal space, especially in a Parisian setting. For one thing, they will have to understand that the French definition of space extends to the home, that many families will feel that guest privileges end outside the student's room and that guests do not have run of the house, whether that means watching television in the living room, raiding the refrigerator, or taking control of the telephone. Students will inevitably compare families and discover that houseparents range from the lenient to the nearly totalitarian. While no student should be subjected to a truly abusive houseparent, it is impossible to lodge students exclusively with "ideal" families—there are simply not enough of such people available in the Paris area. If students are made aware of multiple family models ranging from the near reactionary to the "baba-cool (hip)," from the authoritarian to the permissive, this may not console those who find themselves with less than satisfactory families, but it will at least allow them to place their experience within an overview of the culture rather than losing themselves in its specificity. In the Paris area, students will encounter with increasing frequency single-parent (usually female) families that take in boarders—largely because of economic pressures. Couples are frequently more affluent and more often accept paying guests out of a certain curiosity and enjoyment of a foreign presence.

# Food

Differences in food, mealtimes, and eating habits will make some students unhappy. During instruction or counseling, point out why the French eat less junk food and explain that their more structured eating habits impose a need for a variety of foods to accommodate the progression of the meal. It will also be necessary to make them understand that this is emphatically not a vegetarian culture nor one that is sentimental about the slaughter of animals, included young ones like calves, and "cute" ones like rabbits. You will not be successful in overcoming all student culinary aversions, nor is this necessarily appropriate, as the students' convictions are normally no less rational than those of their hosts. The essential goal is tolerance and a certain understanding of why the French eat as they do and of the social function of eating.

# Getting Around

Navigating within their cities will also be a cultural learning experience for students. Even though the métro has finally abandoned its first-class cars (the last public urban transport system in the world to do so), it still offers rich examples of a high-context culture. (See chapter 8.) Have your students check the decals on the windows to learn about seating priorities; have them try to discover the myriad of different systems of ticket purchasing, and then have them evaluate the graduated fares of the buses. What may seem like perversity at first may later be perceived as a keen sense of precision and a desire for justice. The numerous and, by American standards, verbose regulations posted throughout the system will also illustrate this love of precision through complexity, the desire to explain thoroughly any position from the banal to the complex.

# Homesickness

Student homesickness, usually not severe, is a concern nevertheless. At times, it will be expressed by statements like "I'd just like to go home for the weekend." In other cases, it can result in premature departures. It can be helpful to explain to the students that this is natural, that almost everyone experiences such feelings to a greater or lesser degree. One "cure" is intense immersion in one's own projects and actually seeking enjoyment.

# The French Classroom

Most host institutions that deal with large numbers of foreigners show a certain flexibility and adaptation to their student populations. But one needs to remember that the dominant culture is not simply pushed aside; its more difficult aspects for foreigners are merely attenuated in these circumstances.

Initially, many students misread messages from their French instructors. American students are often not used to being told bluntly that their work is unsatisfactory, that they are lazy and/or irresponsible. They will immediately perceive such behavior as rude. Their French instructors, on the other hand, will dismiss them as lacking in seriousness, as "typically" incompetent Americans. While presumably both have the same objective (achieving fluency or mastering the particular subject), the communications between the two may well lead to the opposite. French instructors will often use sarcasm as a means of playful rebuke. Most American students do not find this amusing and are frequently highly offended by such observations and unimpressed by their instructor's wit. Students will be equally perplexed by the French grading system (based chiefly on 20 points), and will be appalled when they receive 12/20, equating this with 60 percent or a D. Students may also regard the absence of institutionalized student evaluations of instructors as an injustice. Beyond the specific cultural divergences, students will usually be involved in a different course format: frequently, very intensive language courses covering easily three hours per day plus other courses at a more "American" pace. Language courses, because of their time demands and necessity for survival, will usually be perceived as central, while "ancillary" courses on culture, politics, literature, etc., will often be regarded as peripheral. Tensions will arise from these perceptions.

The director of the study-abroad program can help students adapt to these classroom practices by giving a special briefing on them. As a starting point students can be asked to read the section on village education in Laurence Wylie's classic text, A *Village in the Vaucluse*.[2] Although this book describes only a primary school situation, the strictness and concern of the teacher come across very clearly. Her severity is not due to animosity, but to a sense of professionalism and a genuine commitment to the students' welfare. Many students soon realize that their own teachers have inherited that tradition, and they then take a different view of criticism. They also learn that French students expect very direct reprimands from their instructors and realize that they are not being singled out for personal or national abuse.

The program director can then discuss the French educational system more globally, explaining the early channeling and the various gatekeeper examinations that exert considerable pressure on French students. The American group can be asked to compare the general curricula, the amount of abstract knowledge and the reasoning ability required, their own linguistic abilities, etc., with those of their French counterparts in order to make an informed judgment of the merits and demerits of each system. They will also have to understand that the French system does not seek to appeal to the lowest common denominator but to the best in each class and that they must aim in that direction. They will need to learn that marking reflects this exaltation of real distinction and does not serve as a form of encouragement to weaker students, that the French view such behavior as intellectually and

morally dishonest. It is always important and reassuring to inform them—
if such is the case—that the accompanying instructor or the university will
translate their French grades into their American equivalents and that this
does not mean the literal grade they have received! They should also be told
that, while their French instructors undergo no institutionalized student
evaluations, they are subject to evaluation by their superiors–not their
peers—in most language-teaching institutions. Students need to understand that this practice has much to do with French notions of who is
competent to judge, that American evaluation practices are also very far
from perfect—indeed, from the French viewpoint, little better than a
popularity contest.

In the end, these comparisons can lead to valuable discussion on the
goals of education, with students evaluating the achievements of both
educational systems. This evaluation should address American educational hierarchies such as the Ivy League schools and the pride the French
take in what they perceive as their democratic public-education system
where pupil success is based on intellectual merit. Ultimately, they need to
understand the different educational practices as emanating from general
cultural practices rather than as a reflection of superiority of one over the
other. After all, both systems have produced very impressive results.

# Beyond the Classroom

Perhaps one of the greatest problems students will face is socialization
beyond the classroom. This is a feature of the culture and should be part of
your culture course. Making friends in France, especially in metropolitan
Paris, is not an easy task. Students may quickly find themselves isolated and
required to fall back on each other. To some extent, this is natural and
inevitable and should be met with tolerance, especially among those
whose linguistic abilities are very limited.

How can the program director cope with this? When you are placing
students in families or in a dormitory, try to avoid an anglophone environment. Thus, instead of pairing students as roommates for their stay in
France, you might wish to ask your host institution to give them foreign but
nonanglophone roommates. Immediately, French will become per force a
means of communication and, if they befriend their roommates, students
will already have broadened their linguistic and international horizons.

Another strategy, especially as students' language skills improve, is
directing them toward their own interests. A student who likes cycling or

walking may wish to join a French cycling or hiking club. Others may find sporting clubs, ecological groups, theater groups, etc. Some may find French students wishing to pair up with American students for linguistic and cultural exchanges. The essential is to find some connection that will permit socialization. Once the students find themselves in one circle or another, then the main problem will be solved, as they will be in mini-societies.

In a more formal sense, the director should orient the students to utilizing the cultural possibilities offered to them in their locale. Although Paris is literally overwhelming in its cultural options, it does not hurt to review the principal museums, theaters, and concert halls, and to point out specific cinemas, restaurants, and other focal points of high and popular culture. In provinces where local cultural options may be severely limited, a regional orientation helps: what kind of festivals are scheduled during the students' sojourn, what sporting events will occur, etc.? It is important for students to know what the region is like topographically and climatically and for the program director to encourage them to use French guidebooks and the *Syndicat d'initiative*, which gives local tourist information, to plan their own visits.

As students become more comfortable linguistically, it will be time to point out to them formally or informally how the language continuously reflects the culture. Again food can be a good example. The vocabulary for the different parts of a French formal meal (hors d'œuvre, entrée, plat principal, salade, fromage, dessert) is an opportunity to point out to students how insistent the French are about structuring their meals. They can also be made aware of the esthetic transformation worked by language even in areas of strong North American influence. Thus, to continue with food, when discussing changes in French breakfast habits, like eating cornflakes, draw attention to the French translation ("des grains de maïs éclaté dorés au four"). It is very clear that this translation sensualizes an utterly ordinary breakfast food, that it invests it with a special beauty. Ask them to look at some French menu items, to consider how things are normally described on American menus, and to determine what causes the problems in translation of a French menu into English. It should become rapidly evident that an enormous amount of fantasy is operative in a French menu; that much of the difficulty in translation comes from the descriptive garnish that particularizes even the most banal of dishes. They are thus moving into a new awareness of esthetic and sensual perception that is realized concretely on the level of language—practices very different from their own culture.

Students should also be encouraged to read French magazines and newspapers. They can be asked to look at advertisements and compare them with advertisements on similar themes in the United States. Such comparisons will reveal, for example, that the body and bodily functions are treated somewhat more freely than in their own culture. Greater exposure is clearly tolerated in advertising, whether this be in women revealing their breasts or barebottomed babies. This will be the start to understanding why the French view Americans—even very unprudish ones—as representatives of a puritan culture. Students will also realize that the French have a greater sense of ease with their own bodies and considerably less reserve than Americans. This can be related to a different—and again less puritanical—view of nature. Topics like mineral water are the entry point into French mythologies of purification and will enable students to investigate French society's special beliefs in natural remedies, and its own antiscientific spirit in attributing health benefits to water that can be far more "dangerous" than ordinary tap water (because of mineral concentrations and deterioration of plastic containers).

Students will also begin to realize that the expression of feelings is often more "elaborate," more "cloying," more "dramatic," and less "matter of fact" than in their own culture. They will observe that if they translated certain exchanges of affection into English, these exchanges might well seem ridiculous. As this kind of awareness grows, they will understand that using a language is far from being a matter of mere translation, even very accurate free translation.

As the students' stay progresses, they should be developing a sense of linguistic registers and they should start to understand who speaks well and who doesn't and why. The beginnings of notions of class, political intentions, and taste as an expression of the individual's social status and political affiliation should begin to become more evident. Linguistically, the students should become aware of language's role as a social marker, how it poses barriers between distinct social groups.

# The Culture Course Abroad

All the above can be tackled progressively in a classroom situation or through chats, informal talks, and counseling. This in itself represents a major choice. Should the program include a formal culture course or not? Many factors will influence this decision—most notably, the way in which the program is conceived and the skills, interest, and expertise of the teaching staff. If a culture course becomes part of the program, another choice imposes itself: whether to offer it in French or English. When programs include beginning language learners, it is usually not possible to hold the course in French. Although this may seem like a betrayal of language learning, remember that outside the classroom students are immersed in the foreign language and culture. Although beginning students may be barely capable of expressing themselves in the target language, they are nevertheless experiencing a whole array of reactions to their surroundings. Many need immediate assistance in interpreting them. A course in English may initially help them to articulate their frustrations, share their perceptions, and begin the process of interpreting their new environment in a positive context of intellectual curiosity rather than solitary frustration. Even sharing gripes can be a form of catharsis. Some program directors have observed that students taking a culture course in English in such a setting often seem to move toward French expression as the stay wears on; even those with the weakest language skills start resorting to the language because it is the medium in which most of their experiences occur.

When a formal culture course is given, the syllabus should help students observe, analyze, and interpret what they are experiencing in France. Topics, some of which have already been alluded to, would include codes of politeness in personal and institutional contexts, greetings and leave-taking behaviors and gestures like the handshake; the different models of the French family, the importance of intergenerational ties and family life, the notion of the home and its inviolability by strangers; the rituals of eating, the significance of imbibing the totem drink (red wine), and the symbolic values of certain foods (steak and French fries); the educational system from the primary school to the university; a social class or milieu and how this structure differs from American society; the basic political structure of France; aspects of the French economy such as how much the average French man and woman make, how income is concealed for tax reasons and privileges accumulated to enhance economic status,[3] and the national economy in the EC; and the problems and tensions within French society. Students also need a background in the history, topography, and climate of the country so that they do not homogenize France's own diversity.

# Activities

The following activities can be helpful in encouraging students to interact with the new culture.

# Contact with Cultural Objects (the sketchbook or photo album)

One way of engaging students to investigate the special nature of their new environment is to get them to identify objects that, while often part of their own culture, may show distinct modifications in France. One instructor assigned her students to sketch doors in France. This led to considerable research on style that brought an awareness of historical periods and taste and surprising contact with French people who, intrigued by the project, volunteered considerable information. Similar projects can be undertaken by asking the students to compile a sketchbook of housing façades and then requiring that they identify them historically and architecturally. If the students are afraid to draw, they can be asked to photograph examples of doors and façades. Another topic of investigation would be to study shop windows and to make an illustrated collection of the kinds of shops found in the area. This is a positive way to involve students in the discovery of the "particularism" of French life and to increase their vocabulary in identifying shop items and naming shop functions. Such activities can be conducted at any level of linguistic competence and hold out the possibilities of unexpected, very positive encounters with French people.

# A Media Scrapbook

Students compile a collection of articles on recurring themes in French newspapers and magazines. With help from an instructor, depending on their language level, they determine central, recurring themes and the attitudes of the various print media to them. Essentially, they move toward an understanding of political conviction in relation to print. This effort is supplemented, when possible, by intermediate and advanced students reporting on the daily news broadcasts with a list of recurring themes and treatments. Students can be assigned to different television channels and radio stations. One goal of this project would be to create a limited synchronic slice of life in France that would illustrate what items have been presented regularly to the French public during that period. Comparisons with the American media will be inevitable. Important to this project is the fact that the students will also have realia to take home with them.

# An Opinion Poll

Students decide along with the instructor what some of the collective values, general notions, and concerns are in France. After establishing a list, they work out a series of questions related to each value or concern. The instructor can then assign students to function as survey pairs charged with interviewing one or two informants, who can be their houseparents, other instructors, their friends, total strangers, etc. If students of different language abilities are in the class, strong students can be paired with weaker ones to encourage cooperative learning and ensure that the interview is conducted intelligibly and that essential information is gathered. The students can complete the assignment in different manners, according to the time available and their linguistic level. The interviews can be shared and, either individually or collectively, a general report should be prepared. Another option is to make this into a twofold project: each team/individual writes on its own subjects, and each team/individual writes on the group results. Each group may write a separate paper integrating the answers of its respondents into the context of what has been studied.

The overall objective of this project is to conduct a nonscientific but entirely experiential poll that starts the students attempting to interpret and integrate their experience.

# An Impressionistic Overview

Treat your students as impressionists. Ask them to assemble a collage, either visual or verbal or both, that illustrates what France means to them. Clearly, this is a far more poetic, nonrigorous approach to studying French culture, but it can elicit very meaningful discussion because it appeals to deep emotional reactions, many of which will be shared. It can serve as a very lively springboard for the assessment of one's stay.

# The Notebook

You may wish to have your students compile a notebook as described in chapter 5. This time, however, your students will observe at random people's behavior in the surrounding society rather than concentrate on assigned written or video materials. Depending on their level of language competence, the students may keep the notebook in English or French. They will note behavior on one page and attempt to analyze it on the next. You should review their observations in class regularly and encourage collective interpretation of the observed behavior. This kind of activity encourages students to see themselves as interpreters and mediators rather than judges and underscores the value of asking questions rather than leaping to conclusions.

# Program Outcomes

Since study-abroad programs include many diverse student populations, the following are suggested as outcomes for each level of participants in programs of varying lengths.[4]

## Elementary Students

A beginner who stays for a relatively short term can be expected to achieve only limited linguistic/cultural competence. Such a student, besides possessing only a rudimentary, functional competence in French for menu orders, simple banking transactions, minor information requests from authorities, etc., should above all else, take away an appreciation for the difficulties of monolingual people trying to get by in an alien society. One hopes that these students will thus gain a far greater degree of sympathy and understanding for nonanglophone immigrants in U.S. society, that they will make the logical connection between their own difficulties and those experienced by such individuals. In that sense, the key outcome is greater tolerance among these students toward people from other nations.

## Intermediate Students

Culturally, we can hope for the ability to communicate politely basic ideas in a relatively easy manner, a general awareness of the day-to-day organization of life, of the institutions that surround them, and the social expectations of their milieu. They should be able to distinguish between formal and informal registers of conversation and have an understanding of their limitations, of what remains to be learned.

# Advanced Students

These students should have a subtle perception of different language registers and their sociocultural importance and should be able to discuss most subjects with an appreciation of cultural allusions. They should know about the country as a whole, not only their place of residence, and know about France in relation to other francophone countries. They should be generally conscious of the political and social organization of French society and its major political and economic preoccupations. These students should also have some knowledge of the history and values of the country, as expressed in daily transactions and abstract discussion.

# All Levels

At the end of their study-abroad program, students at all levels should feel a sense of achievement. This means the confidence that they can function independently in a foreign country and in a foreign language. To help them achieve this goal, the successful program director will provide them with useful information on *how to do things* rather than doing things for them and will always encourage student initiative. Students who adopt a proactive rather than a reactive approach in the new culture invariably achieve greater benefits from their stay.

A successful cultural program should aim at creating students who are "cultural hybrids," perhaps a more appropriate description than "bicultural." Essentially, it should not be a program goal to turn the students into French people. Learning about another culture should not entail denial of one's own. The degree of biculturalism achieved by any individual is debatable: human beings are not VCRs that can be switched from PAL or SECAM at will. Rather, the original culture is influenced by second culture acquisition so that even the first culture is modified by the loss of its "purity," which depended on ignorance and isolation. The cultural hybrid is thus one who has an experiential awareness of other systems, other modes of behavior, and other solutions to various problems. This individual no longer believes in the primacy and universality of his or her own culture. The cultural hybrid is a concept that represents a movement toward a world citizenry, for it fosters the kind of individual who realizes the world is better because it is not homogeneous.

# Notes

1. The School of Language Studies of the Foreign Service Institute summarizes its experience with students taught in its own classrooms for French as follows: 24 weeks of instruction (720 hours) to reach a minimum of 2 (limited working proficiency) on the Interagency Language Roundtable or a maximum of 3 (professional proficiency) on that scale. See Wilga M. Rivers, *Teaching Languages in College* (Lincolnwood, IL: National Textbook, 1992), appendixes A and B, pp. 393, 395.

   Here we are talking about six months of language study (outside the culture) carried on very intensely by students of relatively high motivation. We therefore suggest that one year is a very safe, conservative figure for advanced language acquisition in French after a year abroad in a francophone country.

2. Laurence Wylie, *Village in the Vaucluse*, 3rd ed. (Cambridge, MA: Harvard Univ. Press, 1981), pp. 55–97.

3. See François de Closets, *Toujours plus* (Paris: Grasset, 1982).

4. Phillis J. Dragonas, *International Homestay Exchange Programs* (Washington, D.C.: CAL/ERIC) 1983. This very useful book explains how to organize exchange visits for high school students in foreign countries.

# CHAPTER X

# FRANCE
# TODAY

The following headings are offered to give some notion of important features of French life in the 1990s and thus to offer a very concise overview that may prove useful in targeting salient features of French culture for development in class. It is important to bear in mind that France, like all countries, is constantly changing and that this overview must necessarily change with the passage of time.

**Demography.** France's metropolitan population currently numbers some 58,000,000 persons. The greatest population concentration is the Paris region, with 2,177,000 inhabitants in Paris proper and 9,878,000 inhabitants in the surrounding area. The population of Paris is actually decreasing, as the French seek better housing and more employment opportunity outside the confines of the capital. Although Paris still dominates economic and political life in France, the decentralization policy of the Socialist government in the 1980s has given considerably more autonomy to the twenty-two regions of France (including Corsica). The large regional cities of Lyon (1,173,000 inhabitants) and Toulouse (354,000 inhabitants in the city proper and about 500,000 when the suburbs are included) are becoming important centers in the broader European Community.

Tensions continue to increase between the French and the resident immigrant populations, most notably the North African population and, increasingly, sub-Saharan Africans. "Les beurs," children born in France of North African parents, often find themselves doubly marginalized as they are outsiders in France and in the country of their parents' origin.

Class structure still persists in France and is often evident in housing patterns; class distinctions, however, are diminishing, and many now prefer the word "milieu" to "classe" in order to indicate differences in social position. Nonetheless the *nouvelle bourgeoisie* forms a powerful grouping with the *cadres dynamiques*, whose success is linked with the flourishing postindustrial French economy. The weekly *Figaro-Magazine* and *Madame Figaro* are a seductive showcase of their tastes and fashions.

France continues to be a land of varied life-styles for different generations and in different regions. The young, who constitute a lsrge percentage
of the population, set trends. At this point, the *soixante-huitards*, students
who participated in the 1968 "revolt," have now reached middle age and
form part of the cultural and power élite. The daily newspaper *Libération*
reflects their attitudes and opinions. The conservative newspaper *Le Figaro*
represents the opinions of the dominant power élite.

**Politics.**   Commentators observe the pivotal attraction of the center (left
and right) and the marginalization of the communists, whose confronta-
tional rhetoric is frequently dismissed as no longer appropriate to current
labor/management relations. The popularity of the radical right has grown
significantly, although not sufficiently to displace the centrist forces. The
March 1993 elections raise many questions but still seem to suggest, even
with the triumph of the right and the collapse of the Socialists, a certain
preference for the center when one considers that both the extreme right,
as represented by Le Pen's *Front National*, and *les Verts*, representing the
ecological left, were unable to retain or gain seats in the *Assemblée Nationale*.

**Intellectuals.**   Intellectuals continue to play a central role in articulating
the problems and challenges to French society in a way not comparable to
anything in the United States. An intellectual (Pierre Bourdieu) was chosen
to direct a project to reform education because of his writings on the
perpetuation of élites; his mission was to put an end to this. French
intellectuals, e.g., Bernard-Henri Lévy, have learned to exploit television as
a medium of communication. Patterns of intellectual discussion such as
those seen on the television programs *Apostrophes* and now *Caractères* and
*Bouillon de Culture* are imitated by many French people.

**New Place in the World.**   Despite some residual resentment, the French
have decided that they are no longer capable of rivaling the English-
speaking world for linguistic preeminence. With an abandonment of this
attempt, a new relaxation and more realistic assessment of France's place
in the world, firmly within the new Europe, have tempered the old linguistic
chauvinism. The general public has reached a clear understanding that
France is not big or powerful enough to change the course of world events
by acting as an isolated nation-state, although there is considerable
nostalgia for the past *grandeur de la France* and national independence.

**Le Rayonnement Culturel.**   Although French ambitions have become less
grandiose, the French government still sees it as its duty to promote the
French language and culture throughout the world. The government

remains the keeper of national values, and culture is understood as very much the domain of state interest. This, of course, represents a fundamentally different notion of culture from that of the United States. Under the socialist government, there was an appointee in the French Ministry of Culture to survey and encourage the development of rock culture, comically known as "M. Rock." It can also be said that France's dissemination of its culture actually makes culture one of its chief exports. This worldwide awareness of French culture does add to France's international importance.

**Business.**  France has rejected both *laissez-faire* and *étatiste* economic traditions and this feeling was stated in the slogan *"ni nationalisations ni privatisations,"* used by François Mitterrand in the successful campaign for his reelection as President for a second term. Nevertheless, the French government has a much stronger interventionist tradition than that of the United States. Five-year economic plans are considered normal procedure, and even businesspeople expect the state to act on behalf of economic development; the notion of a completely indifferent, libertarian state is not part of the French understanding of the state's economic responsibilities. In short, the American model does not obtain for France, for the French people tend to view the state as an efficacious protector of national economic life and national interest whose intervention is not only desirable but indispensable.

Despite the fact that the economic integration foreseen for January 1, 1993, has not been completely achieved, the economies of the EC countries will in all likelihood be fully integrated in the not too distant future.

**The Monumental Image.**  In the long tradition of the French kings, the majority of the presidents of the Fifth Republic have considered it part of their role to bequeath to France public monuments of major architectural significance. Consequently, Paris as capital has seen the *Centre Pompidou* (President Pompidou), the *Musée d'Orsay* (President Giscard d'Estaing), the *Pyramide du Louvre* (President Mitterrand), the *Arche de la Défense* (Mitterrand), the *Opéra de la Bastille* (Mitterrand), and soon the TGB or *Très Grande Bibliothèque* (Mitterrand), which will house much of the collections now at the *Bibliothèque Nationale*. Whatever one's reservations may be about the underlying philosophical and financial implications of such projects, this construction, frequently of extraordinary architectural and sociological importance, contributes to the world repute of the French capital, making it the center of bold experiments in architectural urbanism.

**Decentralization.**  While Paris continues to dominate France politically, intellectually, and financially, this domination is clearly diminishing. The regions have been empowered by the *conseils régionaux*, which now make critical decisions about regional development. At the same time, the Parisian economy has been weaker than that of other areas of France and there has been a net job loss in the region, while areas like the southeast have experienced economic and demographic booms. Paris is also losing population as people move outside the city limits or to completely different parts of the country. The extensive development of rapid rail transport in the Parisian region and through the country has also contributed to suburban and even exurban development.

**Agriculture.**    Despite the ever frustrating problem of excessive food surpluses, France remains a breadbasket. Its agriculture is rich and diverse and ranges from very small, privately owned farms, which are decreasing in number, to vast agribusiness holdings. Psychologically, many French people cling to a rural past. While most are urbanites, they still imagine their own "province," which occupies the place of a mythical home.

**Education.**    The French remain very concerned with their system of public education, which is itself a system very much regulated by competitive examinations whose most significant first barrier is the *bac*, an exam that determines who may or may not enter the university system. Much discussion turns around how to provide a more useful education to undergraduates, and, to a great extent, one's place in society still depends heavily on one's diploma. The graduates of the *grandes écoles* still enjoy a social prestige far higher than an Ivy League graduate in the United States. One might even suggest that diplomas from l'École Nationale d'Administration and l'École Polytechnique have replaced *titres de noblesse*. It seems unlikely that the French education will really change, since, despite all the complaining, parents, students, and educators believe they have a mutual interest in preserving the system as it is.

**France in the World.**    France under Mitterrand has been a nation that believes it has a special responsibility to refugees and to Third World nations. The French have been vocal about the plight of the Boat People, the Kurds, and the Shiites and have preferred negotiated settlements of world disputes—condemning U.S. armed intervention both in Grenada and Panama, although many French people felt compelled to approve the military action against Iraq. France often finds itself in contradictory situations, e.g., the pacific discourse of a socialist president and the dilemma created by being the world's third-largest arms dealer after the former Soviet Union and the United States.

France, of course, maintains a special relationship with her former colonies—most significantly those of the African continent, where it is actively engaged in development projects.

**Energy Policy.** France has chosen to rely heavily on nuclear power. In fact, France is currently the world's number one user of commercial nuclear energy. Although this nuclear policy has been challenged by ecologists, it has never been seriously brought into question. The reasons for this high tolerance to a policy that may engender a disastrous nuclear accident are several: France's need for energy independence from the oil-producing countries of the Middle East, the very grave danger of acid rain from coal and oil usage, and, perhaps, an excessive confidence in French science and government prudence. It is unclear whether this policy will be successfully challenged by France's growing ecology movement or whether the public at large will continue to feel that there is no viable alternative to nuclear energy.

**Mobility/Stability/Family.** Although the French travel widely throughout the world, they tend not to move far from home within France. Indeed, family life is still very important, and the need to attend the Sunday lunch that reunites the extended family is very compelling. Even marriages tend to be endogamous. France's size, relatively small when compared to the United States, ensures that family ties are less easily threatened, as returning home from within the country—even from one extreme to the other—is a shorter and far less costly operation than coast-to-coast travel in the United States.

Despite much concern in the seventies, French sociologists in the eighties concluded that French family ties were very strong and that the family was increasingly united by affection and leisure rather than by work as in the traditional families of the past. The notions of charm, conviviality, family tradition, and *joie de vivre* remain important to the French today.

# Appendix I

# ACTFL Provisional Proficiency Guidelines: French Culture

These are the original guidelines developed by ACTFL in 1982 to measure cultural proficiency. Culture was originally treated as a "fifth skill" that followed a progression similar to that of listening, speaking, reading, and writing. Although the guidelines did not become permanent, they represented a first, widespread professional effort to evaluate cultural acquisition.

## Provisional French Descriptions—Culture

Novice
Limited interaction. Behaves with considerateness. Is resourceful in nonverbal communication, but does not reliably interpret gestures or culturally specific nonverbal behavior, such as physical contacts with greetings, proximity of speaker. Is limited in language (see listening/speaking guidelines), but may be able to manage short phrases of courtesy (*merci, enchanté, s'il vous plaît, pas de quoi, pardon, excusez-moi*) and basic titles of respect (*Monsieur, Madame, Mademoiselle*). Lacks generally the knowledge of culture patterns requisite for survival situations.

Intermediate
Survival competence. Can deal with familiar survival situations and interact with a culture bearer unaccustomed to foreigners. Is able to use conventional phrases when being introduced, such as *enchanté*, as well as proper greetings at different times of day, such as *Bonjour, monsieur; Bonsoir, madame; Salut* (limited to informal occasions with close friends), and leave-takings, *au revoir, à demain*. Shows comprehension of formal and informal terms of address (*vous* vs. *tu*). Can provide background information in a format appropriate to the culture, such as street designation before name (*Rue de la Paix*) and telephone number groupings in pairs in French provinces, i.e., 32-49-63. Is able to express wants in a culturally acceptable fashion in simple situations: *Je voudrais une chambre avec salle de bains. Un coca s'il vous plaît. Je voudrais envoyer cette lettre aux États-Unis. C'est combien?* Understands need to go to specialty shops to buy foods, such as: *la boucherie, la charcuterie, la boulangerie, la poissonnerie, l'épicerie.* Can identify very common products, prices in local currency, and ask questions on conditions of promotion or sale, such as *Combien coûte cette écharpe?* Is aware of the use of the metric system and knows simple phrases, such as *Je voudrais un kilo de pommes.* Is aware of different meal schedules as well as the content of each: *petit déjeuner, dîner* (may be unable to describe the nature of differences between *déjeuner* and *dîner* due to regional or socioeconomic differences). Knows that public transportation has a different structure or organization, i.e., *métro*, classes in subway train systems, conductor vs. driver. Is generally aware that tips are expected in restaurants but are sometimes included in the price (*service compris* vs. *service non-compris* 15%). Also generally aware that tips are expected in hotels, theatres, and other

service situations. Yet may make errors as the result of misunderstanding or misapplying assumptions about the culture, such as not tipping a movie theatre usher or arriving too early for dinner.

Advanced

Limited social competence. Handles social situations successfully with a culture bearer accustomed to foreigners. Though home culture predominates, speaker shows comprehension of general etiquette, such as avoiding taboos and never asking sensitive questions about age, salary, family affairs. Also shows comprehension of guest etiquette, such as complimenting hosts on food and wine, keeping both hands on the table when dining, holding the knife in the right hand, understanding that the kitchen is "off-limits" unless invited, not leaving immediately after dinner, and offering food or cigarettes to others before taking them oneself. Is aware of gifts as an expression of friendship, personal esteem, or gratitude. Knows how to accept gifts graciously. Knows how to apologize using such phrases as: *Je regrette, Excusez-moi, Pardon, Je suis désolé d'être en retard*. Can make introductions in formal and informal situations. Knows how to answer and call on the telephone (*Allô. Qui est à l'appareil? Ne quittez pas.*). Knows how to ask for a third party (*Ici . . . Je voudrais parler avec . . .*) or leave a message (*Pourriez-vous lui dire que . . . lui a téléphoné?*). Occasionally uses polite conditional to make requests (*Pourriez-vous m'indiquer . . .? Je voudrais un aller et retour.*). Knows conversational phrases for accepting invitations (*avec plaisir*) or refusing (*Veuillez m'excuser mais . . . Merci pour l'invitation, mais . . .*). Is able to do routine banking using vocabulary, such as *carnet de chèques, chèques de voyage, compte en banque, compte d'épargne, taux de change*; e.g., *Je voudrais déposer/toucher un chèque de . . .* Knows how to handle routine business at the post office (*Donnez-moi dix timbres par avion s'il vous plaît. Je voudrais envoyer cette lettre 'recommandée.' Je voudrais acheter un mandat postal de 1.000 francs.*). Able to make more specific purchases in small or large stores and/or ask for specific help, such as *Je cherche une chemise de taille 38*. Still makes errors in the use of *vous* and *tu*. Is not competent to take part in a formal meeting or in a group where several persons are speaking informally at the same time.

Superior

Working social and professional competence. Can participate in almost all social situations and those within one vocation. Handles unfamiliar situations with ease and sensitivity, including some involving common taboos, or some that are otherwise emotionally charged. Comprehends most nonverbal responses. Laughs at some culture-related humor, such as imitation of substandard speech, plays on words, etc. In productive skills, neither culture dominates; nevertheless, makes appropriate use of cultural references and expressions, such as colloquial phrases (e.g., *Mon dieu!, sympa, zut!, J'en ai marre, vachement*). Understands more colloquial and idiomatic expressions than is able to use (e.g., *avoir un mal au coeur, dormir debout, boire comme un trou, avoir une faim de loup, ras-le-bol*). Generally distinguishes between a formal and an informal register (correct use of *vous* and *tu*) and proper use of titles of respect. Discusses abstract ideas relating the foreign and native cultures and is aware cognitively of areas of difference, i.e., the importance of family ties, typical French characteristics (*art de vivre*), and some understanding of the role that French history and literature play in the everyday life and attitudes of the people. Realizes the influence of the church, religion, or lack thereof, and the anticleric attitude of many. Is aware of various social classes—*ouvrier, petit bourgeois, grand bourgeois*—and the difficulty in "changing" social classes. Can discuss current events as well as fields of personal interest and support opinions. Is generally limited, however, in handling abstractions. Would know that the French *esprit de contradiction* is a means of animating discussion and that French persons might criticize their own country, but would not accept criticism of France from foreigners. Minor inaccuracies occur in perception of meaning and in the expression of the intended representation, but do not result in serious misunderstanding, even by a culture bearer unaccustomed to foreigners.

Near-Native
Competence

Fits behavior to audience, and French culture dominates almost entirely when using the language. Full social and professional competence. Has internalized the concept that culture is relative and is always on the lookout to do the appropriate thing; no longer assumes that own culture is "the way it is." Can counsel, persuade, negotiate, represent a point of view, describe and compare features of the native and target cultures. In such comparisons, can discuss geography, history, institutions, customs and behavior patterns, and current events and national policies. Perceives almost all unverbalized responses (gestures, emotional reactions) and recognizes almost all allusions, including historical ("L'*état, c'est moi.*") and literary commonplaces ("*Ce siècle avait deux ans.*" "*Rodrigue, as-tu du coeur?*" "*Il faut cultiver notre jardin.*") Laughs at most culture-related humor (*l'esprit gaulois*), such as imitation of regional or ethnic speech patterns (*l'accent méridional*) and allusions to political or comic strip figures (e.g., *Les Frustrés de Bretécher* or *Astérix*). Uses low frequency idiomatic expressions (*J'en ai ma claque. C'est pas demain la veille.*); sayings (*Couper les cheveux en quatre*), or proverbs (*Vouloir, c'est pouvoir*). Controls formal and informal register. Has lived in the culture for a long time or has studied it extensively. Is inferior to the culture bearer only in background information related to the culture such as childhood experiences, detailed regional geography, and past events of significance.

Native
Competence

Native competence. Examinee is indistinguishable from a person brought up and educated in the culture.

# APPENDIX II

# AATF: The Teaching of French— A Syllabus of Competence

This Report of the Commission of Professional Standards of the American Association of Teachers of French, published as a special issue of the *National Bulletin* of the American Association of Teachers of French (volume 15, October 1989), "defines what the level of language proficiency of French teachers ought to be, and also sets standards for the range of their knowledge in linguistics, culture, literature, and methodology" (Foreword). It contains chapters on Language Proficiency, Culture, Literature, Applied Linguistics, Methodology, FLES, Professional Concerns, and Curricular Implications. We reproduce here chapter 2 on Culture. The Chair of the Culture Subcommittee was Howard L. Nostrand.

Copies of the complete report are available from the American Association of Teachers of French, 57 East Armory Avenue, Champaign, Illinois 61820.

## 1. The Place of Culture in Language Teaching

The social and cultural context is essential for communicative competence, for understanding a language as a system of meanings, and for the full appreciation of the literature that is the autobiography of a people.

Furthermore, the curiosity of students in our time to know about different ways of life offers the principal means of interesting them in a language and literature. From the standpoint of American education as a whole, a foreign language and culture hold the main chance of strengthening several weak dimensions. One of these is the skillful use of language, based on knowledge of how to analyze and shape verbal expression. Another is the capacity for mutually beneficial social and economic relations with the world that lies outside the English-speaking countries. A third is self-understanding, which requires a perspective from a point outside our culture, for it involves awareness of how one's culture influences the way one thinks and feels. While it is not proposed that proficiency in one's own culture be evaluated as part of the competence defined here, foreign-language teaching certainly should make its whole unique contribution to human development.

## 2. The Meaning of Cultural Competence

A consensus on the essentials of this competence has developed over the past forty years among the educators who have given it the most thought. Acceptance will have to be field-wide, however, before adequate national tests can be constructed.

The consensus is based on the concept of a culture as an organic whole made up of values, a grid through which one sees the world, habits of thought and feeling, and habits of interacting with certain social institutions and customs. The present evolution of a culture is strongly influenced by its past, including its proud achievements.

Within a culture area, different national societies lead to different sociocultural systems, yet they share important central patterns of culture. This is true of the more than forty countries or regions where French is the first or second language (*Dictionnaire général de la francophonie*).

Cultural competence can best be defined as a combination of three interrelated parts: the sociolinguistic ability to communicate, certain areas of knowledge, and certain informed attitudes. The three parts will be described at two levels of competency, **Basic** and **Superior,** at the end of these introductory considerations.

Cultural competence has the same meaning for a teacher as for anyone else. It is quite separate from pedagogical competence, the techniques for imparting one's skills, understanding and enlightenment to others. And while those techniques vary greatly from pre-school to graduate school teaching, the cultural competence of the teacher remains the same. At each age level, even early childhood, one can impart some elements of an adult understanding, as Jerome Bruner has shown; and the quality of a teacher's or a parent's understanding inevitably reflects itself in the quality of a young learner's development.

Fortunately, an adult understanding of a culture requires only a certain core of the vast existing knowledge about the French culture area. It is the specialist in a field of research, international negotiation, or the like, who must add to the core in one direction or another.

Cultural competence does however include a body of knowledge and attitudes that supplements the understanding of a single culture area and its component societies.

To be more than an amateur observer, one needs to know how to relate the heterogeneous surface manifestations to underlying core elements. (Nostrand 1977, and the "Index socio-culturel" in Nostrand 1988). One needs also a kit of methods and conceptual tools for observing and analyzing a culture:

- field study, direct and remote—pen and tape pals, sister cities; the complementary roles of inside and outside observers;

- the differentiation of subcultures—regional, socioeconomic, age groups (Stoetzel);

- the analysis of space and time concepts—the monochronic and polychronic ways of "living" time; and the distinction between high-context and low-context cultures (Hall);

- contrastive analysis—notably the identification of key cross-cultural variables (Hofstede) and the analysis of the contact points between cultures (Carroll).

To avoid overgeneralizing about "national traits," one must distinguish three levels of useful generalization: about humanity as a whole; about a single culture or subculture; and about individual differences.

Informed attitudes are like the conceptual tools in that once acquired in studying any culture, they apply to all (Seelye, chapter 11). The following, ranging from rudimentary to sophisticated, are all desirable for the **Basic** cultural competence, and are indispensable at the **Superior** level:

- curiosity about discovering similarities and differences between one's home culture and French culture; the determination to be sensitive to the ethnic heritage of all one's students and associates;

- intellectual awareness that "different" does not mean "wrong"; and applied to language, that the French Canadian pronunciation, for example, is not "inferior" to the Parisian;

- without losing one's own identity, a basic desire to accommodate to the norms of the foreign society;

- the determination to avoid overgeneralization and stereotyping;

- an appreciation of the fact that each culture makes sense in its own terms, and that no one culture is privileged to possess an absolute criterion for judging the others;

- awareness of the fact that one's perceptions and judgments are patterned by one's home culture, and are subject to temporary influences such as the phases of culture shock (Valdes 35–39);

- a critical approach to statistics and opinion polls; a concern to know the date, the size of the sample and the scope of the evidence, even if one is not able to judge the credibility of the agency;

- a fair-minded, relativistic appreciation of cultural differences to the point of being able to present objectively some judgments that foreigners make concerning one's home country.

## 3. Consensus and Diversity

Consensus on a core competence, sufficient for the purposes of education and evaluation, is compatible with wide diversity in local and individual variation beyond the core.

Diversity is imposed first of all by the fact that the two components of understanding, "experience of" and "knowledge about," develop differently at the different age levels. In childhood the former, the sociolinguistic performance, advances ahead of "knowledge about." At later age levels, any knowledge or attitude can be taught to beginners, and has educational value long before it may be needed for performance abroad. Adult learners, moreover, have specific personal or vocational objectives on which their motivation depends, and they differ in attitudes and appreciations. A critical appreciation and an enthusiastic one, reasonably defended, can be equally valid forms of cultural awareness.

## 4. The Evaluation of Cultural Competence

The definition of a competence entails provision for evaluating it (Valette; Crawford-Lange and Lange 169–170).

Sociolinguistic performance is inextricable from communicative competence. The ACTFL interview test of the speaking skill inevitably includes cultural elements. The same type of interview can therefore yield a separate score for the sociolinguistic skills based on a sampling of critical elements such as the use of tu/vous, the formal and informal ways of speaking and behaving, and the nonverbal factors that make for ease and rapport with an interlocutor.

Unlike the behavior involved in oral communication, knowledge and attitudes can be evaluated in writing. The dominant attitudes of a person can be brought out, despite the virtuous self-image so often induced in such testing, by a combination of instruments, notably the Osgood semantic differential; opinion questions on a 5- or 7-point scale; and the critical-incident question. A test combining these approaches is exemplified in the *Manuel du professeur* accompanying *Savoir vivre en français* (Nostrand 1988).

ACTFL is addressing the problem of defining the cultural framework one needs in order to understand an authentic text—step one toward a full test of cultural competence; and the National Teacher Examination already includes some culture items.

The following descriptions of the **Basic** and **Superior competence** are presented in the form of examples, which come closer than do generalized statements to the operational definition of standards needed for evaluation, teaching, and curriculum design. The details given must be used nonetheless as illustrations of the needed competence: they are neither its only nor its indispensable concrete manifestations.

# 5. Basic Cultural Competence

**Basic** cultural **competence** ("Minimal Social Competence")

### 5.1 Sociolinguistic Ability (Heny; Crawford-Lange and Lange)

A person at this level of cultural competence

- can meet all the demands for survival as a traveller: can reach an intended destination via public transportation; secure lodging for the night; order and pay for food and drink; cash a check; make a simple purchase; conduct a simple phone conversation and take notes on information such as price, location, and departure time; can explain public signs and such common symbols as the abbreviations used in classified ads.

- in addition to the survival-level skills, can understand most announcements made over public address systems, gather the gist of a newscast if free to listen intently, and after specific preparation, can grasp the main points of a lecture and take notes; can explain the terms commonly used in culture-related texts such as menus and wedding or death announcements.

- can handle any common social situation with an interlocutor accustomed to foreigners: make requests politely, offer and receive gifts and invitations, apologize, make introductions, and discuss some current events or policies, a field of personal interest, a leisure-time activity of one French-speaking country; can participate in a conversation if conducted in "français soigné," perhaps asking to have some expressions repeated or paraphrased.

- comprehends, though may not use, the common unconscious and symbolic French gestures and facial expressions (Wylie; Nostrand 1988, 138–41).

- prompted by an example, shows awareness that compliments can arouse a reaction different from what would be expected in the home culture.

### 5.2 Knowledge (Michaud; Ardagh; Duby; Seelye; Verdié; Knox)

A person at this level of competence

- can interpret simple menus, timetables, schedules, maps; manipulate the currency; knows which kinds of shops sell what kinds of merchandise, and knows where to go for information on such subjects;

- beyond the survival level, knows about the phases of "culture shock" and how they may affect perception (Valdes 35–39); can identify the truth or untruth implied in the stereotypes of his or her home culture and of French culture;
- can discuss the present significance of the historic periods, prominent personalities and cultural achievements in France since the Middle Ages, and in the French-speaking world since the 18th century; can define such twentieth-century expressions as la Résistance, collaboration, the Algerian war, and May '68 as they relate to present attitudes;
- can name at least two present political parties in France, and two or three major contemporary issues;
- can describe or give examples of qualities prominently sought in French education, such as clear expression and organization of ideas, knowledge of French history and geography, and literature;
- can list ten, including three in Africa, of the more than forty countries or areas where French is the first or second language; can locate them on a map, name their capitals, and add a sentence about their society or economy or international situation;
- can describe in broad outline the main geographical regions, the political institutions, the public education system, and the mass media of France or another French-speaking country; can produce a few proverbs or stock phrases which reflect a world view often encountered there;
- can say how that country's institutions, regulations, and customs such as attitudes toward behavior and appearance in public, may affect him or her as a foreign traveler (or student, trainee, business person); and can name the official agencies which may hold the foreigner responsible for compliance with the regulations;
- can identify, in a literary or a journalistic text, examples of elevated style and of familiar and popular expressions, and in reading, can point out some of the verbal indications of attitudes, hidden quotations or allusions; can read classified ads containing the customary abbreviations;
- can describe a favorable and an unfavorable French attitude toward the United States or its people. (Servan-Schreiber; and present-day journalism).

# 6. Superior Cultural Competence

**Superior** cultural **competence** ("Working Social and Vocational Competence")

At the **Superior level** the person has additional skills and knowledge which enable a teacher to give a fuller experience of the culture, as well as to build upon individual motivation by relating to a wider variety of student interests.

### 6.1 Sociolinguistic Ability

At this level of cultural competence, a person

- uses cultural references and idioms, comprehends puns, uses the main unconscious and symbolic French gestures (Nostrand 1988, 138–41); interacts with the rhythm of the interlocutor (Hall 1983) and keeps the French distance between persons—"proxemics" (Hall 1959); consistently distinguishes between a formal and an informal way of speaking and behaving. (As an example of formal vs. informal behavior between speakers: if called upon to simulate meeting an old friend after a lapse of time, can judge whether an *embrassade* or handshake is appropriate, depending on the situation, social milieu and ages of the persons);

- finds comic some culture-related French humor, e.g., a passage from Pierre Daninos, and can tell what a French person finds amusing in a situation involving culture-related humor: for example, an unwarranted pretense to *intellectualité*, a self-satisfaction that clashes with the value of *la simplicité*, or an incongruous cultural allusion; in a joking or teasing situation, can explain the danger of offending;

- can describe a type of compliment likely to be misinterpreted or embarrassing in French culture;

- can participate in a formal meeting, or an informal discussion where several persons talk at the same time; and can infer the underlying intent of a speaker from what is said. (These abilities are important both as goals and as criteria for defining this level. The first two can be tested by combining part of a one-on-one interview with a background of recorded speech, and then testing the interviewee's comprehension of it. The ability to infer a speaker's intent can be judged by how well one "reads between the lines" of a written dialogue.)

### 6.2. Knowledge

At this level of competence, a person

- can discuss abstractions in fields of prior study: a vocation, a hobby, an aspect of one French-speaking area: its main institutions, social stratification, and mobility, the place of private organizations and unions, informal customs, sex- and age-group differences, current cultural and social changes.

- can write a simple social letter or a business letter that does not require technical (e.g., legal) language, with beginning and ending appropriate to the given situation, though the style may be obviously foreign; on seeing such a letter, can interpret the evidences of formality or informality.

- in response to questions, can comment on a feature of French culture such as a major value (art of living, friendship, realism, intellectuality), a habit of mind (abstract expression, quest for the "très précis" and the delimited field—e.g., "de A à C, en passant par B", a widespread assumption (the sharp contrast between friend and outsider, or between work and leisure, the inseparability of fact from context), the space and time concepts which bear on social and business relations (Hall, 1978; 1983; 1959 or 1984).

- can list twenty of the forty francophone countries or areas; can locate fifteen of them on a map, name their capitals, and add a sentence about their society or economy or international situation.

- can write about an aspect of France and one additional French-speaking area to the extent of three or four substantial paragraphs. In the case of a developed country, knows the point of view of a few current political figures and periodicals, knows about the electoral procedure, and can discuss some recent cultural achievements in film, song, art, architecture, or literature including TV and cartoon serials; in the case of a sub-Saharan or Caribbean area, for example, can write on topics such as the status of women, literacy, Islamic militancy, opposition between subcultures, terrorism, dictatorship, the political and economic relations between the Third World and the developed countries. For the second French-speaking country selected, can name two or three present political parties and describe two or three contemporary issues; can produce a few proverbs or stock expressions one encounters there.

- can discuss the metaphorical nature and cultural role of myth, à propos of a given text such as an African legend.

- can explain features of his or her home culture that puzzle a French-speaking inquirer.

Many non-native teachers of French aim still higher, at levels 4 and 5 on the Government's ILR (Interagency Language Roundtable) scale of five. In the case of cultural competence, these two categories cannot be conceived as "Near-Native" and "Native," but simply as "Near-Optimal" and "Optimal," for the outsider never will match the native's childhood experience, nor the unconscious use of face muscles. On the other hand, the outsider, while conforming to the customs of the society, has a capacity for an eclectic approach to French values and habits of mind which is hard for the native to imitate. These levels, moreover, require a broader knowledge of the French culture area as a whole than most natives ever attempt.

## 7. The Projected Sequel to These Definitions

In time it should be possible to choose and arrange empirically the main behavioral and cognitive elements of cultural competence: what is really needed for survival in a society and for successive levels of social and vocational adequacy seems bound to become determinable in the light of examined experience. Until such experience exists, however, the choice and sequencing of elements can only be hypothesized as the best approximation achievable in the present state of the art.

A three-stage process is projected: (1) revision, including coordination where possible with the criteria for the language skills, (2) experimental use, with feed-back, and (3) validation of a later draft by a team of researchers.

# Appendix III

## The Levels of Cultural Competence: Guidelines Applied to France and *La Francophonie*

These guidelines represent a concerted collective effort of the AATF to establish national standards of cultural competence. Once again, this effort has been led by Howard L. Nostrand.

The document below is the January 1992 revision of work still in progress. As this document is a revision of Howard L. Nostrand's appendix to "Basic Intercultural Needs: Breadth and Depth" in Ellen S. Silber, ed., *Critical Issues in Foreign Language Instruction* (New York: Garland, 1991): 153–59, we publish the guidelines with the permission of Garland Press and urge the reader to consider this book for Professor Nostrand's article as well as the works of its other contributors.

The references cited are those in the original, but the numerical intercalations have been normalized for the reader's convenience. Many of the author's bibliographic notes have been deleted.

### Cultural Guidelines Applied to France and *La Francophonie*

### Novice–High: Progress toward Survival Competence (= 0+ on the scale of the ILR, the Interagency Language Roundtable of the U.S. government)

#### Sociolinguistic Ability

A person at this lowest level of useful ability

A1— can accompany a few memorized formulae with appropriate body language (handshake, *l'embrassade*), but understands responses only within memorized patterns.

A2— has limited understanding of the behavior of interlocutors (especially, of nonverbal cues); often interprets according to the code of the home culture.

A3— can be understood, but with difficulty, by a native speaker acquainted with the home culture involved.

A4— can create a rapport of good will via tone of voice and nonverbal means.

#### Knowledge of the Culture Area

A5— understands conventional signs such as P for parking area, and simple official instructions and warnings such as on trains and in parks or public buildings.

A6— has limited knowledge of the culture area and of cultural analysis, but demonstrates some of the types of knowledge requisite for survival.

# Intermediate: Survival Competence (= ILR 1 and 1+)

Note: Each level includes all the abilities of the prior levels.

## Intermediate–Low: Minimal Survival Competence (= ILR 1)

### Sociolinguistic Ability

A person at this level can act acceptably in most everyday survival situations, for example,

B1— can meet minimal courtesy requirements, travel and shopping needs; e.g., greeting, leave taking, politely asking a stranger for information, using background knowledge to limit the scope of the request.

B2— can be understood by native interlocutors accustomed to such learners, but even in that case, miscommunication is frequent.

B3— demonstrates knowledge of the aspects of the culture related to everyday survival needs, such as the currency, official regulations, and the difference between restaurant, café, and brasserie; hotel and *pension; drugstore, pharmacie,* and *droguerie.*

### Knowledge of the Culture Area

B4— can describe one or more major values, common assumptions about human nature/society, or habits of mind which the outsider is likely to encounter. (See the annotations on Reference #28.)

## Intermediate–Mid: Above-Minimal Survival Competence (= ILR 1+)

### Sociolinguistic Ability

At this stage, the person

B5— can resolve two or more of the seven survival-level problems listed below under Intermediate–High.

B6— understands most conventional public signs.

B7— understands and demonstrates conventional gestures such as thumb and index finger indicating "2."

B8— comprehends, though may not use, most of the common unconscious and symbolic gestures of the culture. (For the two kinds of gesture, cf. Reference #28, vol. I, *Culture et communication,* pp. 138–41.)

B9— uses the French handshake (a single descending stroke, ending without jarring).

B10— makes an effort to keep the proper conversational distance between person |"proxemics"| (Reference #17).

### Knowledge of the Culture Area

B11— can find France and several other Francophone countries on a world map.

B12— for one country of the language area, can place several main cities and regions on an outline map, or can locate one city and point out a few main landmarks.

B13— can describe briefly two or three major values, a widespread assumption and a characteristic habit of mind (see the annotations on Reference #28)—and can recognize these when evident in a text or in behavior.

B14— can describe several main social conventions, such as those that govern dating, invitations to meals, giving and receiving compliments (recognizing that accepting praise, e.g., of one's dress may be considered vain).

B15— can say which kinds of stores sell what kinds of merchandise, and knows where to go for information on such subjects.

## Knowledge of Cultural Analysis (References #27, 28)

B16— can describe the phases of "culture shock" and how they may affect one's perception of the intercultural experience. (Reference #28, pp. 292–93 & 304; Reference #34, pp. 35–39)

B17— is aware that successful oral communication in a culture involves interacting with the rhythm of the interlocutor (Reference #15) and keeping the proper distance between persons ["proxemics"] (Reference #17).

# Intermediate–High: Full Survival Competence (= ILR 1+)

## Sociolinguistic Ability

A person at this level

B18— shows sufficient knowledge of the culture and society to avoid irritating an interlocutor with importune questions, in fulfilling the requirements for survival as a traveler to (1) obtain the information to reach an intended destination via public transportation; (2) secure lodging for the night; (3) select, order and pay for food and drink; (4) cash a check; (5) make a purchase; (6) take notes on information such as price, location, departure time; (7) understands the telephone dial tones, and can use the Minitel directory.

B19— can explain the terms commonly used in culture-related texts such as menus, wedding or death announcements, and the abbreviations in classified ads.

B20— can choose an acceptable formula for a social letter.

## Knowledge of the Culture Area

B21— for one Francophone country can say how that country's institutions, regulations, and customs (such as attitudes toward behavior and appearance in public) may affect him or her as a foreign traveler (or student, trainee, business person); and can name the official agencies which may hold the foreigner responsible for compliance with the regulations.

B22— can describe several major values (six would be about half of the basic value system), and more than one of the habits of mind and prevalent assumptions (see the annotations on Reference #28) and can recognize any of these when apparent in a text or in behavior.

B23— demonstrates some knowledge of one Francophone country's contribution to one or more of the arts.

### Knowledge of Cultural Analysis

Same as for Intermediate–Mid (B16, B17)

## Advanced: Limited Social Competence (= ILR 2)

### Sociolinguistic Ability

This person

C1— can offer culturally appropriate compliments, gifts, and invitations.

C2— discuss knowledgeably a current event or policy, a field of shared personal interest, a leisure-time activity of one Francophone country.

C3— can participate in a conversation if conducted in the standard (not colloquial) language, though may ask to have cultural allusions explained.

C4— now interacts part of the time with the rhythm of the interlocutor (Reference #15) and keeps the proper distance between persons ["proxemics"] (Reference #17).

### Knowledge of the Culture Area

C5— can locate on a world map a dozen or so of the 40+ countries or areas where French is the first or second language. For several of these, can name their capital or a major city, and can add a sentence about the society, economy or international situation.

C6— concerning one Francophone country (1) can name the President or national leader; (2) can discuss some of the country's historic periods, prominent personalities and cultural achievements.

C7— can discuss at least one proverb or stock expression which reflects a cultural characteristic.

C8— can give examples of differences among subcultures: regional, socioeconomic, ethnic/ religious and by age groups.

C9— can write a short essay on the place of, e.g., cuisine, sports, or the French language, in one Francophone country.

C10— can write in culturally acceptable terms a simple social letter, or a business letter that does not require legal or other technical language, with a beginning and ending of the proper formality; the style may however be obviously foreign. On seeing such a letter, can discuss the degree of formality required by the occasion.

### Knowledge of Cultural Analysis (References #27, 28)

C11— can list a few cultural characteristics one may look for in observing the culture directly (as visitor or through such contact as a sister-city relation), and from a distance (through pen, tape and video pals, electronic mail).

C12— can describe the complementary roles of inside and outside observers (Reference #28, pp. 29, 294–304).

C13— can distinguish between describing a fact and proposing possible explanations or interpretations.

## Advanced Plus: Improved Social and Limited Vocational/Professional Competence (= ILR 2+)

### Sociolinguistic Ability

Here the person

C14— can usually detect emotional overtones conveyed by intonation and body language, but may not detect these in a written text.

— has the background knowledge to understand most announcements made over public address systems, and to gather the gist of a newscast if free to listen intently.

C15— after specific preparation, can grasp the main points of a culture-related lecture and take notes.

### Knowledge of the Culture Area

C16— can identify the truth or untruth implied in stereotypes concerning the home culture and French culture.

C17— demonstrates awareness that one must overcome the *méfiance* toward strangers by establishing a personal rapport before undertaking business or negotiation.

C18— in reading, recognizes commonplace historical or literary allusions, and evident elevated or popular expressions.

### Knowledge of Cultural Analysis (References #27, 28)

C19— can discuss the proposition that there are three levels of useful generalization, radically different in scope: generalizations about humanity, about a given culture or subculture, and about different individuals; can justify assigning a proposed generalization to one of the three levels.

## Superior: Working Social and Vocational/Professional Competence (= ILR 3)

### Sociolinguistic Ability

The person at this level of competence

D1— uses cultural references and idioms, comprehends puns; uses the main unconscious and symbolic gestures of the culture (cf. Reference #28, pp. 138–41).

D2— consistently behaves with the appropriate degree of formality or informality. (For example, if asked to simulate meeting an old friend after a lapse of time, can judge whether a handshake or an *embrassade* is called for by the situation, social milieu and ages of the persons.)

D3— finds comic some culture-related humor: for example, a violation of a cultural value, or an incongruous cultural allusion. In a joking or teasing situation, can explain the danger of offending.

D4— can discuss, in the context of at least one field of prior study (one's vocation, a hobby), some aspect of one Francophone country: its main institutions, social stratification/mobility, the place of private organizations and unions, informal customs, sex- and age-group differences, showing awareness of any important cultural or social changes currently under way.

D5— can point out nuances of written style, but cannot vary writing style to fit accurately a variety of styles or audiences.

## Knowledge of the Culture Area

D6— for one Francophone country, can write on the main social institutions in terms of their underlying values and assumptions: for example, (1) family types in relation to the status of women and children; (2) friendship and *méfiance* toward outsiders; (3) religion and political parties or factions as affected by traditions of totalitarianism or pluralism; (4) the economy in its relation to government, and to the distinction between work and leisure; (5) business relations as affected by the conception of time and space; (7) education and the access to wealth and power; (8) the tastes reflected in the arts and in the media; (9) ecology and attitudes toward the environment.

D7— can list or locate on a map half of the 40+ countries or areas where French is the first or second language. For many of these, can name the capital or a major city, and can add a sentence about their society, economy, or international situation.

D8— can explain features of the home culture that puzzle an inquirer from the other culture.

D9— can discuss the manifestations of any of the culture's major values, prevalent assumptions or habits of mind which appear in a literary text, a social institution or an instance of social behavior.

D10— can discuss the metaphorical nature and cultural role of myth, à propos of a text in the language, such as an African legend.

## Knowledge of Cultural Analysis (References #27, 28)

D11— can discuss intercultural differences in the conception of space (Reference #16) and time: the monochronic and polychronic ways of "living" time (Reference #15, Index), and the distinction between high-context and low-context cultures (Reference #14).

# Near-Optimal: Optimal Except for Circumscribed Limitations (= ILR 4)

## Sociolinguistic Ability

At this level the person

E1— behaves in such a way as to win acceptance as an outsider equivalent to a bearer of the culture in most respects that matter for social or vocational relations, as evidenced in a simulated situation.

E2— can describe the institutions of one country, relating them to cultural values and assumptions.

E3— can fashion writing to fit a variety of styles and audiences.

E4— can participate in an association which uses the culture's parliamentary procedures.

## Knowledge of the Culture Area

E5— can write three or four substantial paragraphs on an aspect of one Francophone country or area, e.g., a current social or political issue. In the case of a developed country, knows the point of view of a few current political figures and periodicals; knows about the electoral procedure; and can describe briefly some recent cultural achievements—in film, song, art, architecture, or literature including TV and cartoon serials. In the case of a developing country, can write on topics such as the status of women, literacy, religious militancy, opposition between subcultures, terrorism, dictatorship, political and economic relations between the Third World and the developed countries.

### Knowledge of Cultural Analysis (References #27,28)

E6— can describe and apply the concept of contrastive analysis, including the identifying of key cross-cultural variables (Reference #19) and the approach of focusing on conflicts at the point of contact between cultures (Reference #9).

## Optimal: Competent as an Educated Native Well Informed about the Francophone World (= ILR 5)

### Sociolinguistic Ability

This person

F1— behaves in such a way as to permit acceptance into any group or clique in at least one Francophone country or area; or as a test, can demonstrate the requisite sociolinguistic features.

### Knowledge of the Culture Area

F2— is informed on most of the matters listed, plus those which a native typically retains from a secondary education.

### Knowledge of Cultural Analysis

F3— same as for Near-Optimal.

# References

1. AATF (American Association of Teachers of French). "The Teaching of French: A Syllabus of Competence. The Report of the Commission on Standards." AATF *National Bulletin* 14 (Special Issue, October 1989).

2. American Council on the Teaching of Foreign Languages. *Provisional Proficiency Guidelines.* Yonkers, NY: ACTFL, 1982. *Guidelines* [the cultural component omitted]. Yonkers, NY: ACTFL, 1986.

3. _____. Faculty Workshop on the Use of Authentic Texts to Develop Cultural Understanding in Foreign Language Programs. Yonkers, NY: ACTFL, 1987.

4. Allen, Wendy W. "Toward Cultural Proficiency." *Reports of the Northeast Conference on the Teaching of Foreign Languages* (1985): 137–66. (Bibliography, 165–66.)

5. Allen, Wendy, Keith Anderson, and Léon Narváez. "Foreign Languages across the Curriculum: The Applied Foreign Language Component." *Foreign Language Annals* 25 (1992): 11–19.

6. Boyer, Ernest L. "For Education: National Strategy, Local Control." *The New York Times,* 26 September 1989, A19.

7.  Byram, Michael. *Cultural Studies in Foreign Language Education*. Avon, Eng.: Multilingual Matters #46, 1989. Available through Taylor & Francis, Bristol, PA.

8.  Byrnes, Heidi. "Proficiency [Test Results] as a Framework for Research in Second Language Acquisition." *Modern Language Journal* 71 (1987): 44–49.

9.  Carroll, Raymonde. *Évidences invisibles: Américains et Français au quotidien*. Paris: Éditions de Seuil, 1987. Translated as *Cultural Misunderstandings: The French-American Experience*. Chicago: Univ. of Chicago Press, 1988.

10. Crawford-Lange, Linda M., and Dale Lange. "Doing the Unthinkable in the Second-Language Classroom: A Process for the Integration of Language and Culture," pp. 139–77 in Theodore V. Higgs, ed., *Teaching for Proficiency, the Organizing Principle*. ACTFL Foreign Language Education Series. Lincolnwood, IL: National Textbook Co., 1984.

11. Damen, Louise. *Culture Learning: The Fifth Dimension in the Classroom*. Second-Language Professional Library. Reading, MA: Addison-Wesley, 1987.

12. Gaudiani, Claire. *Strategies for the Development of Foreign Language and Literature Programs*. New York: Modern Language Association of America, 1984.

13. *A Guide to Proficiency-Based Instruction in Modern Foreign Languages for Indiana Schools: Generic Competencies, Levels I–IV*. Lorraine A. Strasheim and Walter H. Bartz, eds. Indianapolis, IN: Indiana Public Schools, 1986.

14. Hall, Edward T. *Beyond Culture*. Garden City, NY: Anchor, 1976.
    This perceptive anthropologist's contribution of tool concepts—here, chiefly "high and low context cultures," "monochronic and polychronic time"—would have won acceptance quite apart from his engaging style of presentation. Chapter 15 is devoted to the subject of self-identification.

15. _____. *The Dance of Life: The Other Dimension of Time*. Garden City, NY: Anchor, 1983.
    ". . . time as culture, how time is consciously as well as unconsciously formulated, used, and patterned in different cultures." (p. 3) Among the cultural differences is the synchronizing of rhythm between interacting persons. A Glossary, pp. 209–13, defines many of Hall's tool concepts.

16. _____. *The Hidden Dimension*. Garden City, NY: Doubleday, 1966.
    The cultural differences in the conceptualizing of space, including proxemics (personal distancing) and the layout of houses and towns.

17. _____. *The Silent Language*. Garden City, NY: Doubleday, 1959.
    This first of his books explored the field of kinesics: gestures and body language.

18. Heny, Frank. "Theoretical Linguistics, Second Language Acquisition, and Language Pedagogy." *The Annals of the American Academy of Political and Social Science. Foreign Language Instruction: A National Agenda*. Richard D. Lambert, special editor (March 1987): 194–210.

19. Hofstede, Geert. *Culture's Consequences: International Differences in Work-Related Values*. Newbury Park, CA: Sage, 1980.

20. Kraemer, Alfred J. *Development of a Cultural Self-Awareness Approach to Instruction in Intercultural Communication*. Washington: Human Resources Research Organization, 1973. (HumRRO Technical Report 73-17.)

21. Lambert, Craig. "Optical Disks in the Attic." *Harvard Magazine* (September–October 1989): 4,6.
    Videodisks and CD–ROM now enable a student to call up together the plan of the Acropolis, a view of the Parthenon, Attic vases, and texts of history, literature and mythology, foreshadowing the future of the language and culture textbook.

22. Lange, Dale L. "The Language Teaching Curriculum and a National Agenda." *The Annals of the American Academy of Political and Social Science. Foreign Language Instruction: A National Agenda.* Richard D. Lambert, special editor (March 1987): 70–96.

23. Lehmann, Winifred P., and Randall L. Jones. "The Humanistic Basis of Second Language Learning." *The Annals of the American Academy of Political and Social Science. Foreign Language Instruction: A National Agenda.* Richard D. Lambert, special editor (March 1987): 186–93.

24. Lewald, H. Ernest. "Theory and Practice in Culture Teaching on the Second-Year Level in French and Spanish." *Foreign Language Annals* 7 (1984): 660–67.

25. Met, Myriam. "Learning Language through Content: Learning Content through Language." *Foreign Language Annals* 24 (1991): 281–95.

    The focus is on FLES, yet the policy of balancing language in its cultural context with further language practice, and the corollary of coordination with other subjects, apply as well to higher age levels. In the same issue, Carol Ann Pesola devotes a substantial article to "Culture in the Elementary School Classroom," pp. 331–46, Marcia H. Rosenbusch formulates criteria for strong FLES programs, pp. 297–314, and Helena Curtain summarizes methods for orienting FLES toward communicative skills, including sociolinguistic ability, pp. 323–29.

26. Nostrand, Howard L. "Authentic Texts and Cultural Authenticity: An Editorial." *Modern Language Journal* 73 (Spring 1989): 49–52.

    Argues that unless a student is enabled to see a text or situation against its authentic cultural background, the authenticity is lost.

27. _____. "The 'Emergent Model' (Structured Inventory of a Sociocultural System) Applied to Contemporary France." *Contemporary French Civilization* 2 (1977): 277–94.

    Based on a reconciliation, explained in an introduction, between the anthropologist Morris Opler's "main themes" description, specific to a given culture, and the sociologist Talcott Parsons's organization of data into subcultures, designed to apply to all sociocultural systems.

28. _____, Frances B. Nostrand, and Claudette Imberton-Hunt. *Savoir vivre en français.* New York: John Wiley & Sons, 1988.

    Definitions of major values, habits of mind and prevalent assumptions of the French culture area are based on the research then available. Examples are pointed out in the language, the arts, behavior patterns, customs and social institutions. An *Index socioculturel,* pp. 413–18 of vol. I, *Culture et communication,* outlines the references to France and the Francophone world, as well as to methods and concepts for cultural analysis, and international career interests.

    Among the major French values, Claudette Imberton-Hunt has proposed *l'Amitié, l'Amour, la Patrie* (whose irrational and emotional elements are similarly limited, she points out, by a realistic sense of limitations), *l'Art de vivre et le souci esthétique du goût, l'Individualisme/Liberté, l'Intellectualité et le Réalisme, la Conscience et le souci de la Justice sociale, la Fraternité et l'Esprit humanitaire, la Sécurité et le souci de la Justice répressive.*

    Important assumptions one meets in the European version of the culture are: *la primauté de l'individu sur le collectif, la conception de l'espace comme étant ou public ou privé; la qualité précise du temps futur proche.*

    Pervasive habits of mind are: *la réserve, la méfiance, l'auto-critique national. En définissant un objet d'attention, le souci de prendre en compte son contexte comme partie intégrale de la définition (le "relationnisme"), ainsi que l'asservissement à des catégories préconçues qui est caractéristique des cultures à contexte riche ("high-context"—le compartimentage). Dans le discours, l'insistance à préciser les limites du propos, et la fierté de raisonner à la manière cartésienne.*

29. _____, Gerald Richard Upp. *Databases: Our Third Technical Revolution*. Champaign, IL: American Association of Teachers of French, 1991.

(The two earlier "revolutions" were audio and AV models.) Over 100 databases, in France (including the Départements d'Outre-Mer), Canada, Germany and the U.S. constitute the main sources for research-based knowledge of the French-speaking world. The monograph includes information on access to the databases. Information on France including the DOM can be updated through ERIC, FRANCIS, and La Mémoire de l'Education (CNDP); the rest of *la Francophonie* through SDM (Montreal), and BIEF (Ottawa). Pedagogical research is covered in ERIC, La Mémoire de l'Education, and the Informationszentrum für Fremdsprachenforschung at the Philipps Universität (Marburg).

30. Omaggio, Alice C. *Teaching Language in Context: Proficiency-Oriented Instruction*. Boston, MA: Heinle & Heinle, 1986.

31. Robinson, Gail L. Nemetz. *Crosscultural Understanding*. New York: Prentice-Hall, 1988.

32. Seelye, H. Ned. *Teaching Culture: Strategies for Intercultural Communication*. Lincolnwood, IL: National Textbook, 1984. Third ed. in preparation for 1993.

33. Silber, Ellen S., ed. *Critical Issues in Foreign Language Instruction*. New York: Garland, 1991.

34. Valdes, Joyce Merrill, ed. *Culture Bound: Bridging the Cultural Gap in Language Teaching*. New York: Cambridge Univ. Press, 1986.

35. Vallette, Rebecca. *Modern Language Testing*. 2d. edition. New York: Harcourt Brace, 1977, pp. 262–81.

# APPENDIX IV

# The "Emergent Model"

This article, fully entitled "The 'Emergent Model' (Structured Inventory of a Sociocultural System) Applied to Contemporary France," by Howard L. Nostrand, is published with the kind permission of *Contemporary French Civilization*.* Here Howard L. Nostrand presents an inventory of French culture in an effort to organize its essentials for classroom presentation.

## The "Emergent Model"
## (Structured Inventory of a Sociocultural System)
## Applied to Contemporary France

### Howard Lee Nostrand
### University of Washington

One may certainly question in the first place whether knowledge about a culture is worth the trouble. Good will (and the health to sustain it) might assure the peace on earth that is required for the pursuit of happiness. But good will has not been a match for the hazard of misunderstanding, even between historically related peoples, where the pitfalls are the more treacherous because they tend to be underestimated.

If, then, we decide to seek descriptive knowledge of a culture, we face a series of questions. What is to be its purpose? Let us suppose it to be cross-cultural understanding and communication. By what criteria shall we select, out of the infinite whole, what is essential to be described? How define the essential elements, and on what standard of evidence? How organize the essentials into an adult understanding? And finally, how unfold the result for a given type of learner?[1]

The present article will answer only a part of the question, How to organize the essentials. There appear, in fact, to be six approaches to this problem: (1) free-wheeling, personal *aperçus*, which are precious because they are free of the structuring imposed by systematic method; (2) an inventory; (3) a model of structure and function; (4) organization around main "themes"; (5) history; and (6) cross-cultural comparison. It may be possible in time to combine these approaches, using the *aperçus* as hypotheses, transposing the inventoried data to a model of their interaction, relating the whole to central "themes," adding the diachronic dimension of culture change, and placing the one culture in the context of others similarly described. Each approach has its own strengths, weaknesses and ideal specifications.

The inherent specifications for an inventory, in addition to its being convertible to a model, are comprehensiveness of the essentials, applicability to all cultures, economy of items, and proper emphasis, which for our purpose means the amenability to a teachable understanding.

* *Contemporary French Civilization* II (ii, Winter) 1978, (11) 277–299.

The present inventory grew out of several U.S. Office of Education projects which provided for advisers from sociology, anthropology and social psychology. The first project laid the "Groundwork," 1964, and the last applied the inventory to France in *Background data for the teaching of French* (EDRS numbers ED 031 964 and ED 031-989), 1967. The "emergent model" has continued to evolve, expanding to provide places for more observations, both before and after it was published in *The American foreign-language teacher* (4, iii) 1974.

The best of the existing inventories failed to meet most of the specifications. The ingenious grid of Edward Hall and George Trager, with its 100 intersections of ten elements such as Learning and Play, proved to have the added disadvantage of ambiguity: Did the intersection mean the learning aspect of play, or vice versa? The same would be true of the alternative set of ten very different elements later proposed by Nelson Brooks (*Foreign Language Annals* 1, iii, 1968, pp. 204–217). The Human Relations Area Files came nearest to the specifications, and it remains attractive by reason of the 200 cultures already analyzed. But it is far from economical. Its emphasis on things and social structure leaves the value system undeveloped as a subcategory of "Ethos." And its list of 79 major headings lacks any articulation to favor the emergence of a model.

The most promising start toward a comprehensive model was the identification of several subsystems within the sociocultural system, each marked off by natural boundaries, as proposed by the Harvard sociologist Talcott Parsons. The best economy and emphasis, on the other hand, had been achieved in the "themal" description elaborated by the Cornell anthropologist Morris Opler from the too simplified, one-theme description of Ruth Benedict in *Patterns of Culture*.

Opler and Parsons have never accepted that their approaches are reconcilable. In discussions while Opler was a visiting professor at Harvard, Parsons objected that main themes, always specific to one culture, did not permit the universality science must seek; Opler countered that universalized concepts such as "a value" were insensitive to real cultures, where the main preoccupations include fears and anxieties that would escape the researcher seeking a value system.

Nonetheless, I contend that the virtues of the two structures can be combined. Opler's culture-specific themes can be equated with Parsons' values, provided one recognizes that a value may sometimes be expressed negatively, as a disvalue; and provided one amplifies the definition of each value to include the habits of mind, and assumptions about reality, which one must know in order to grasp the value as it is felt by bearers of the culture.

Thus section 1.A of the present outline, amplified by the relevant items from 1.B and 1.C, constitutes a themal description within the comprehensive inventory; and this juxtaposition of themes and behavioral manifestations of the culture and society helps to avoid the settling into cliches which was the fate of the "national traits" descriptions of the 1930's. How much better we can do than that generation is explained by Anthony Wallace in a fascinating essay, "The new culture-and-personality."[2]

The inventory presented here is far from final, but its basic structure enables it to satisfy the specifications our purposes require. It organizes 32 main features of a sociocultural system into four component (sub)-systems.

The 32 main headings, written in capitals ( 1.A, 1.B, etc.), and the four systems in which they are grouped, are applicable to the life style of any population. The same is true of certain of the minor headings. The four systems have been adapted from Talcott Parsons, who distinguishes "four levels of organization," successively broader in range of inclusion: the human organism; the personality; social relations; and the culture patterns.

The first two Parsonian levels, limited to the individual, are here combined in Section V. The social and cultural systems are borrowed intact, except that the social system (Section II) is divided into the familiar social institutions, more useful for our purposes than Parsons' division into "imperatives." A subsection II.M serves in this inventory to collect data on social conflicts. This subsection would be absorbed when the inventory is converted into a model of interacting forces; or it might have to be expressed as a coherent counterculture. A whole Section III is reserved for an eventual bringing together of all the patterns of behavior, cultural as well as societal, which form the antithesis of the established system. An ecological system is added, on the hypothesis that it evolves in partial independence from the others. Attitudes toward other cultures and international organizations have been collected into a separate Section VI, so that the other sections may deal entirely with the one culture and society as seen by bearers of the culture and by outside observers.

The best chance of transmitting a lifelong specialist's insight to observers who have limited time for the subject probably lies in relating *experience of* a culture's concrete manifestations to *knowledge about* the first three topics in the "Culture" (sub)system inventoried here: Values, Habits of Thought, and World Picture. These three elements of a sociocultural system summarize the concrete manifestations collected into the remainder of the inventory. They constitute the culture's "ground of meaning": the basis of "what makes sense" to bearers of the culture; and for the outsider, a vantage ground from which to understand the meaning which an act or event takes on in that culture.

A working concept of the ground of meaning can be further unified: if we add to each major value the habits and assumptions of fact essential for a full perception of the value, we arrive at the culture's main themes. These themes, with their interaction of mutual support or conflict, are probably the most concise of all descriptive knowledge that is true-to-fact enough to be useful. Seen in historical perspective, as a present stage evolving from a known past toward the resolution of current stresses and imbalances, the main themes of a contemporary people's life give insight into a culture in both its meanings: everyday behavior and historic achievements.

The "themal" description developed by the anthropologist Morris Opler (now of the University of Oklahoma) is thus integrated into a sociological model. While the basic model applies to all cultures, each culture has its own set of themes, which can be discovered inductively from manifestations throughout the sociocultural whole. In the Anglo culture, for example, achievement-success and pragmatism emerge as main themes, individualism is replaced by self-reliance, and intellectualism is omitted. No culture appears to have more than a dozen main themes: proliferation is countered by simplification, perhaps because an added theme multiplies painful value conflicts.

Once a culture's main themes have been approximated, it is useful to define each theme under these aspects:

(a) its central value, with the variations according to social classes, age groups, and geographical regions,

(b) its typical manifestations, beginning with section I.D,

(c) its relation with the other themes which it supports or restricts,

(d) its relation to the habits in section I.B,

(e) its relation to the relevant assumptions in section I.C,

(f) the forces which are causing the theme to evolve,

(g) the changes in the theme that are consequently under way,

(h) constructive proposals for directing or exploiting the changes.

The cultural subsystem, including the themes, is common to an entire language area, but a sociocultural whole, in which that subsystem interacts with local social institutions and ecological problems, is limited to a part of the language area, such as a single nation. Within the nation, subcultures must be distinguished, by region, social class, age groups, and ethnic loyalty.

The French example which illustrates here the expansion of the universal inventory suggests how it will need to be supplemented so as to serve for the storing of data peculiar to subcultures or to other cultures, while the headings in common still serve for later purposes of cross-cultural comparison.

Underlying issues and decisions, such as the justification for distinguishing between culture and society, are examined in "Describing the sociocultural context of a foreign language and literature," pp. 1–25 of Albert Valdman, ed., *Trends in language teaching*, McGraw-Hill, 1966. How themes can be derived: "Theme analysis in the study of literature," pp. 182–97 of Joseph Strelka, ed., *Problems of literary evaluation: Yearbook of comparative criticism*, Penn. State U. Press, 1969. Later references, including writings of Morris Opler, are listed in "Empathy for a second culture: Motivations and techniques," pp. 263–327 of Gilbert A. Jarvis, ed., *Responding to new realities: The ACTFL review of foreign-language education*, vol. 5, National Textbook Co., 1974.

# I. The Culture

GENERAL: The people's self-concept and foreign views of the culture (Alphabetically by nationality)

I.A     MAJOR VALUES (The culture's value system and the tensions within it)—Cf. V.D.

GENERAL: Relations among the major values

Each theme centers around a major "value," in the broad sense of a pervasive or recurrent motive, need, aspiration, or other preoccupying concern. The main themes form two clusters, which define the two ideals of the good person and the good society. In the French system, these clusters largely overlap: only the first two values below are qualities of the individual alone; and not one of the twelve is exclusively a societal feature. (Cf. I.C.4, the primacy of the individual over the collective!)

.1 The art of living: enjoyment of the lifestyle one has chosen

.2 Intellectuality and "être raisonnable"

.3 Individualism and civil liberty (including acquisitive ambition)

.4 Realism and good sense (including health care and sensitivity to material conditions and conveniences)

.5 Friendship

.6 Love

.7 Family

.8 Religion

.9 The quest for community (within a subculture), and loyalty to a province or region: regional movements

.10 Patriotism and its object

.11 Distributive justice (including an increasing humanitarian concern and sensitivity to the deteriorating environment)

.12 Law and order (including retributive justice, "la justice répressive")

Note: Security is not a single value, since its different directives conflict among themselves. It is one element of each main theme except distributive justice, with which it usually conflicts.

I.B        HABITS OF THOUGHT not markedly valued or disvalued: cognitive style, and modes of procedure including administrative style (for habits of feeling—affective style—see I.A.)

GENERAL: Relations among the mental habits, notably unresolved oppositions such as between traditionalism and bold imagination, conformity and periodic revolt (cf. I.B.5)

.1 The concern to analyze relationships and to achieve form. (Edmund S. Glenn: 'a relational culture, on the continuum between the case-oriented mentality exemplified by the U.S. and the universalistic mentality exemplified by Russia'.)

.2 Imaginativeness, capacity for abstract thought

.3 Ocontological emphasis (i.e., on how one *ought* to act), disciplined conformity, cautious traditionalism

.4 Importance of the mouth: language (I.F, G), gastronomy (I.E.6)

.5 Rather widespread: a low threshold of exasperation and impulsiveness

.6 Generally realistic attitudes toward the human body, including sexuality

.7 Survival of certain traditional patterns, including, for some, superstitions

I.C  WORLD PICTURE (Beliefs, assumptions of fact)
GENERAL: Relations among beliefs
(HUMAN NATURE:)

1. The self as a detached entity; and as a creation resulting from one's own actions

.2 Humanity as a quality that must be learned

.3 Appearances contrasted with inner reality: hence distrust, "méfiance"

(SOCIAL RELATIONS:)

.4 Primacy of the individual over the collective

.5 A social structure still predominantly vertical

.6 Marked distinction between friends and "others" (in-group & out-groups)

.7 Mistrust toward authority

.8 Acceptance, periodically, of authoritarian reformers

(MAN IN NATURE, including attitudes toward Life and Death:)

.9 Adaption to natural forces, seen as necessary for exploiting them

(TIME CONCEPT:)

.10 The present in a context of past and future

.11 History as a storehouse of models from which the individual may choose

(SPACE CONCEPT:)

.12 Public and private contrasted, malaise in ambiguous areas

.13 Radial organization of space

.14 France as a frame of reference

.15 Current broadening perception of the international context

I.D  VERIFIABLE KNOWLEDGE from the sciences and humanities (For research institutions, see II.F. For applied sciences, see IV.)

I.E  ART FORMS, folk and elite

.1 Literature, opera and cinema, "comic" strips

.2 Music and the dance

.3  Painting and sculpture

.4  Architecture and interior decoration (Urban planning is included in IV.E, Settlement and territorial organization.)

.5  Clothing and adornment (including haute couture)

.6  Cuisine (Gastronomy)

.7  Humor (Recurrent patterns)

I.F     LANGUAGE

.1  Phonology, morphology, syntax, and lexicon

.2  Levels of discourse, including slang

.3  Change, including neologisms; language planning

.4  Instructional grammar

.5  Central place of the French language in the culture

I.G     PARALANGUAGE AND KINESICS

.1  Vocal communication other than words, including intonation, accentuation, breaks

.2  Visible expression including facial expressions, gestures, postures and body motions, and proxemics (conventional distances between persons interacting socially)

# II. The Society

Defined as interpersonal and intergroup relations; and its institutions, defined by their component roles and the norms governing the roles. (These situation-specific norms are also components of the culture's generalized values, or main themes.)

GENERAL: Bibliography; Periodicals; General History; Recent Social Change. (For Administrative Style, see I.B.)

II.A     THE FAMILY (OR THE COMMUNAL MILIEU)

.1  Origin of the affective, mother-child-centered family, scarcely antedating the eighteenth-century beginnings of Romanticism

.2  Differentiation by social class and urban or rural setting

.3  Current affective and legal changes

II.B     RELIGIOUS INSTITUTIONS

.1  The Roman Catholic majority; liberalization

.2  The minority religions (*Qua* religion; see II.L)

.3  Decline of political alignment by faiths

II.C ECONOMIC-OCCUPATIONAL INSTITUTIONS

   .1 Business and industrial organizations; the uneven modernizing of management

   .2 Government planning

   .3 Poverty

   .4 The consumer; defense of the consumer

   .5 The economic aspect of regionalization

   .6 Economic provision for retirement

   (For unionism, see II.1. For technology including agriculture, see IV.)

II.D POLITICAL AND JUDICIAL INSTITUTIONS, including the police and military establishments

   .1 The electorate and parties analyzed into six categories: the Left and Right, the smaller Extreme Left and Extreme Right, the Center, and the usually inactive fraction, at times a third of all potential voters, called "le Marais" (the swampland)

   .2 The elected officials

   .3 The resistant, rule-bound bureaucracy

   .4 The juridical system; paternal features of the State

   .5 The police

   .6 The military

   .7 Attitudes toward political regionalization; grassroots democracy

   (For demographic control, see IV.C)

II.E THE EDUCATIONAL INSTITUTIONS

   .1 Centralization, since Napoleon

   .2 Recent dissatisfactions at each age level

   .3 Current attempts to decentralize and to innovate; vested interest in traditional privileges

   .4 Nursery school

   .5 Primary grades

   .6 Secondary school

   .7 Higher education

   .8 Technical training

   .9 Adult education

II.F THE INTELLECTUAL-ESTHETIC AND HUMANITARIAN INSTITUTIONS

   .1 The Ministry of Culture: State initiative in the arts. The Académie Française

   .2 The Centre National de la Recherche Scientifique: State support of research

.3  Private artistic production and awards, e.g. in literature (Cf. II.H.2)

.4  Private organizations devoted to research, the arts, philanthropy (See also II.C.4 and II.G.4)

.5  Museums and libraries

(Prestige of intellectuals: see I.A. 2)

II.G    LEISURE AND RECREATION

.1  Growing popularity of sports, camping and travel

.2  Vacations and holidays

.3  The Government's Maisons des Jeunes et de la Culture

.4  Private recreational organizations, including a new type of discussion club to which couples belong

II.H    THE MASS MEDIA

.1  Newspapers and magazines

.2  Book publishing and readership

.3  The State-controlled television; radio

.4  The film (For the cinema as art form, see I.A.11)

II.I    STRATIFICATION AND MOBILITY

.1  Social classes. The eleven or more socio-occupational groupings needed for some purposes may be combined into four or five classes: the upper class, or *haute bourgeoisie* (which includes the old aristocracy); the middle class including landed farmers; the *petite bourgeoisie*, including shopkeepers and low-paid office workers; the factory workers; and the farm laborers. (Cf. I.C.5)

.2  Unionism. Closed shops rare, hence trade unions bargain as unstable coalitions. The union of business executives( Le Patronat Français); of doctors; unions of educational personnel

.3  Transitional mixture of job-related, working-class identification and at the same time, a growing feeling of upward mobility, as member of a large middle class.

(For international mobility, see II.L)

II.J    SOCIAL PROPRIETIES (Le Savoir-vivre)

An exacting set of rules, long maintained by a strict socialization of children, is yielding at those points where it comes to seem repressive, or incompatible with the tempo and efficiency of modern life.

II.K    STATUS BY AGE GROUP AND SEX

.1  Men—decline of the autocratic husband and father

.2  Women—increasing economic and social independence

.3  Adolescents—increasing autonomy of the age group

.4  Children—traditionally seen as incomplete adults, beginning to be recognized as having developmental tasks and satisfactions peculiar to each stage of growth

.5  The elderly—their plight attracting notice, as part of an expanding humanitarian concern (I.A.11)

II.L    ETHNIC, RELIGIOUS AND OTHER MINORITIES

.1  Algerian, Portuguese, and Common-Market-country immigrants

.2  Protestants and Jews

.3  A subtle racial discrimination

(For loyalty to a province of region, see I.A.9)

II.M    INTERPERSONAL AND INTERGROUP CONFLICT

.1  Strikes: cf. II.I.2

.2  Protest: May 1968; the Left; students

.3  Altercations: the important role of verbal skill

# III. Conflicts

This section has been reserved to replace and expand sections II.M and V.D (Intrapersonal conflict), in the event that the study of conflict requires an elaborated description of the conflicts both between and within the categories of the other sections. (Section III would thus need many of the present categories plus additional headings for conflicts between them.) The uninstitutionalized conflicts—those for which the system provides no mechanism capable of resolving them—escape the system and so constitute to some degree an antisystem, a mirror image. At the extreme of the uninstitutionalized conflicts are those where neither side admits the legitimacy of its antagonist. When the inventory is successfully converted into a model, however, the sections on conflict within a single culture or subculture will be eliminated, as the conflicts are absorbed into the expressions of interaction that distinguish the model from an inventory. This section would then be concerned only with relations between the models of cultures or subcultures.

# IV. The Ecology and Technology

Ecology is defined as the relationship of the population to its physical and biological environment; technology includes artifacts and products that free, constrain, and so shape behavior.

GENERAL: Measures for control of pollution: integration of the efforts described in the subsections of IV.

IV.A      EXPLOITATION OF PHYSICAL RESOURCES

          GENERAL: Applied physical geography, organized by ecological regions
          .1   Sources of energy
          .2   Mining
          .3   Industry (automobile, chemicals, textiles, electrical equipment . . .)
          .4   Aerospace
          .5   Household equipment, appliances
          .6   Private telecommunication: mail service, telephone, telegraph

IV.B      EXPLOITATION OF PLANTS AND ANIMALS

          GENERAL: The rural population
          .1   Agriculture, including wine production
          .2   Fisheries
          .3   Animal husbandry and hunting
          .4   Forestry

IV.C      DEMOGRAPHIC CONTROL (Action affecting natality and immigration) (For
          research, see I.D; for research institutions, see II.F)

IV.D      HEALTH CARE AND ACCIDENT PREVENTION
          .1   Nutrition
          .2   Disease patterns, including alcoholism, drug abuse, and mental
               illness
          .3   Medicine, dentistry, psychiatry
          .4   Nursing
          .5   Hospitals
          .6   Medical insurance
          .7   Accident prevention and insurance

IV.E      SETTLEMENT AND TERRITORIAL ORGANIZATION

          GENERAL: The urban population
          .1   Housing: dwelling types
          .2   Urbanization and urban planning
          .3   The diminishing contrast between Paris and "la province" (the rest of
               France)
          .4   The continuing attachment to one's region, and the demand for
               decentralization, vs. patriotic devotion and apprehensions: I.A.9, .10)

IV.F     TRAVEL AND TRANSPORTATION

      .1  The geographical conditions to be met

      .2  The response: radiation from cities (cf. I.C.13)

      .3  Railroads

      .4  The highway system (*routes nationales*)

      .5  The rivers and canals

      .6  Aviation

      .7  The increasing travel in and beyond "the hexagon"

      .8  Transportation of goods: postal service; the private express company, Sernam

# V. The Individual

V.A     INTEGRATION OF THE PERSONALITY FOR SELF-CONTROL AND PURPOSEFUL ACTION

See I.A, .B, .C for the core of shared traits that constitutes the "basic personality" and the mode (the range of variation containing the bulk of the cases) of each trait, which is the basis for defining the population's "modal personality." This section V concentrates upon the internal organization and variability of an individual, and upon his reactions to the shared patterns and institutions—reactions of conformity, revolt, or exploitation to achieve ends other than the professed purpose. Thus, studies tracing the life cycle of individuals can best be inventoried in V.C, but the generalizations to be abstracted from such studies will belong in the sections on shared patterns. The same is true of individual professions of faith, (V.A), to be synthesized in I.A, .B, .C.

V.B     INTEGRATION AT THE ORGANISMIC LEVEL

      .1  Biological, including genetic, factors in behavior (For nutrition, see IV.D.1. For disease patterns, see IV.D.2)

      .2  Dreams, as self-adjustment of the organism

V.C     INTRAPERSONAL VARIABILITY

      .1  The life cycle of the individual

      .2  Short-range variation and vacillation

V.D     INTRAPERSONAL CONFLICT

      .1  Conflicts resulting from individual versions of the value system and institutional norms. (This inventory assigns to I.A the tensions among main themes, which in France focus around the conflicts between individual indulgence and the social restraints; between old kinds of security and the adaptation to new conditions; and as part of the latter, the conflict between the jealous guarding of privacy and a need for community: a need for the kinds of fulfillment once afforded by the village or the urban neighborhood.)

.2  Responses to intrapersonal conflict: Mechanisms of adjustment and defense. A rather wide discrepancy between the attitudes one feels free to avow in public, among intimates, and to oneself. (This spread is narrowing, as young people find ways to overcome the hypocrisies and reticences of their predecessors.)

.3  Avoidance of conflict: Expiation of guilt and shame; escapism through the arts or reductivism (far-west movies; *Jours de France*, a successful magazine avoiding problems; Mme. Soleil, popular astrologist). L'horreur du face-à-face: avoidance of confrontation with authority which threatens one's feeling of individual autonomy.

V.E      INTERPERSONAL VARIATION (Individual differences)

# VI. The Cross-Cultural Environment

Attitudes toward other cultures and toward international and supranational organizations, arranged in a single alphabetical list. Data are stored under the headings of the five sections above and their subsections. For example, French views of the values of another people or of a cross-cultural organization are stored under VI: 1.A.

As the French-speaking areas outside France are inventoried under the same headings as for France, a comparison of the separate inventories will one day make it possible to extract the features that are demonstrably common to the whole culture area.

Contrastive analyses of cultures, though extraneous to a model of a culture, may be stored in an inventory, re-using the subsystems outlined here.

# Notes

1. These questions are examined in Albert Valdman, ed., *Trends in language teaching* (McGraw-Hill, 1966).

2. In *Anthropology and human behavior* (Anthropological Society of Washington, [D.C.] 1962), pp. 1–12.

# Appendix V

# Empathy toward Other Cultures and Perspective on One's Own

The draft document, completed in 1992 and presented here in edited format, is the product of Group VI ("Empathy toward Other Cultures and Perspectives on Our Own") of the Cultural Competence Committee of the AATF Commission on Proficiency. The Group VI Subcommittee, chaired by Claire J. Kramsch, also included Pauline R. Nelson, Gail Nemetz Robinson, Ross Steele, and Andrew Suozzo. The draft report was written by Claire Kramsch. We are most grateful to the subcommittee members for their permission to reproduce this document here.

Increasingly contextual complexity is used as an organizing principle for the progression of the pedagogical tasks in this section. The philosophy behind the pedagogic tasks in this document and the concept of contextual progression are explained comprehensively in Claire Kramsch's book's *Context and Culture Language Teaching* (Oxford, Eng.; Oxford University Press, 1993).

## Preliminary Considerations

1. "Empathy toward other cultures" has three aspects: cognitive, affective, and behavioral.

### Cognitive

To be aware of, sensitive to differences; to distinguish, recognize, describe differences between cultures; to resist overgeneralization; to show curiosity; to have an outsider's perspective on the home culture; to see the target culture in terms of its own context

### Affective

Fair-minded tolerance, ability to describe calmly and objectively; to be skeptical about stereotypes and generalizations; to be open, accepting, considerate

### Behavioral

To adjust actions and behavior to others and to the perceptions of self by others; to act and to react according to one's understanding of the target culture (e.g., consistency between words and deeds)

2. Perspective on one's own culture can be cultivated more effectively as the correlate of specific insights into a foreign culture then as an added generalization

(such as "How do the French view Americans?"), which runs the risk of reinforcing stereotypes.

3. Given the sensitive nature of measuring empathy, it is preferable to define cultural competence in terms of positive accomplishments, rather than negative stereotypes (e.g., "can identify and name differences," rather than "views different behaviors as weird and threatening").

4. Empathy differs from language proficiency, and even from the other components of cultural competence, in that its elements cannot possibly be arranged in a sequence of levels. The ACTFL proficiency levels are meant to reflect a linguistic progression; in no way can they be taken to reflect the development of empathy toward other cultures. Empathy does not correlate with linguistic ability. For example, sophisticated cultural attitudes may precede the acquisition of simple skills, and, vice-versa, superior linguistic ability may be accompanied by very low empathy. Furthermore, there is no evidence that one grows into an empathetic attitude according to harmoniously sequenced stages of development, as one grows biologically into adulthood.

The evidences of empathy are part of a psychological ensemble, or *Gestalt*, which must be developed and tested as a whole. They cannot be reduced to what one should say or do during an oral proficiency interview. They have to be identified by the tester across all other domains—during the role-play portion of the OPI, for example—or documented in other ways by the testee (such as in the form of a portfolio).

5. What *can* be sequenced, here and in any other matter where the objectives form such a *Gestalt*, are pedagogical tasks, which can be arranged in a progression from the less to the more difficult—according to the amount of contextual and cultural knowledge the learners have to draw upon and according to the age and background of a given group of learners.

The Guidelines in this case are therefore presented in the form of an ensemble of objectives, followed by three "telling examples" of French culture patterns and an illustrative sequence of pedagogical applications.

# Gestalt Indicators of Empathy toward Other Cultures

## Cognitive Competence

1. Is curious about similarities and differences between the home and the target culture with regard to such phenomena as physical objects, customs, daily life, conversational topics, styles, ways with words, opinions, mindsets, values. Shows eagerness to understand differences and discover diversity amid apparent similarity.

2. Can identify and conceptualize areas of difference between home and target culture.

3. Is able to compare phenomena in the home and in the target cultures on the same level of conceptualization.

4. Is able to distinguish between differences due to national, regional, or individual characteristics, social class, gender, or ethnicity.

5. Contextual awareness. Can link observed phenomena to others in the greater social context and/or place them in historical context when appropriate.

6. Is aware of his/her own cultural perspective and how this perspective influences his/her perception of phenomena.

## Affective Competence

1. Given an embarrassing situation or a cross-cultural conflict, shows evidence of fair-mindedness and calm in trying to solve the problem.

2. Is sensitive to the complexity of cross-cultural understanding and resists easy generalizations.

3. Has given some thought to the problem of conforming to the norm of a foreign society while maintaining one's own values and identify.

## Behavioral Competence

1. Adjusts behavior and conversation according to the situational context and to the expectations of participants.

2. Shows interest in the target culture by questioning, listening, and other outward signs of an active search for understanding.

3. Can act and react in a culturally appropriate way while being cognitively aware of one's "otherness."

# Pedagogical Applications

The following sequence of tasks is meant to foster empathy toward other cultures and to help the language student gain an outsider's perspective on his/her own culture. These tasks all have at least three components: cognitive, affective, and behavioral. From the novice to the superior level, each of the three pedagogical-task components is viewed on a continuum from lesser to greater pedagogical difficulty.

1. Cognitive tasks: development of the learner from

- punctual, informational knowledge    to    relational thinking
- fixed rules of use    to    variable rules of use
- no metareflection    to    use of metareflection
- equating C1–C2 concepts    to    dissociating C1–C2 concepts

2. Affective tasks: development from

- exclusively C1-centered    to    C2-centered
- true/false concept of learning    to    multiple truths
- awareness/tolerance of difference    to    relativizing self and other

3. Behavioral tasks: development from

- reproductive, monovalent    to    context-sensitive, polyvalent
- obligatory contexts of use    to    variable contexts of use
- context is given    to    context is created
- little or no interaction    to    high degree of interaction

## Sample Pedagogical Applications

Topic: "The French view the meal as a major event in family and social life."

## Novice-High Level (little or no C2 context yet available to the student)
### Cognitive Tasks

1. Visionnez et observez a. un spot publicitaire pour une eau minérale (e.g., Contrex) ou pour une bière (e.g., Heineken), ou b. un documentaire (e.g., la récolte des truffes au Périgord): mise-en-scène, montage, séquences, scénario. Cochez sur une liste préétablie tous les mots qui ont trait à la saveur, la couleur, aux rapports entre la nourriture et la sexualité, au rôle que jouent les femmes, les hommes.

2. Allez à la découverte! Faites une liste à votre supermarché de tous les produits gastronomiques français que vous pouvez trouver. Classifiez-les en catégories de produits d'importation (e.g., fromage, vin). Quelles catégories manquent à votre liste?

### Affective Tasks

1. Comment réagissez-vous en tant qu'Américain(e) à ce spot publicitaire?
    amusant
    intelligent
    idiot
    ennuyeux
    trop court
    n'a rien à voir avec le produit
    trop d'allusions que je ne comprends pas
2. Observez comment un(e) Français(e) exprime la colère, la surprise, la joie, l'impatience, l'hésitation, etc. Transcrivez ce que vous entendez. Comparez avec la manière dont vous-même exprimez ces sentiments en anglais. Faites une liste de phrases usuelles et pratiques avec leur équivalent anglais.

### Behavioral Tasks

1. Jouez un rôle. Reproduisez en classe le spot publicitaire que vous avez visionné: imitez le comportement, l'intonation, les gestes des personnages aussi exactement que possible.

2. Dans le contexte de cette situation, simulez la colère ou la surprise, utilisant les expressions idiomatiques appropriées à la situation et au rang social des interlocuteurs.

## Intermediate Level (some C2 context available to the student)
### Cognitive Tasks

1. Spot publicitaire (cf. ci-dessus): Découvrez les relations entre deux informations données à l'avance (couleur/produit, qui dit quoi?).

2. Visionnez le film *Le charme discret de la bourgeoisie* de Buñuel. Observez les différences dans la manière de parler des divers personnages du film, leur manière de s'habiller, de manger, l'attention qu'ils portent à la nourriture et aux repas. Comment ces personnages se différencient-ils des paysans périgourdins que vous avez vus dans le documentaire *La récolte des truffes au Périgord*? Comment Buñuel caractérise-t-il la bourgeoisie française? Lesquelles de ces caractéristiques avez-vous déjà rencontrées jusqu'à présent dans vos études de français?

3. Faites une enquête parmi vos camarades de classe sur les habitudes gastronomiques dans leur famille: heures des repas, menu, sujets de conversation, interaction à table, etc.

## Affective Tasks

1. Comment trouvez-vous les personnages du film et leur conversation à table? Comparez avec les conversations et les repas dans votre famille.

2. Vous êtes un(e) étudiant(e) français(e) de bonne famille bourgeoise, en visite dans une famille américaine. Vous écrivez une lettre à vos parents sur les habitudes gastronomiques de cette famille.

## Behavioral Tasks

Faites un repas "à la française" pour vos camarades de classe. Après avoir préparé le repas, invitez vos camarades de classe à dîner. Chacun devra adopter pendant le dîner les manières de table et de conversation que des étudiants français adopteraient s'ils dînaient ensemble chez l'un de leurs camarades.

# Advanced Level (substantial C2 context available to the student)

## Cognitive Tasks

1. Contextualisez la manière de manger et de parler des personnages du film de Bunuel. Comparez avec des affiches de publicité, des descriptions dans les guides gastronomiques, des recettes de ELLE, des menus de restaurants.

2. Après avoir vu le film de Buñuel, vous décidez de faire un film semblable sur les habitudes de la vie quotidienne de la bourgeoisie américaine. Quelle manière de vivre choisirez-vous comme sujet de votre film? Ecrivez une esquisse de scénario.

## Affective Tasks

La famille chez laquelle vous habitez en France ne parle que de politique à table et les repas durent généralement une bonne heure. Dans votre journal, écrivez vos réactions à des habitudes de manger et de conversation de table qui sont différentes des vôtres aux Etats-Unis.

## Behavioral Tasks

1. Le film *Trois hommes et un couffin* a été refait par Leonard Nimoy pour un public américain sous le titre *Three Men and a Baby*. Le remake a l'avantage d'être en anglais et de présenter des situations familières à des spectateurs américains tout en restant fidèle au thème de l'original. Faites un remake de certaines scènes du film de Buñuel pour un public américain. Rédigez le scénario ou faites vous-même un enregistrement vidéo.

2. Un des personnages du film de Buñuel vient vous rendre visite aux Etats-Unis. Où l'emmènerez-vous manger? Décrivez le restaurant et le menu.

3. Une famille de la haute bourgeoisie parisienne se reconnaît dans le film de Bunuel et intente un procès au réalisateur. Jouez le procès en classe (procureur, avocat de la défense, tribunal).

## Superior Level (full social and historical C2 content available to the student)

### Cognitive Tasks

1. Créez un collage de textes et documents variés destinés à expliquer à des étudiants américains les habitudes de repas et de conversation de la bourgeoisie française.

2. Récrivez certaines scènes du film pour un autre contexte: milieu ouvrier, paysan, petit commerçant, étudiant.

3. Vous êtes critique de films. Ecrivez une critique du film que vous avez fait (cf. ci-dessus) sur la bourgeoisie américaine pour des lecteurs français.

### Affective Tasks

Vous êtes Japonais(e), immigré(e) récemment aux Etats-Unis et vous apprenez le français. Vous voyez donc la culture américaine et la culture française de l'extérieur. Comparez les repas et les conversations à table dans des familles américaines et françaises.

### Behavioral Tasks

Imaginez que vous ayez été invité(e) à la soirée dépeinte dans le film de Buñuel. En tant qu'étranger(ère), vous pouvez choisir le comportement que vous voulez, mais vous devez en prévoir les effets. Comment vous seriez-vous comporté(e)?

# APPENDIX VI

# AATF Culture Commission's Testing Procedures: Recent Modifications

In 1993 the AATF Culture Commission drafted a provisional document called "The Cultural Component of Foreign Language Learning: A Common Core of Cultural Understanding and Knowledge of the French-Speaking World." It points out that the core needs to include more than understanding of main French-speaking areas and practice in their forms of verbal and nonverbal communication. Equally essential is a certain understanding of how to observe and analyze a culture as well as the ability to deal with cultural differences in a constructive spirit. This provisional document abandons previous attempts to match the successive levels of cultural competence to the eleven levels of the ACTFL Language Proficiency Guidelines. Instead it proposes four general levels of cultural competence for learners: (1) "Novice," progress toward the Intemediate level with emphasis on observation; a beginning knowledge of selected French-speaking areas and first skills in intercultural communication. (2) "Intermediate," progress beyond the traditional concept of the ability to survive in the foreign society toward a basic understanding of the different aspects of cultural competence; basic knowledge of selected French-speaking areas and essential skills for intercultural communication. (3) "Advanced," a more complete understanding that, with sociolinguistic as well as language skills, is sufficient to function adequately with limited social capability; well-developed skills in intercultural communication. (4) "Superior," extensive knowledge, skills, and sensitive understanding of cultural phenomena that assure the capacity to assume socioprofessional responsibility. The Superior level lies beyond the usual undergraduate major program. The four levels that make intercultural competence an essential part of cultural competence promote the integrated teaching of culture and language. As the learner progresses beyond behavioral abilties, the cultural component becomes increasingly the substance of communication in the language. To test the cultural component, fifteen types of test questions that probe further than the retention of facts have been identified and are presented on pages 131 to 135.

# BIBLIOGRAPHY

This bibliography is in addition to the very useful books and articles in the reference list in Appendix III.

The pedagogical practice of teaching culture is principally documented in articles and book reviews published in *Contemporary French Civilization, The French Review, Foreign Language Annals, The Modern Language Journal*, and *Le Français dans le monde*. Readers should consult these journals to keep abreast of new research and applications in the teaching of culture.

Altman, Rick. *The Video Connection: Integrating Video into Language Teaching*. Boston: Houghton Mifflin, 1989.

Barthes, Roland. *Mythologies*. Paris: Éditions du Seuil, 1957.

Béacco, Jean-Claude, and Simonne Lieutaud. *Mœurs et mythes*. Paris: Hachette, 1981.

_____. *Tours de France*. Paris: Hachette, 1985.

Bellah, Robert N., R. Madsen, W. M. Sullivan, A. Swidler, and S. M. Tipton. *Habits of the Heart: Individualism and Commitment in American Life*. New York: Harper and Row, 1985.

Benadava, Salvador. "De la Civilisation à l'ethnocommunication." *Le Français dans le monde* 170 (juillet 1982): 33–38.

_____. "La Civilisation dans la communication." *Le Français dans le monde* 184 (avril 1984): 79–86.

Besse, Henri. "Eduquer la perception interculturelle." *Le Français dans le monde* 188 (octobre 1984): 46–50.

Bourdieu, Pierre. *La Distinction*. Paris: Editions de Minuit, 1979.

Brooks, Nelson. "Teaching Culture in the Foreign Language Classroom." *Foreign Language Annals* 1 (1968): 204–17.

_____. "The Analysis of Language and Familiar Cultures," pp. 19–31 in Robert C. Lafayette, ed. *The Cultural Revolution in Foreign Language Teaching*. Lincolnwood, IL: National Textbook, 1975.

Byram, Michael, and Dieter Buttjes, eds. *Mediating Languages and Cultures*. Avon, Eng.: Multilingual Matters, 1991. Available from Taylor & Francis, Bristol, PA.

_____, and Veronica Esarte-Sarries. *Investigating Cultural Studies in Foreign Language Teaching*. Avon, Eng.: Multilingual Matters, 1991. Available from Taylor & Francis, Bristol, PA.

Cain, Albane, ed. *Enseignement/Apprentissage de la civilisation en cours de langue (Premier et second cycles)*. Paris: Institut National de Recherche Pédagogique, 1991.

Cathelat, Bernard. *Les Styles de vie des Français 1978–1998*. Paris: Stanké, 1977.

Closets, François de. *Toujours plus*. Paris: Grasset, 1982.

Cottenet-Hage. "Enseigner la langue et la culture," *Le Français dans le monde*. 250 (1992) 66–69.

Courtillon, Janine. "La Notion de progression appliquée à l'enseignement de la civilisation." *Le Français dans le monde* 188 (octobre 1984): 51–56.

Daninos, Pierre. *Les Carnets du major W. Marmaduke Thompson; découverte de la France et des Français*. Paris: Hachette, 1954.

_____. *Les Nouveaux Carnets du major W. Marmaduke Thompson*. Paris: Hachette, 1973.

Dean, Sherry. "French Popular Music." AATF *National Bulletin* 17,2 (November 1991): 2.

Debus. "Culture, civilisation, société *Centre International* d'Etudes Pédagogiques de Sèvres. 63 (1991).

Elliot, Jacqueline C. "Analyzing French Culture and Interpreting Some of Its Manifestations," pp. 49–56 in Robert C. Lafayette, ed., *The Cultural Revolution in Foreign Language Teaching*. Lincolnwood, IL: National Textbook, 1975.

Frommer, Judith G. "Language Learning, Cultural Understanding, and the Computer." *Papers from the Georgetown University Round Table on Languages and Lingusitics* (1989): 332–43.

Gallison, Robert. *De la langue à la culture par les mots*. Paris: Clé International, 1991.

*Le Français dans le monde*. "D'une culture à l'autre." Numéro coordonné par Geneviève Zarate. 181 (novembre–décembre 1983)

_____. "Civilisation encore." Numéro coordonné par Salvador Benadava. 188 (octobre 1984).

*Francoscopie: Les Français: Où sont-ils? Où vont-ils?* Paris: Larousse, 1986, 1993.

Geertz, Clifford. *The Interpretation of Cultures*. London: Hutchinson, 1975.

Jarvis, Donald K. "Making Crosscultural Connections," pp. 151–77 in June K. Philips, ed., *The Language Connection: From the Classroom to the World*. Lincolnwood, IL: National Textbook, 1977.

Kimmel, Alain. *Vous avez dit France*. Paris: Hachette, 1992.

Knop, Constance K. "On Using Culture Capsules and Culture Assimilators." *The French Review* 50, 1 (1976): 54–64.

Knox, Edward C. "Pour un Deuxième Cours de civilisation." *The French Review* 52 (1978): 255–60.

_____. "Propos d'un usager." *Études de linguistique appliquée* 47 (juillet–septembre 1982): 8–20.

_____. "Bibliography on the Teaching of French Civilization." *French Review* 58,3 (1985): 426–36.

_____. "Bibliography on the Teaching of French Civilization." *The French Review* 61,2 (1987): 239–46.

Kramsch, Claire. *Context and Culture in Language Teaching*. Oxford: Oxford Univ. Press, 1993.

_____. "The Cultural Discourse of Foreign Language Textbooks," pp. 63–88 in A. J. Singerman, ed., *Toward a New Integration of Language and Culture*, Northeast Conference on the Teaching of Foreign Languages. Middlebury, VT: Northeast Conference, 1988.

_____. "Culture and Constructs: Communicating Attitudes and Values in the Foreign Language Classroom." *Foreign Language Annals* 16 (1983): 437–48.

_____. "New Directions in the Study of Foreign Languages." ADFL *Bulletin* 21,1 (Fall 1989): 4–11.

_____. "New Directions in the Teaching of Language and Culture." National Foreign Language Center Occasional Paper (Washington: NFLC, 1989): 1–12.

_____. "Redrawing the Boundaries of Foreign Language Study," pp. 203–17 in Merle Krueger and Frank Ryan, ed., *Language and Content: Discipline- and Content-Based Approaches to Language Study*. Lexington, MA: D.C. Heath Co., 1993.

Lange, Dale. "The Language Teaching Curriculum and a National Agenda," pp. 70–96 in Richard D. Lambert, ed., *Foreign Language Instruction: A National Agenda*. Special issue of *The Annals of the American Academy of Political and Social Science* 490 (1987).

Luce, Louise Fiber, ed. *The French Speaking World: Anthology of Cross-Cultural Perspectives*. Lincolnwood, IL: National Textbook, 1990.

Mariet, François. "Un Malaise dans l'enseignement de la civilisation." *Études de linguistique appliquées* 64 (octobre–novembre 1986): 64–74.

Meade, Betsy, and Genelle Morain. "The Culture Cluster." *Foreign Language Annals* 6 (1973): 331–38.

Melvin, Bernice S., and David Stout. "Motivating Language Learners through Authentic Materials," pp. 45–58 in Wilga M. Rivers, ed., *Interactive Language Teaching*. Cambridge, Eng.: Cambridge Univ. Press, 1987.

Michaud, Guy, Georges Hacquard, and Georges Torres. *Nouveau Guide France: manuel de civilisation française*. Paris: Hachette, 1977.

_____, and Alain Kimmel. *Le Nouveau Guide France*. Paris: Hachette, 1990.

_____, and Edmond Marc. *Vers une Science des civilisations*. Brussels: Hachette, 1981.

Moirand, Sophie. *Une Grammaire des textes et des dialogues*. Paris: Hachette, 1986.

Morain, Genelle. "Commitment to the Teaching of Foreign Cultures." *The Modern Language Journal* 67,4 (1983): 403–12.

Nora, Pierre. *Les Lieux de mémoire*. Paris: Gallimard, 1986.

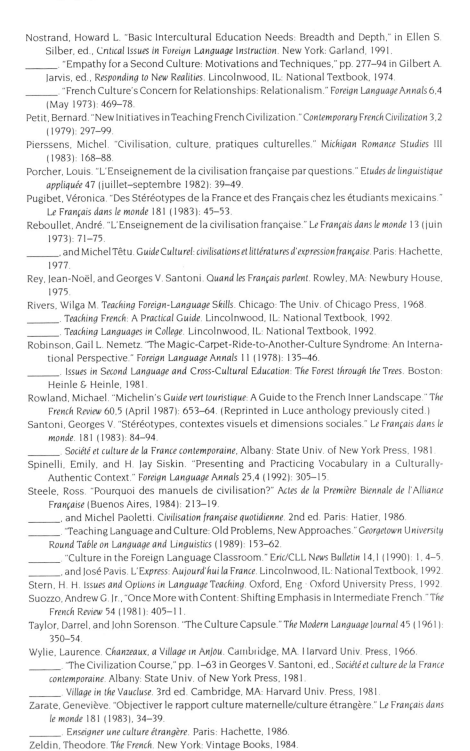

Nostrand, Howard L. "Basic Intercultural Education Needs: Breadth and Depth," in Ellen S. Silber, ed., *Critical Issues in Foreign Language Instruction*. New York: Garland, 1991.

———. "Empathy for a Second Culture: Motivations and Techniques," pp. 277–94 in Gilbert A. Jarvis, ed., *Responding to New Realities*. Lincolnwood, IL: National Textbook, 1974.

———. "French Culture's Concern for Relationships: Relationalism." *Foreign Language Annals* 6,4 (May 1973): 469–78.

Petit, Bernard. "New Initiatives in Teaching French Civilization." *Contemporary French Civilization* 3,2 (1979): 297–99.

Pierssens, Michel. "Civilisation, culture, pratiques culturelles." *Michigan Romance Studies* III (1983): 168–88.

Porcher, Louis. "L'Enseignement de la civilisation française par questions." *Etudes de linguistique appliquée* 47 (juillet–septembre 1982): 39–49.

Pugibet, Véronica. "Des Stéréotypes de la France et des Français chez les étudiants mexicains." *Le Français dans le monde* 181 (1983): 45–53.

Reboullet, André. "L'Enseignement de la civilisation française." *Le Français dans le monde* 13 (juin 1973): 71–75.

———, and Michel Têtu. *Guide Culturel: civilisations et littératures d'expression française*. Paris: Hachette, 1977.

Rey, Jean-Noël, and Georges V. Santoni. *Quand les Français parlent*. Rowley, MA: Newbury House, 1975.

Rivers, Wilga M. *Teaching Foreign-Language Skills*. Chicago: The Univ. of Chicago Press, 1968.

———. *Teaching French: A Practical Guide*. Lincolnwood, IL: National Textbook, 1992.

———. *Teaching Languages in College*. Lincolnwood, IL: National Textbook, 1992.

Robinson, Gail L. Nemetz. "The Magic-Carpet-Ride-to-Another-Culture Syndrome: An International Perspective." *Foreign Language Annals* 11 (1978): 135–46.

———. *Issues in Second Language and Cross-Cultural Education: The Forest through the Trees*. Boston: Heinle & Heinle, 1981.

Rowland, Michael. "Michelin's *Guide vert touristique*: A Guide to the French Inner Landscape." *The French Review* 60,5 (April 1987): 653–64. (Reprinted in Luce anthology previously cited.)

Santoni, Georges V. "Stéréotypes, contextes visuels et dimensions sociales." *Le Français dans le monde*. 181 (1983): 84–94.

———. *Société et culture de la France contemporaine*, Albany: State Univ. of New York Press, 1981.

Spinelli, Emily, and H. Jay Siskin. "Presenting and Practicing Vocabulary in a Culturally-Authentic Context." *Foreign Language Annals* 25,4 (1992): 305–15.

Steele, Ross. "Pourquoi des manuels de civilisation?" *Actes de la Première Biennale de l'Alliance Française* (Buenos Aires, 1984): 213–19.

———, and Michel Paoletti. *Civilisation française quotidienne*. 2nd ed. Paris: Hatier, 1986.

———. "Teaching Language and Culture: Old Problems, New Approaches." *Georgetown University Round Table on Language and Linguistics* (1989): 153–62.

———. "Culture in the Foreign Language Classroom." *Eric/CLL News Bulletin* 14,1 (1990): 1, 4–5.

———, and José Pavis. *L'Express: Aujourd'hui la France*. Lincolnwood, IL: National Textbook, 1992.

Stern, H. H. *Issues and Options in Language Teaching*. Oxford, Eng · Oxford University Press, 1992.

Suozzo, Andrew G. Jr., "Once More with Content: Shifting Emphasis in Intermediate French." *The French Review* 54 (1981): 405–11.

Taylor, Darrel, and John Sorenson. "The Culture Capsule." *The Modern Language Journal* 45 (1961): 350–54.

Wylie, Laurence. *Chanzeaux, a Village in Anjou*. Cambridge, MA. Harvard Univ. Press, 1966.

———. "The Civilization Course," pp. 1–63 in Georges V. Santoni, ed., *Société et culture de la France contemporaine*. Albany: State Univ. of New York Press, 1981.

———. *Village in the Vaucluse*. 3rd ed. Cambridge, MA: Harvard Univ. Press, 1981.

Zarate, Geneviève. "Objectiver le rapport culture maternelle/culture étrangère." *Le Français dans le monde* 181 (1983), 34–39.

———. *Enseigner une culture étrangère*. Paris: Hachette, 1986.

Zeldin, Theodore. *The French*. New York: Vintage Books, 1984.

# INDEX

# NTC ADVANCED FRENCH TEXTS AND MATERIAL

**Cultural History**
Tableaux culturels de la France
Le passé vivant de la France
De la Révolution à nos jours

**Contemporary Culture**
L'Express: Ainsi va la France
L'Express Learning Package (includes text, 3
  audiocassettes, interview transcript)
Le Nouvel Observateur: Arts, idées, spectacles

**Cross-Cultural Perspectives**
The French-Speaking World

**Text and Audiocassette Learning Packages**
Practice & Improve Your French
Practice & Improve Your French Plus
Sans Frontières

**Handbooks and References**
Guide to French Idioms
Guide to Correspondence in French
French Verbs and Essentials of Grammar

**Dictionaries**
NTC's New College French and English Dictionary
NTC's Dictionary of *Faux Amis*
Plus a large selection of Imported Pocketbook Classics

For further information or a current catalog, write:
National Textbook Company
a division of *NTC Publishing Group*
4255 West Touhy Avenue
Lincolnwood, Illinois 60646-1975 U.S.A.